W9-DDC-789

Praise for Now Is Too Late

"Gerald Baron's new book is a must-read by Academe, voters, news consumers, marketers, business leaders, and politicians. Baron provides a cogent, insightful snapshot of today's media landscape. Ignore this book's lessons at your own peril—McLuhan's Global Village is here to stay, and how!"

—Tim O'Leary, Manager, Media and External Affairs, Shell Oil Company

"Having lived in Europe at the time of the Erika oil spill off the coast of France, as well as the Concorde crash outside of Paris, and then returning to the United States just prior to the September 11 disaster—all this within just two years—there's no doubt that my personal life has been impacted by 'real time' news distribution. But as Executive Vice President of a global communications agency, my professional impact is even greater—as clients are forever in a heightened state of paranoia about whether they, and more so their global customers, can survive the fury of being heard amid a world in turmoil. Gerald R. Baron eloquently captures the essence of this dilemma in *Now Is Too Late,* and through thoughtful analysis, he provides a clear vision of how communicators can strategically plan for, and effectively manage, '24/7' soundbyte streams. A must-read for anyone in the media delivery business ... a should-read for those on the receiving end!"

—Barron T. Evans, Chicago

"Suffice it to say that I'd like to reprint most of *Now Is Too Late* in my newsletter. But they won't let me. So you'll have to buy it."

—Jonathan Bernstein, Editor/Publisher, "Crisis Manager" Ezine, President & CEO, Bernstein Communications, Inc.

"Gerald R. Baron takes his readers to the front lines of crisis management in public relations. This useful book will help executives, PR professionals, entrepreneurs, and anyone who wants to know how to better navigate a changing media environment."

—Jon Talton, Business Columnist, The Arizona Republic

"Gerald R. Baron has authored an absolutely essential guide for understanding and surviving the 'Instant News World.' This book is essential for any executive or communications leader wishing to protect the reputation of their products and organizations."

—Kevin G. Sawatsky, Dean, School of Business at Trinity Western University

NOW IS TOO LATE

ISBN 0-13-046139-3
90000
9 780130 461391

FT Prentice Hall
FINANCIAL TIMES

Pearson
Education

NOW IS TOO LATE

Survival in an Era of Instant News

GERALD R. BARON

An Imprint of PEARSON EDUCATION

Upper Saddle River, NJ • New York • London • San Francisco • Toronto
Sydney • Tokyo • Singapore • Hong Kong • Cape Town
Madrid • Paris • Milan • Munich • Amsterdam

www.ft-ph.com

Library of Congress Cataloging-in-Publication Data

Baron, Gerald R.

Now is too late : survival in an era of instant news / Gerald R. Baron

p. cm.

Includes index

ISBN 0-13-046139-3

1. Journalism, Commercial. I. Title

PN4784.C7 B37 2002

070.4'4965--dc21

2002027858

Editorial/Production Supervision: *Carol Moran*
Cover design director: *Jerry Votta*
Cover design: *Nina Scuderi*
Interior design: *Gail Cocker-Bogusz*
Manufacturing buyer: *Maura Zaldivar*
Editor-in-chief: *Tim Moore*
Editorial assistant: *Allyson Kloss*
Marketing manager: *Bryan Gambrel*

Publishing as Financial Times Prentice Hall
Upper Saddle River, New Jersey 07458

Financial Times Prentice Hall books are widely used by corporations and government agencies for training, marketing, and resale.

For information regarding corporate and government bulk discounts please contact: Corporate and Government Sales (800) 382-3419 or corpsales@pearsontechgroup.com.

Printed in the United States of America

10 9 8 7 6 5 4 3 2 1

ISBN 0-13-046139-3

Pearson Education Ltd.
Pearson Education Australia Pty, Limited
Pearson Education Singapore, Pte. Ltd.
Pearson Education North Asia Ltd.
Pearson Education Canada, Ltd.
Pearson Educación de Mexico, S.A. de C.V.
Pearson Education—Japan
Pearson Education Malaysia, Pte. Ltd.

FINANCIAL TIMES PRENTICE HALL BOOKS

For more information, please go to www.ft-ph.com

Dr. Judith M. Bardwick
Seeking the Calm in the Storm: Managing Chaos in Your Business Life

Gerald R. Baron
Now Is Too Late: Survival in an Era of Instant News

Thomas L. Barton, William G. Shenkir, and Paul L. Walker
Making Enterprise Risk Management Pay Off: How Leading Companies Implement Risk Management

Michael Basch
CustomerCulture: How FedEx and Other Great Companies Put the Customer First Every Day

J. Stewart Black and Hal B. Gregersen
Leading Strategic Change: Breaking Through the Brain Barrier

Deirdre Breakenridge
Cyberbranding: Brand Building in the Digital Economy

William C. Byham, Audrey B. Smith, and Matthew J. Paese
Grow Your Own Leaders: How to Identify, Develop, and Retain Leadership Talent

Jonathan Cagan and Craig M. Vogel
Creating Breakthrough Products: Innovation from Product Planning to Program Approval

Subir Chowdhury
Organization 21C: Someday All Organizations Will Lead this Way

Subir Chowdhury
The Talent Era: Achieving a High Return on Talent

Sherry Cooper
Ride the Wave: Taking Control in a Turbulent Financial Age

James W. Cortada
21st Century Business: Managing and Working in the New Digital Economy

James W. Cortada
Making the Information Society: Experience, Consequences, and Possibilities

Aswath Damodaran
The Dark Side of Valuation: Valuing Old Tech, New Tech, and New Economy Companies

Henry A. Davis and William W. Sihler
Financial Turnarounds: Preserving Enterprise Value

Sarv Devaraj and Rajiv Kohli
The IT Payoff: Measuring the Business Value of Information Technology Investments

Nicholas D. Evans

Business Agility: Strategies for Gaining Competitive Advantage through Mobile Business Solutions

Nicholas D. Evans

Business Innovation and Disruptive Technology: Harnessing the Power of Breakthrough Technology…for Competitive Advantage

Kenneth R. Ferris and Barbara S. Pécherot Petitt

Valuation: Avoiding the Winner's Curse

Oren Fuerst and Uri Geiger

From Concept to Wall Street

David Gladstone and Laura Gladstone

Venture Capital Handbook: An Entrepreneur's Guide to Raising Venture Capital, Revised and Updated

Marshall Goldsmith, Vijay Govindarajan, Beverly Kaye, and Albert A. Vicere

The Many Facets of Leadership

Robert B. Handfield, Ph.d, and Ernest L. Nichols

Supply Chain Redesign: Transforming Supply Chains into Integrated Value Systems

David R. Henderson

The Joy of Freedom: An Economist's Odyssey

Faisal Hoque

The Alignment Effect: How to Get Real Business Value Out of Technology

Harvey A. Hornstein

The Haves and the Have Nots: The Abuse of Power and Privilege in the Workplace…and How to Control It

Philip Jenks and Stephen Eckett, Editors

The Global-Investor Book of Investing Rules: Invaluable Advice from 150 Master Investors

Charles P. Jones

Mutual Funds: Your Money, Your Choice. Take Control Now and Build Wealth Wisely

Thomas Kern, Mary Cecelia Lacity, and Leslie P. Willcocks

Netsourcing: Renting Business Applications and Services Over a Network

Al Lieberman, with Patricia Esgate

The Entertainment Marketing Revolution: Bringing the Moguls, the Media, and the Magic to the World

Frederick C. Militello, Jr., and Michael D. Schwalberg

Leverage Competencies: What Financial Executives Need to Lead

Robin Miller

The Online Rules of Successful Companies: The Fool-Proof Guide to Building Profits

D. Quinn Mills
Buy, Lie, and Sell High: How Investors Lost Out on Enron and the Internet Bubble

Dale Neef
E-procurement: From Strategy to Implementation

John R. Nofsinger
Investment Blunders (of the Rich and Famous)...And What You Can Learn from Them

John R. Nofsinger
Investment Madness: How Psychology Affects Your Investing...And What to Do About It

Erica Orloff and Kathy Levinson, Ph.D.
The 60-Second Commute: A Guide to Your 24/7 Home Office Life

Tom Osenton
Customer Share Marketing: How the World's Great Marketers Unlock Profits from Customer Loyalty

Richard W. Paul and Linda Elder
Critical Thinking: Tools for Taking Charge of Your Professional and Personal Life

Matthew Serbin Pittinsky, Editor
The Wired Tower: Perspectives on the Impact of the Internet on Higher Education

W. Alan Randolph and Barry Z. Posner
Checkered Flag Projects: 10 Rules for Creating and Managing Projects that Win, Second Edition

Stephen P. Robbins
The Truth About Managing People...And Nothing but the Truth

Fernando Robles, Françoise Simon, and Jerry Haar
Winning Strategies for the New Latin Markets

Jeff Saperstein and Daniel Rouach
Creating Regional Wealth in the Innovation Economy: Models, Perspectives, and Best Practices

Eric G. Stephan and Wayne R. Pace
Powerful Leadership: How to Unleash the Potential in Others and Simplify Your Own Life

Jonathan Wight
Saving Adam Smith: A Tale of Wealth, Transformation, and Virtue

Yoram J. Wind and Vijay Mahajan, with Robert Gunther
Convergence Marketing: Strategies for Reaching the New Hybrid Consumer

I gratefully dedicate this to my family. To my beautiful wife and helper Lynne, who chose willingly to walk this life with me. To Chris, Geoff, Amy, and Ashley, who are the great blessings of that walk together. Above all to Him, to whom all honor is due.

Contents

INTRODUCTION

"A lie is halfway around the world before you can get your pants on."

—Winston Churchill

In a heart's beat of a faster and faster pace, it's suddenly becoming a more dangerous world. Although much attention has been focused on security—personal, national, transportation, and business—in the months following the September 11, 2001 terrorist attacks, this book focuses on another type of security risk, the new risk to reputations.

Corporate and organizational reputations are more at risk than ever, not because of a cataclysmic event such as the al-Qaeda offensive, but because of the significant changes in how the news indust operates and how the public gets its information. To compete in an increasingly crowded media environment, news organizations have turned increasingly to "infotainment." Activists have learned how to exploit old and new media to push their agendas. The news public is becoming increasingly cynical. Digital, satellite, and other technologies are increasing the rush toward "breaking news," meaning that reputations can be severely impacted before a communication team can be assembled. Primarily, the news and public information world is changing because of the Internet. If a lie could travel halfway around the world before the prime minister could get his pants on before, in the early days of the new century that lie can travel around the multiple times world, causing irreparable damage before the great gentleman would have time to put down his cigar before pulling on his pants.

Many public relations professionals, communication managers, and business and organization leaders are becoming aware of these escalating risks. The average tenure of CEOs has been declining and a review of news headlines shows a strong correlation between a public reputation problem and a short career for a CEO. In the weeks following September 11, 2001, executives were asked if they felt their organizations were prepared to handle a large-scale crisis, and the overwhelming majority said no. Crisis communication professionals are reporting that more company leaders are expressing interest in communication plans. Public relations and communication managers are struggling with the variety of issues involved in protecting their organization's brand value and reputations in a world of increasing risk.

This book is essentially about the need for leadership in reputation management. CEOs and executive directors are the ones who fall when the public turns against a company and the organization loses its public franchise. Leadership at this level is critical if an enterprise is to survive a rapid and voracious attack on everything that it is and does. Innovative and aggressive communication managers are taking a higher profile in companies and organizations when they demonstrate they can provide concrete solutions to reputation protection. There is a strong need for leadership from both the executive level and the communication leaders.

To address this new "instant news" environment, communicators and leaders must have an understanding of the conditions that create the risk and a clear picture of what can be done to protect against the threats. That is what is offered here: an analysis of the new public information environment and the strategies needed to protect reputations and enhance brand value while operating in this new environment.

While the war on terror was waged in far corners of the world, Americans were "entertained" with stories about the demise of several giants in the world of business. Two of the country's largest bankruptcies occurred when Enron, and then Global Crossing, needed protection from creditors. Although the greed, dishonesty, and shady internal politics revealed by both news media and a Congressional investigation of Enron should have provided sufficient diversion, attention was soon focused on the respected global accounting firm, Arthur Andersen. First, there was concern about Andersen's role in potentially illegal accounting practices. Then the news broke that an Andersen partner was shredding documents and destroying evidence that investigators were seeking concerning Enron's financial dealings. A reputation crisis of the first order took over the headlines, the attention of the business world, and the global news audience.

Although many reputation crises are played out on the national or international media stage, a far greater number involve smaller companies in local or regional markets. Not all companies have the reach of Firestone, ValuJet, or Exxon. But for these less prominent companies, the impact on their futures is just as great, even though the audience may be smaller. Local newspaper articles, local television broadcasts, and localized activist attacks are every bit as significant. Manufacturing companies, oil and chemical companies, health organizations, government agencies, nonprofit organizations, politicians, and other individuals whose public stature is vital to their future are at risk in the new environment of instant news.

However, it is not all bad news. Along with the new risks come new opportunities. In the Internet-connected global village, everyone has the potential of being a broadcaster or publisher. This is being demonstrated every day. Today, new voices on the Internet are gathering audiences that rival those of some daily newspapers. Some of them are doing it from their spare bedrooms with almost no investment except their own time, ideas, and energy. Activists and corporate opponents are clearly demonstrating the power of the new media tools to forge opinion and create public and political action: It's one of the significant risks. However, these same tools and methods are available to companies and organizations needing to build their enterprise and protect their investment. The question is whether or not they will be as quick to learn, adapt, change policies, invest in needed technologies, and meet the challenge.

With all the new voices, the acceleration of news delivery, and the growing importance of public information in policy making around the world, the noise level is rising. From this cacophony a key question emerges: Who is to be believed? Credibility has always been an essential element for people and organizations operating in the public sphere, but in the instant news world, when everyone is shouting to be heard, credibility takes on a new urgency. Protecting the organization's voice and public franchise becomes the real role of executive and communication leadership. Today, there are so many ways to lose believability that anything remotely resembling a cover-up is certain to destroy a solid reputation. Yet another way to lose credibility in this news era is simply to be too slow. Crisis communication case studies of the last few years, Andersen's prominent among them, offer one example after another of providing too little, too late.

Speed, direct communication, and credibility are the keys to survival in this risky public information environment. Understanding these needs thoroughly and doing what it takes to prepare to meet the challenges these demands pose is the only real protection against the frightening discovery that now is too late.

For more information about crisis communication trends and updated information about crisis communication technologies, please visit *www.nowistoolate.com*. Make sure you register on the mailing list to receive the latest tips and updates.

CHAPTER

1 Discovering the New World of Instant News

Mid-June in the far upper corner of the Pacific Northwest is a time of anticipation. Long spells of dreary rain begin to give way to the piercingly bright blue of summer and, when the sun does emerge, the days are long with the sun setting shortly before 9 p.m.

June 10, 1999 was one of those promising days. Two 10-year-old boys were playing in the park right below their homes. Not like most city parks, this park is a typical Northwest rain forest, although right near the heart of a city of almost 70,000 people. Trails cut narrow swaths through a dense and dark forest. Whatcom Creek runs through the center of the park and immediately after it exits the park it flows through downtown Bellingham: past the big car dealership, past a number of office buildings, right below the jail windows, right past City Hall, and past the Whatcom County Courthouse. The stream starts at

Lake Whatcom, a 12-mile lake at the eastern edge of the city. After plunging down a beautiful waterfall with a drop of about 30 feet, the 50-foot-wide creek meanders through towering firs and hemlocks, finally exiting into Bellingham Bay right near the Georgia-Pacific pulp and chemical plant.

The downtown stream was a favorite of fishermen as well. Around 4 p.m., an 18-year-old who had just graduated from a local high school the week before was enjoying early summer by fly fishing on the creek. He was about a half-mile upstream from where the boys were playing.

What happened next began a series of events that changed my understanding of what was happening in the world, much as September 11, 2001 changed the understanding of many others around the world.

Returning from a speaking engagement in Spokane, a six-hour drive east along Interstate 90 from Bellingham, I received a phone call at about 5 p.m. My wife was frantic. "What was that?" she shouted in my ear. My wife is a remarkably calm and strong woman. Hearing the fear and uncertainty in her voice immediately put me on high alert.

"What do you mean, 'What was that?'" I asked.

"It looks like half the town has blown up!" she said.

From her point of view, it was not an exaggeration. From the front yard of our house she saw a wall of black smoke a mile and a half long that would quickly tower to 30,000 feet. I asked if it was Mount Baker. The nearly 11,000-foot mountain was a semiactive volcano and after Mount St. Helens, everyone in the region is aware of the risk of sudden volcanic activity. She didn't know. She had to check on the kids and so she was gone off the phone.

My kids—there were three of them—were my main concern, and I took a mental inventory. One was safely in college in Chicago. My second son was in an apartment about a half-mile north of us—right in the direction of the plume. My daughter was safely at home.

"Turn on the radio," I snapped at my young employee who was driving the car. We tried to get a Seattle station that might have some news, but we were on the edge of their coverage area. Not long after the aborted phone call we picked up a breaking news story on the radio: A pipeline explosion in downtown Bellingham. A huge plume of black smoke. No more details.

In our area there are four oil refineries. It's a natural location for them given the enclosed waters of northern Puget Sound and the proximity to the Alaska North Slope oil fields. The millions of gallons of fuel produced by these four refineries flowed primarily through a fuel products pipeline. All the jet fuel used by the busy SeaTac airport came directly from the refineries to the airport via pipeline.

The pipeline was built in 1965 and ran from the Cherry Point area about 10 miles northwest of Bellingham where two refineries were located, through what was then the outskirts of Bellingham, south toward Mount Vernon, where the lines from the two refineries near Anacortes connected with it at a point called Bayview.

I had become quite familiar with one of those Anacortes refineries because it had become a major client of mine. The refinery had experienced a devastating accident and I was assisting with rebuilding community relationships and assisting with ongoing media coverage.

Shortly after hearing from the scratchy radio about some enormous explosion just a mile or so from my house, and trying to keep myself calm while I repeatedly tried to get my wife on her cell phone, which was now continually busy, I received another call from Houston. On the phone was a communication manager who was a contact point for my work with the refinery. He calmly informed me that the "Away Team," a group of professionals designated to deal with major incidents for their company and related companies, was on the way to Bellingham. "Why?" I asked. It was then I found out that two major oil companies owning refineries in the area, including the one I worked with, were involved in ownership of the pipeline.

Until I received that call, I was a member of the audience, affected by the events and with a high demand for information, so high that I was presumptuous enough to call the manager of the local radio station on the phone to get more information because I was still too far away to get the local radio signal. However, with that phone call from Houston, my position changed. I was no longer an audience member impatient for any bit of information. I became part of the team that tried to meet that demand—a team that faced innumerable obstacles to getting the right information to the right people when they wanted it. The realities of the new world of instant news were about to make themselves evident.

The two 10-year-olds were good friends. Both were active in sports, particularly baseball. They played together a lot and a favorite place was the creek, which dropped down a deep gully behind their homes. Something must have seemed strange to them that day: a strong smell, an overpowering smell like gasoline. As strong as it was, it didn't deter them from playing near the stream and playing with a barbeque lighter they carried with them.

Upstream from them, a little below the city's water treatment facility, stood the 18-year-old fly fisherman. He too must have noticed the smell. Quickly it became overpowering. As he started to try to get away from it, it overwhelmed him. Before he could climb out of the fast-flowing stream, now flowing not just with water but with some of the 229,000 gallons of gasoline spilling from a 27-inch wide gash in the underground pipeline, he fell into the gasoline and water mixture and drowned.

Fumes were now rising from the stream into the canopy of heavy trees that covered both sides of the stream and the steep sides of the canyon through which it flowed. The barbeque lighter, just an interesting toy to the boys, lit off the gasoline choking the stream, and a rolling explosion began in two directions at once. It thundered downstream to the point where it meets the Interstate 5 bridge that crosses the creek just before entering downtown. It also rolled a half-mile upstream, flashing up Hannah Creek, a small tributary, until it reached the point of the leak just yards below the city's water treatment facility.

The boys, with horrific burns over 90 percent of their bodies, managed to climb up the steep bank to be met by horrified friends and family members. They were rushed to the local hospital, then to a burn center, but their lives ended early the next day.

On a larger scale of events, this might not rank with major, earth-shattering news events such as September 11 or even major industrial disasters, such as Exxon *Valdez* or Bhopal. However, to Bellingham citizens, and particularly to those directly affected by this event, it marks a milestone by which time, history, and lives are measured. "Where were you June 10?" makes as much sense in our town as it does asking where you were November 22, December 7, or September 11. Almost everyone in the area has personal stories about where they were, what they were doing, and how they heard. How they first heard, and how they got subsequent information that was important to them, is the relevant question we are dealing with here.

We could take any event like this and look at how the information about it would flow in various times and cultures. For most of human history, information about life-changing events would be personal and direct: You tell me what you know and I tell the next person or perhaps a group. That is definitely not mass media. The written word made possible some extension of this, but the fact that each document needed to be handwritten represented definite limitations. It could not be considered mass media. The first thing that might be considered close to mass media was the town crier. As villages and towns emerged, news and commercial announcements were conveyed by a person with a loud voice calling out from a tower. This method could get the word out to perhaps a small village or at least a large group. A small village might stretch the definition of mass audience, but the crier was definitely a medium—an intermediary who carried the message from the person or event serving as the source to an audience presumably hungry for the story.

Gutenberg's printing press led to ever faster and cheaper production of the written word. Newspapers emerged and made it possible for a great many people to get essentially the same information relatively quickly. Mass media was born. It took on a greater immediacy with radio, and achieved an even greater impact with the immediacy combined with the real-time visual images of television.

For the past 300 years, people have been living in a world of expanding public information dominated by the media: a "media world." In a media world there are two sources of information: direct and indirect. Direct information is still very much limited to personal observation or talking directly to someone else by phone or personal, face-to-face conversation. Indirect information via media is provided by those who control the means of distribution—the printing presses or broadcast transmitters. This is the way things have worked for a long time, and most people have been pretty content with this arrangement. However, things are no longer quite so simple, because now there is a new way of communicating that blends the personal with the impersonal, and at the same time destroys the monopoly that media have held on mass public information. The Internet provides the immediacy, visual impact, and information content of the best of other media, but it delivers that content directly to individual members of the audience. This immediacy, directness, and depth result in profound changes in expectations. This change—the adoption of the Internet—is but one of several significant technological and cultural changes that has altered how the world gets its information. That change represents new risks and new opportunities for businesses and organizations that may find themselves, willingly or not, in the news.

When the ground beneath us moves, when sea changes occur, the reaction is not necessarily immediate. On June 10, 1999 I was living in the instant news world but didn't know it or comprehend it. As a result, my behavior and actions, as well as those of my colleagues working hard on the information response to the pipeline tragedy, was a response to a world that had changed. Only in looking back on the things we did well and those things that could have been improved did I begin to more thoroughly understand that we are living in a fundamentally different era.

The Gatling gun—a rudimentary machine gun—was introduced during the U.S. Civil War. Close formation charges against overwhelming artillery or machine gun firepower made absolutely no sense, but tactics do not change readily. The tried and the true methods in most things are relied on until they are clearly and unquestionably proven to no longer be useful. The battle of English longbowmen against the massed glory of French knights is another example. Agincourt would have been an easy victory for the French if they had more thoroughly understood how the strong arms and powerful bows of the English peasantry could defeat their formerly undefeatable armor.

Providing public information is not exactly a war, although for those on the front lines it can feel uncannily like a genuine battle. The consequences can be quite serious—for the reputation of the company or organization, as well as for the impact on a great many lives. Certainly, the September 11 events and their aftermath have made clear that providing the right amount of accurate public information at the right time is a fundamentally strategic issue as far as national security and national welfare are concerned. The point here is that tactics need to change when there has been a fundamental shift in the ground rules. The ground rules of public information have changed forever. The way the media gathers, prepares, and distributes the news has changed. Perhaps more important, the role of the media as the sole provider of mass public information is no more. We will not return to the days when soldiers marching in lockstep toward a well-entrenched enemy who has the firepower to wipe them all out is the strategy of choice. Nor will we return to the days when corporate and organization executives and their communication staffs and experts can focus exclusively on their work with the media to convey the facts, information, and priorities of a news story or an item of pressing public interest.

That the media continue to be a primary means of public information is beyond question. However, the traditional media are changing as well, in part to meet the new challenges represented by the Internet. The changes in traditional media combined with the use of the Internet as a direct means of public information require substantial change in policies, people, and technology for those concerned about reputation protection in this new news era.

Information Response

Early on the morning of June 11, 1999, the basement of the Whatcom County Courthouse was quickly turned into a response command post. The Bellingham Fire Department was in command during the immediate response, and during the night they closely monitored the progress of fumes throughout the city's sewer system. As the afternoon turned into uneasy night in the small city, most residents were unaware that a city-wide evacuation was actively considered but eventually determined to be unnecessary.

The Sheriff's Search and Rescue team began conducting a thorough search of the "hot zone" while the ground near the rupture site still flamed. It was then they discovered the body of the 18-year-old fly fisherman. At that time it was unknown if there were more fatalities or injuries.

Responders began arriving from all over. Soon there were more than 40 response agencies and more than 300 people crowding into the small offices and corridors of the courthouse basement. An information team was loosely organized and we began to develop the information needed for the press of media standing outside the door of the command center and calling by phone. While the response commanders got themselves organized, the Bellingham Fire Department spokesperson continued to speak for the response. Company officials, along with the response commanders, decided to hold a press conference at 11:00 a.m. on the morning of June 11. The top company official on scene, the vice president in charge of operations for the pipeline, would be the one to face the cameras and reporters.

Earlier, a sheriff's department helicopter attempted to land near the city water treatment plant about an hour after the explosion occurred. As it was seeking a clear place to land, another helicopter swooped in and landed. The sheriff's department helicopter landed nearby. Furious with the intrusion, the sheriff's deputy strode up to the people exiting the other chopper: the executive team arriving from the pipeline company's offices in Renton, Washington, near Seattle. The deputy recalled later how the helicopter's passengers emerged, tears streaming down their faces. His intention to issue his complaint disappeared. He realized, as he recounted later, that there was tragedy all around that day. The company had operated for 34 years without so much as a serious injury before this.

At 11:00 a.m. the company executive stood before the press in front of a large mahogany dais where the Bellingham City Council normally met. Satellite trucks lined the street outside City Hall. Perhaps two dozen reporters waited inside with about six television crews. The executive started out, "This is the blackest day in our history." That quotation provided the headline for the next day's local daily. He hadn't slept during the night; he was visibly shaken and shocked. The press conference did not go well. The Fire Department and Bellingham Police officials gave solid summaries specific to the search and rescue efforts, the damage to the creek, the extent of the fire and explosion, and the current state of the hot zone. The executive received questions about cause, what the company could have done to prevent it, whether or not the company was accepting responsibility, and why in the world the pipeline was crossing a creek that flowed right into downtown.

An enduring image I have of that day is the lead public relations manager for the company with his arms around his friend, the company vice president, as they walked from City Hall following the difficult press conference back to the emergency operation center or command post in the basement of the county courthouse. The PR manager had been brought out of retirement to help with the response, and through his long history and extensive contacts in the oil industry, had gotten this manager his job a number of years earlier. The two were old friends, now brought together again under circumstances that probably seemed unimaginable when, years earlier, they celebrated this executive landing his new job.

For the next three weeks, the emergency operation center, or EOC as it came to be called, was the center of my life. Fortunately, I was in my own hometown and could go home at night after a long day in the EOC, unlike my compatriots who called one of the local hotels home. A routine slowly emerged:

- Collect the facts by attending the Unified Command briefings or going around the to the key players in the fire department, sheriff's office, or Department of Emergency Management to find out what was going on.
- Assemble the facts into the next version of the fact sheet being prepared for issue to the media. Get a sign-off from the commanders on the fact sheet.
- Coordinate with the various agencies such as the Department of Ecology, Environmental Protection Agency, police, fire and sheriff's office for the next press conference.
- Always, constantly, attempt to stem the tide of reporters calling by phone, collecting outside the door, and attempting to catch anyone who might emerge from the safety of the EOC.

As the long, long days turned into weeks, the focus expanded to include the various people in the community who wanted to know and had a right to know what was going on. Phone calls, meetings, broadcast faxes, mailings, and public meetings were all used to get information out about the response, the unfolding story of the horrific damage to the park and the environment, and the very limited information emerging about how this sort of thing could have happened.

It was in reflecting on the experience in dealing with the pipeline incident, along with several other situations of high public interest, that my realization grew that we are living in a very different world. The new era of instant news has created very different expectations from the news media and the audiences—expectations about speed and directness of information. Reviewing the coverage in the newspapers and television reports demonstrated something I had been increasingly aware of: News is often designed to fit a predetermined formula that is not dictated by the information, but by the media's understanding of the audience's need to be entertained. It is a blending of information and entertainment that results in public information being packaged in a way that resembles melodrama, complete with white hats and black hats. It seems to intentionally ignore the complexities of real life and real events. In the new era of instant news, information demands are growing exponentially and audiences are quickly developing whole new expectations regarding events or facts that affect their lives.

In many respects, although the communication team did an admirable job, we were living in an era that had passed by. We had entered a postmedia world, but were operating as if it was still a media world. We operated in a time frame and with measured steps that reflected a public information world that no longer existed. The subsequent viewpoint expressed by some in the community that the public information effort was bungled was not an indictment against the effort made, but more a reflection that change had occurred, and the paradigms we operated within did not take that change into account. The team members, who came from government agencies, the companies involved, and public relations and communications firms did a credible and professional job. However, like the massed columns advancing in the Civil War or the inglorious charge of the French mounted knights, we were fighting a battle with outmoded tactics and technologies. This became clear only after the battle was long over.

A Noninstant News Response

Not everyone is afforded the luxury of a wake-up call that a new day has dawned. My wake-up call came on reflection of what was done well and what could be improved. It was then that my realization came that things had changed. The evidence of an instant news world surrounded us, but was not clearly visible or understandable until we realized the ways in which we missed the mark. At the time it appeared there were no choices or options. Later, those options became more visible and with them, an understanding that an entirely new way of thinking about providing public information was needed.

The following are some of the key elements that were identified as indicators that change was needed:

1. No "golden hour" response
2. Inadequate internal communication
3. Antiquated information distribution
4. "Scratchpad" method of database development
5. Handcuffed without email
6. Separate Web team to update site
7. Behind the curve on media response
8. The "media first" mistake
9. The approval process slowdown
10. No inquiry and response tracking
11. No way to easily update new reporters

No "Golden Hour" Response

Although definitions might vary, most crisis communication experts consider the first hour of response the "golden hour." Why focus on this first hour? Because in most newsmaking events, the initial reports emerge in this first hour and the story begins to be told and written. As the old saying goes, "You only have one chance to make a first impression." Every subsequent news story will either follow the line of the initial story or contradict it. Every reporter is influenced by the initial information emerging and the initial public reports, as is every member of the audience. The information that is available, the way it is prioritized and presented, who it comes from, who it does not come from, the context of the information, and the history of similar events are all critical items normally included in the first reports emerging from an incident.

In the pipeline incident, there was no effectively coordinated golden hour response. The initial reports coming from a company spokesperson nowhere near the scene later turned out to be quite incorrect. The company had little to no visibility until late the next morning at a press conference. The inability to very quickly "push" information to the media and other stakeholders about the company, its background and history, and whatever information about the incident was known at that time did not bode well for the ongoing information response. Subsequently, in talking with a number of communication professionals, it has become clear that this inability to meet new information demands is very common. Although some companies and industries with a high risk of major public events have extensive preparations in place, many do not. Many communicators seem to believe that a communication team has hours or even days to put the infrastructure in place, organize the information process, and get to work. However, events such as September 11, 2001 and the Enron–Andersen story demonstrate that the communicator's understanding of "now" means they will probably be too late.

Inadequate Internal Communication

In a real news-making event, the communication team has a great many responsibilities. Effective internal communication is certainly one of them. September 11, 2001 demonstrated to many executives that they were unprepared to quickly reach employees at their workplaces or homes, particularly in a major crisis when telephone service was affected.

Internal communication means effectively gathering the needed bits and pieces of information and being the source of reliable information for internal audiences. Those audiences include corporate management, employees, other company communication team members, the immediate response team, and other agencies or organizations involved in the response. The reality is that many of these people who need to have the latest and most accurate information about what is going on are not likely to be on scene. It seems like an impossible situation—and without the proper planning, policies, and technologies it really is impossible. However, effective internal communication is also critically important—and the task of communicating with these internal audiences and sources of information falls on the communication team.

In the emergency center after the pipeline accident, the communication team on scene was focused on preparing and distributing information to the media. That was the task the team understood that it was assembled for. All other efforts were secondary, ad hoc, and uncoordinated. The impacts of this can be very significant, one of them being the confidence or lack of confidence in the entire response team by the corporate and agency leaders who are not on scene. If the organization leaders who are not there don't have good, timely information about what is happening, they cannot evaluate the effectiveness of the response. They need this information to determine whether or not additional resources are required and whether or not to begin second-guessing those who are extremely busy dealing with the rapidly evolving situation.

Antiquated Information Distribution

Technology has revolutionized business and government in the past many years. Unfortunately, there's a good chance if you find yourself in a command post responsible for managing an overwhelming crush of reporters and information-hungry stakeholders, your most important tools may be random scratch pads, barely operational phones, and perhaps a single fax machine.

At the very time when the dot-com explosion was dominating the business scene, the pipeline accident communication team did not even have a fax machine to support the communication effort. There were a few computers scattered around the EOC, but the process of getting them adequately connected to working printers was a tremendous challenge. Internet connection was not a reality until several days into the event, and then it was strictly through dial-up connections. A few employees brought laptops with them, but without a real network, data was transferred by floppies. In the basement of the county courthouse, cell phones were mostly unusable.

The information process as it evolved was fairly simple: Someone would write a draft of an updated information release and get it to the computer that was connected to the printer—an excruciatingly slow printer. The draft was given to the Unified Commanders and others who had direct knowledge of the latest information. The changes were then incorporated and then it went back through the process. When the release was approved (usually three or four drafts later), it was rushed to my office about six blocks from the EOC. There, one of my employees would stand by the fax machine and send it out to the rapidly growing list of reporters who were eagerly awaiting the latest dispatch from the incident's Joint Information Center.

"Scratchpad" Method of Database Development

In an event of significant public interest, a large number of people are going to want and expect the latest information. The most important of these are the family members and close friends and associates of anyone possibly hurt or killed in the incident. The list quickly grows to neighbors closest to the event, employees, company leaders, local elected officials, people from the various agencies responding to the event, prominent people in the community who hold their place because others consider them continually "in the know," and—oh, yes—reporters: local reporters, regional reporters, national and international reporters, industry reporters, stringers, publishers, broadcast executives, and so on.

As mentioned earlier, our method of distribution was to answer questions on the phone and to send our updated fact sheet to an outside office where someone stood for an ever increasing amount of time faxing it out and manually adding to the rapidly growing fax list. Within a few days, it took two hours to send the broadcast fax. Now, if you were on the tail end of the two hours, and you were a reporter, you would probably not rely on the faxed fact sheet. When you got the new one, you'd probably call in and see what was new since the fax broadcast had started.

The growing list was developed very simply. Any one of perhaps 10 or more people in the EOC assigned to take media or community calls would answer the phone, and if a reporter asked to be put on the fax distribution list or wanted a call back for a later answer, the responder would take down the name, and phone or fax number on any old piece of paper lying around. If it was to be added to the fax list it would usually make its way to me and I would take it back to the office along with the next update. From there my administrative assistant would load it into the fax machine. There was no way of knowing whether the question was answered, whether the person got the information he or she needed, and no way for the communication leaders or information officers to know who had called, for what reason, and whether a response had been properly offered. Management of the message was definitely handled by walking around.

Handcuffed Without Email

Connection junkies that we are, when separated from our cell phones, text pagers, and certainly email, we become almost panic stricken. In the pipeline incident's EOC, most cell phones had very weak to no signal and because Internet connections were almost nonexistent, email was out of the question. In "old-world" crisis communications planning, the information center is designed to be a place where all those participating in the information function can gather together. Reality is not so neat. There are a number of people critical to the information function who cannot be physically present, but who need to participate in the information function—company and agency leaders, lawyers, experts with critical information, on-scene responders, and so on. Take some of the routine methods of communication away, and everything tends to slow and lose efficiency. Take email away and replace it with phones that need to be shared with a lot of others who all have an urgent need for communications and you have instant frustration and inefficiency.

We have all become accustomed to working at our comfortable workstations. We have the tools at hand that we rely on to get things done. However, in a crisis incident with a defined command and information center, we find ourselves removed from that comfortable and efficient world. When the demands for efficient and accurate work are higher than they can possibly be in our normal routines, we are asked to do without the very things we rely on for quality communication. There are only two solutions to this very significant challenge—either we find a way to work from our well-established workstations or, the tools we use to communicate, including email, PDAs, wireless phones, and so on, must be completely accessible at the information center regardless of where it is located.

Separate Web Team to Update Site

It is quickly becoming commonplace that in any situation involving significant public interest, a Web site must play a key role. The effectiveness of a Web site as a critical information tool is dependent on the degree to which the communication manager or managers have direct and immediate control. Since 1999, there have been tremendous advances in the technologies that enable Web content to be managed "on the fly" by nonprogrammers or noncode writers—in other words, the rest of us.

All things considered, in mid-1999 we were fortunate in the early stages of the response to a have a Web presence for the event. It featured photos that were taken by the hazmat-trained photographer authorized to take photos to be shared by all news organizations. No one was allowed into the "hot zone" without training on operating in environments where hazardous materials are present. Because of this, the only photos or videos used came from helicopter shots or those provided by the fire department-authorized photographer. In addition to the photos, the Web site included all the latest fact sheets, usually posted within an hour or two of being approved.

However, the Web site used for the incident provided only a fraction of the potential benefit for the information response. It was managed by one person, which meant it was limited by her availability and her work schedule. She was a county employee taking orders from the County Department of Emergency Management director. This represented few significant problems, but it became clear that as far as the Web was concerned it was this person who managed information flow. The Web address was that of the county and it was almost impossible for anyone to remember. Because it was the county's property and under their control, information items of interest to reporters or an interested public on things such as the company's safety record or background information on the company, and the ability to respond to questions or post frequently asked questions were simply were not considered.

As a result, after the emergency response began to evolve into a more long-term restoration effort, we developed a Web site for the company. Previously it did not even have a Web presence, being one of those companies not normally in the public eye. The company considered it an advantage to "fly under the radar." Why bring yourself to attention when everything is going along swimmingly? A Web site was therefore built to provide company information of interest to the public, the emerging activists, and the media. Only now, the information focused on this one large event that would probably forever define the company in the minds of the public.

Behind the Curve on Media Response

Few executives, or even communication professionals, can adequately prepare for the crush of eager, insistent reporters that automatically comes when a company or organization finds itself in the maelstrom. The media training experienced by many people who may find themselves under the hot lights or behind the microphones is valuable, but rarely comes close to putting stress on people like the real thing. This is particularly true when the person who steps in front of the camera knows that the questions may be intentionally aggressive, and the media may have already tried the company or organization in their own private courtroom, delivering a guilty verdict.

As in most real situations, the press conferences were only the tip of the iceberg in the pipeline incident. It started out with the reporters there trying to get the latest information from anyone that would talk to them. Then, it changed to phone calls, often repeatedly from the same reporter, and then from new reporters from the same publication or broadcasters who needed to be taken through the whole sequence of events one more time. It was not unusual for the same reporter to call the information center several times with the same question looking for different responders to provide different answers. Then it evolved into private and individual interviews by phone or in person with reporters intent on getting scoops or pursuing their special angles.

Each stage of the process involved a different type of reporting, and, as a result, should have received a different kind of media response. However, despite the best efforts of everyone involved, it seems in hindsight we were continually one step behind the reporters. When they shifted to a new game, we were still playing the old one. Unable to take a strong step forward in information management, the information center continued in a highly reactive mode rather than taking the opportunity to anticipate and keep pace.

It was my strong sense at the time that we were doing a good job of handling the crush. It is true, the team worked well together, and responded as efficiently and effectively as possible given the constraints we had. In retrospect, and particularly from the company's standpoint and with the advantage of hindsight, I later understood we were continually playing catch up. Aside from the effort to reach out early to the community influencers, there was little effort to get ahead of the curve and take proactive steps to directly communicate key information and anticipate the direction of coverage and public interest. It is a situation that perhaps many people would consider normal or acceptable, but as will become clear later, getting behind the media curve is frequently deadly in this new era of instant and direct communication.

THE "MEDIA FIRST" MISTAKE

How can putting the media first be a mistake to a communications professional, particularly a public information officer? Simply because there are a number of stakeholders who expect and believe they have a right to the absolute latest and most up-to-date information. If you give them unadulterated and truthful information before or at least simultaneous with the media, you gain appreciation and support. If you give it to them through the media, you are considered unresponsive or uncaring.

Some of these people have been mentioned already. They include anyone with a close connection to individuals who may have been personally and directly affected by the incident—family members, neighbors, coworkers, and relatives. They also include local elected officials, community leaders, and agency managers, such as the heads of state environmental regulatory agencies or the head of the local Red Cross. With an incident of sufficient scope, these people include the governor, U.S. senators, and state elected officials. When you start making a list, particularly when you think about these things in advance of an incident, you understand that there are quite a few people who have a reasonable expectation of getting direct and immediate information about what is going on. However, you only have a small crew to work with and there are all those reporters out there.

As in most situations like this, the communication team in this incident was involved primarily in meeting the needs of the media. One of the best things that we did, from the company perspective, was fax a letter from the president of the company to a list of local elected officials and community leaders within a few days of the incident occurring. This direct, personal, and relatively immediate information was very well received. It was in observing the value that was placed on this limited direct communication that helped me understand that most of the opportunities for such communication were passed up because they were impossible in our situation. Thorough direct communication would seem impossible to most in situations like that. Yet, in this new era of direct communication that task cannot be treated as impossible because the stakeholders do not see it as impossible. The new understanding going into such situations is that the media is one group among a whole number of groups of equals. That is a big change.

At the same time the information center was working hard to communicate with the media, a local activist group was communicating directly through a growing network of contacts. The environmental disaster, in addition to the human tragedy, awakened passions of many in the community, easily spurred on by the direct communication being conducted by the activist group who spotted an opportunity to provide leadership in a new cause: pipeline safety. The momentum built by this group proved to be a potent force in the weeks and months that followed and demonstrated that those involved in such incidents need to have and use the same direct communication methods as those who wish to take advantage of such situations to pursue their own agendas.

The Approval Process Slowdown

Now, now, now! Reporters and all those others looking for information aren't content with later and tomorrow. Urgency has always been a critical element of effective reporting, but with the advent of 24-hour instant news coverage, "now" takes on a more urgent meaning. After the best available information was collected and word-smithed into a new statement for the press, it needed to be "vetted" for approval. The final authority in a situation managed under the Incident Command System is the Unified Command. The Incident Command System, as we will see later, provides a highly structured and effective approach to crisis management. At the top are the Unified Commanders, unified in title at least. In this case, the Unified Command comprised leaders from state, federal, and local agencies, as well as a company Incident Commander. The Unified Commanders all needed to review and approve any public information prior to release. Getting their approval was one critical task, but the main issue was gaining the approval of attorneys. Even in the earliest days of the response, company attorneys were there, participating as part of the "away team." The proximity of a company attorney in the EOC made approvals relatively easy; things got much more difficult when multiple attorneys in different cities also needed to review information prior to release.

In the pipeline incident, the entire public information process, and particularly the approval process, was made considerably more challenging because of criminal investigations.

Within a half-hour after the explosion occurred, the company, at its headquarters in Renton, Washington, was informed by the U.S. District Attorney's office in Seattle that a criminal investigation had been launched. By law, the company was obligated to inform all its employees who could be subjects of the investigation that they should seek their own counsel and that the company, again as provided by state law, would not provide attorneys for them but would pay for the attorneys they chose. Soon, in addition to the company attorney or his or her replacements in Houston needing to approve public statements, a variety of executive attorneys from Seattle to Anchorage needed to review information before it could be released.

Some of the most difficult situations involving timing of press reports were a result of the time lag involved in getting approval from communication team members, including attorneys, who were not physically present at the information center. This difficulty, an exceptionally common problem in fast-paced information management, is a primary reason today's instant news environment requires a thorough change in policies and communication technology.

No Inquiry and Response Tracking

"Who was *that*?" we'd ask the communication team member who was handling a call from a particularly aggressive caller. That is how information about the inquiries coming in was shared. There was no way of keeping track of who was calling, what information they wanted, who provided the information to them, what was said, or even whether or not their questions had been answered or all promised responses had been fulfilled.

In such a situation, responders include staff from many of the agencies involved in the response. A public relations person from the company involved may find himself or herself sitting next to a public information specialist from the Coast Guard, the state environmental agency, or the Environmental Protection Agency (EPA). The ability to respond well and work together as a team is dependent on forming some level of group cohesion. Operating well together means talking to each other about the calls that are coming in, sharing information, asking questions, and learning from everyone else's experience.

This highly informal process would be much aided and strengthened by better inquiry tracking. Some communication plans require responders to fill out two-part forms logging each inquiry, the time it arrived, who responded, what was said, when the response was completed, and so forth. This is very helpful and aids significantly in quality control. However, as we will see, it only solves part of the problem. It is useful to those who are physically part of the response team in one place at one time, but does nothing for those members of the team who are not actually there.

No Way to Easily Update New Reporters

It is common to think that when a major news event occurs, you can't throw enough bodies at it. The problem with that thinking is the more bodies you throw at the response, the more difficult it is to operate with efficiency and control. The real answer isn't simply increasing the number of people handling the response; the answer is in controlling the work that the team needs to do and making the few highly efficient. One of the ways to control that work and enhance efficiency is to understand what creates much of the work.

A crisis communication team might receive hundreds of phone calls in a few hours or days, but that does not mean there are hundreds of reporters. Most calls come from the same media outlets, which call repeatedly. There are two reasons for this. First, the reporters want to make certain they are continually updated. It became a standing joke in the EOC when one of the more persistent and sneaky reporters made his hourly phone call: "It's Bernie [not his real name]. He wants to know if there's anything new." He was constantly looking for an edge on the other reporters and felt by keeping up a continual effort and talking to a different responder each time he could procure some information that would prove a scoop.

The second cause of the high volume of phone calls was the fact that reporters work on shifts, too. They didn't necessarily consider it their job to brief the reporters taking the next shift on the background to the accident and the latest information. That became the job of the hard-pressed information staff. This was where the lack of control over the Web site really hurt, because it could have been used considerably more effectively to provide background information. A technique that was used in this response did help considerably, and that was using a rolling fact sheet. As new information emerged, it was added to the previous version of the fact sheet, so reporters could see the progression of information over time and therefore get a better picture of the chronology of the event.

Despite this, it became clear that an effective information response required a much more efficient means of updating reporters new to the story as well as satisfying those looking for the latest information in a way that discouraged them from making their routine "Anything new?" calls to the EOC. If reporters knew that the very best place for them to be was at their computers watching their email and that no one was going to get any newer or better information than what came to them via email, it would do much to cut down on the number of calls coming into the command center. The more repetitive and unnecessary work that is eliminated, the higher the response quality will be from the limited resources available.

A New Approach Needed

There were important lessons to be learned from this and from every incident involving the news media, but the most important lessons go far beyond techniques, tactics, and strategies. There are three critical elements of a communication response to a public issue or newsworthy incident: people, policies, and technology. Interdependent and intertwining, each element needs to be effective and aimed at the single objective of protecting or building the organization's public trust through accurate, timely information.

As members of the public looking at a news story, we do not typically see the people hard at work behind the scenes, but they are people with all the dynamics of personality, turf battles, personal agendas, ambitions, and fears. One of the people I knew during the pipeline incident EOC experience was a woman who was a sometime competitor in the local public relations business. Clearly, she didn't like me. She was a volunteer with the local Department of Emergency Management and was helping out with the information process in the early stages. It was obvious in a very short while that she deeply resented and took some personal offense to my even being in the EOC. On more than one occasion when I was performing my duties she would aggressively challenge me, "Who authorized you to do that?" Instead of getting into an unnecessary turf battle that had nothing to do with the response, I just shrugged my shoulders and walked away. Fortunately, she was gone in a day or two.

There were a considerable number of personal battles going on. One public relations staff member for one organization felt another one was intruding on her territory, and in the midst of the craziness of trying to respond to the information demands, organization leaders had to make decisions about who should go and who should stay. Contract workers maneuvered and positioned to increase their roles and thereby lengthen their tours of duty. Sometimes the inherent distrust between corporate people and government agency staffs showed itself, and too often—not just in this instance, but in several others I personally observed—the tendency of some government agency people to engage in power games became painfully obvious and obstructed the work at hand.

Not only do personalities and personal agendas affect how the response is handled, but individual work styles and comfort levels do as well. This is particularly true when technology beyond pen and paper is employed. Even in this age, there are more than a few who say, "I'm comfortable with writing everything down on paper," and they simply cannot cope with any other way. This also applies to nontechnology issues. How media calls are handled and how the interaction works among team members depends to a considerable degree on the individuals who suddenly find themselves thrown together in an extremely high-stress situation.

Policies also determine outcomes. Has the company determined that it is its goal to be the first and best source for information? One of the most important factors is whether or not there are written policies for handling crucial decisions. Similarly, if there are written policies but they are not available to those who need to make decisions, they might as well not be written. In this particular incident, I was not aware of any written policies or crisis communications plan. Policies emerged, no doubt, and those policies began to set the course for public information strategies and decisions. However, they were policies based on the personal experience and approach of the person who emerged as the designated manager of the public information and public affairs efforts. As specific issues are explored, such as involvement of the legal team, timing issues, and dealing with mounting criticism, you will see how these policies were articulated and how they resulted in some of the perception and reputation difficulties that emerged.

We have already discussed the impact of technology on the response. That clearly is one of the central themes of this book. As we delve into that in greater detail, the relationship between people, policies, and technology cannot be forgotten. That was one of the most important things I learned in the weeks and months following June 10, 1999.

CHAPTER

2 Toward a Postmedia World

September 11, 2001 is one of those dates in American history that will be seen as a turning point and a defining moment. It may well be seen as the moment in which the Internet came into its own as a critical communication medium. If so, September 11, 2001 might be marked as the date in which we first entered the postmedia world, in which the monopoly long held by traditional mass media was broken.

We have come to take it for granted that news and information about the world will come to us via traditional media. Traditional media is expensive; the cost of entry is high. This is one reason why it holds such power. Few can afford the investment needed to build the transmitters, printing presses, and the infrastructure needed to deliver information quickly to thousands and millions of viewers or readers. The power of the media to control public opinion and influence the events of history is most clearly demonstrated by the fact that despotic governments have two main concerns: controlling the military and controlling the media. Company and organization leaders are very well aware that media have tremendous influence over the future of their enterprises. Positive coverage in the press or on national television can catapult a small company to instant success, whereas negative stories can bring even the most well-established and respected giants to sad endings in short order.

Traditional media are highly competitive. Audiences are the product they deliver to their customers, the advertisers. Audiences want and demand ever faster, more vivid, more exciting, more relevant information. Those in the news business employ the technologies, strategies, and infrastructure needed to meet this accelerating demand. Hence, the era of instant news. However, there is a vital element of the new era of instant news that is threatening the dominance of traditional media as the primary conveyors of public information. The Internet has quickly become a vital tool for the news organizations and an important means of distribution. However, unlike the printing presses and transmitters, the news organizations do not control the Internet. They do not make the rules, and they do not manage the application and use of the Internet. It has proven wild, uncontrollable, and resistant to almost all efforts to corral its use and misuse.

The Internet provides audiences with access to vital information at the speed of light. It provides a depth of information to the average viewer that was previously not possible. The Internet allows publication of information in all forms—audio, video, and text—at a cost that is unmatched by any other major media. It also provides the audience with one of the things they want most: control.

More than offering the audience what it wants, the Internet has a lot to offer broadcasters or publishers. All major traditional media have embraced the Internet as a critical adjunct to their broadcasting and publishing efforts. Much more than that, the Internet offers the ability to publish or broadcast to virtually anyone with a computer and a connection. The sources of news are multiplying. People with messages to send, with agendas to pursue, and with vital information to offer have discovered that they too have control.

Traditional Media and the Global Experience

An argument can be made that Internet use for public information on September 11, 2001 demonstrated that we are moving into an era of instant news dominated by this powerful new medium, but many argue that point. After all, September 11 is when virtually the whole world shared the unutterable shock of watching two of the greatest symbols of American prestige crash to the ground, taking with them the lives of more than 5,000 innocent people. They shared this experience via global television. This event made the global village idea a reality to much of the world in a way few other events have or could. The overwhelming sense of shock, horror, and sadness was felt in real time around the globe as people of many nations and cultures gathered around the nearest available television to stare numbly at the fireballs and clouds of dust. Those who found reason to exult in the collapse of these proud symbols of American economic, political, and military power also shared the experience. The pictures of exultation in the streets of Palestinian villages brought home to many in the complacent West the visceral power of hatred and wrath.

Good friends of ours were traveling in Europe at the time. After visiting the cemetery of forefathers in a small town in Switzerland, they heard of the events in New York and Washington. Without a television in their room, they found a lobby where Cable News Network (CNN) was broadcast. There they shared not only with strangers from Switzerland, but all of us back home, the same emotions of fear and disbelief. When we discussed this with them a week or so later, it was if we had both been at the scene together because we did indeed see it together. The same images, the same sounds, the same information, and the same emotions were separated by 7,000 miles of land and water.

In the days before the attack, approximately 160 million people were online around the world according to the Internet traffic analysis firm comScore Networks.[1] On September 11, 2001 that number declined by almost 30 million. Analysts suggest this decline was because many were spending time with traditional media, proof it seems, that September 11 was a high point of the media world, not the postmedia world. However, we must look a little deeper to see to what degree the Internet as means of interpersonal communication as well as a means of gaining immediate public information had already penetrated the hold the traditional media had on information.

Use of the Internet on September 11

A young woman from our community was working at the Pentagon on the morning of September 11. Like many others, for her the Internet had become a way of working and in some respects, a way of living. Someone in the hall said something about a plane hitting the World Trade Center. She immediately went to her normal news sites, but she couldn't get on. There was no access available to any of the common news Web sites she normally reviewed. Before she had the time to seek alternative sources, her world went dark as the third hijacked airliner crashed into her building just a few offices away. She escaped through the darkness and confusion.

Her experience of turning to the Internet was not unique and neither was her experience that day of finding most news sites inaccessible. The Internet is used every day for a wide variety of purposes: hobbies, entertainment, commerce, socializing, research, and so on. Gathering information about important events is only one use. On September 11, that changed. The millions of people normally using the Internet for all kinds of reasons suddenly rushed to the news sites and any other site that could give them the information they were seeking relating to this event. In fact, although the number of Internet users on September 11 declined, according to comScore Networks, the number of site visits jumped 240 percent, from 1 billion to 3.4 billion. The number of page downloads jumped 272 percent, from 5.7 billion to 21.2 billion. The number of minutes spent online jumped 245 percent, from 8.2 billion to 28.3 billion.

There is no question that television was the primary means by which Americans, as well as the rest of world, gained information about the terrorist attacks. Seventy-nine percent of Americans said television was their primary information source and Internet users reported an even higher dependence on television: 80 percent. One chat room contributor even suggested that computers should be turned off that day: "This is definitely a case where online sources are going to lag well behind TV. It's on all the major channels. I think all Americans should be let out of work/school to watch; it's major history. What I mean is that this is one of those times to abandon your computer and go turn on a TV. Any TV."

That so many did exactly that and yet the news sites, government sites and company sites involved became overburdened is the significant point here. During normal times, about 22 percent of the more than 100 million American Internet users gain some news via the Internet every day. According to an AOL/RoperASW Cyberstudy poll,[2] more than 75 percent of Americans who use the Internet use it regularly to gain news. By comparison, French online users are considerably more news hungry, with 96 percent using the Internet for news. On September 11, 50 percent of American Internet users went in search of news related to the event; of these, 57 percent were men and 43 percent were women. The use of the Internet to obtain news of the incident also resulted in the sharp decline in non-news use of the Internet. Dollar sales on the Internet dropped 58 percent that day and most other non-news uses saw similar drops. Interestingly, by September 20, most of these non-news uses of the Internet were back up to their pre-September 11 numbers, and some even showed increases.

The impact on news sites was very significant. Table 2–1 provides a quick summary of sites, numbers of visitors, and increases over normal use.

The young woman in the Pentagon who had come to rely on news sites to help keep her informed found those sites unusable on the morning of September 11. It was not just because millions of people were hitting these sites; their use of them was particularly burdensome. Fifteen percent of American Internet users got audio or video streamed to their desktops from these sites on that day, and 7 percent requested automatic email alerts that would provide them with up-to-the-minute information. Given this kind of use, it is not surprising that a great many people who turned to the Internet for information simply couldn't get it.

Keynote, which measures Internet performance and availability, reported that the major news sites were largely unavailable between 9 a.m. and 10 a.m. Eastern Daylight Time on September 11.[3] *CNN.com*, *NYTimes.com*, and *ABCnews.com* all showed 0 percent availability. USA Today, less hard hit than the others, showed 18.2 percent availability, and *MSNBC.com* showed 22 percent availability. To improve access, CNN reduced the size of its home page from a normal size of 255 kilobytes (Kb) to just 20 Kb. When these numbers are looked at in comparison with the large hit rate and the number of viewers accessing streaming audio and video, this question

TABLE 2.1 Increase in News Web Site Usage on September 11, 2001

Site	Millions of Unique Visitors	Percent Increase
CNN.com	11.7	680%
MSNBC.com	9.5	236%
CBS.com	1.7	819%
NYTimes.com	1.7	206%
Washingtonpost.com	1.2	225%
USAtoday.com	1.2	174%

arises: How many more people would have logged on if the performance had not been so degraded?

One indication is the number of people who gave up going to the news and other informational sites they were seeking. Among Internet users, 43 percent said they had trouble getting to the sites they wanted. Of those, 40 percent of those kept trying and eventually got there, 39 percent went to alternative sites, and 20 percent of those reporting trouble simply gave up on using the Internet to get the information they wanted.

The news sites were not the only ones to be hard hit. This is particularly significant because our interest here is directed at companies, organizations, and agencies that might some day find themselves at the center of strong public inquiry. The New York/New Jersey Port Authority Web site had a greater than 7,000 percent increase in unique site visitors. The Red Cross disaster relief portal had a 2,300 percent increase, and the FBI Web site had a 1,300 percent increase. What was the impact on performance? Normal site access time for the FBI site is less than one second. On September 11, it jumped to 180 seconds—three minutes. Not many people in today's broadband environment are going to wait three minutes for a page download. So the question again arises, how many more people would have used these sites at these critical times if performance had been better? What did those users of the Port Authority or Red Cross or FBI sites feel, when they expected that at all times they would be able to get the help they needed from their government agencies or the organizations who were supposed to be there to help them?

What about those who turned to American Airlines or United Airlines? After I returned to my office from SeaTac airport, where I was just boarding a flight to Los Angeles when the announcement came that all flights were cancelled, I personally tracked the performance of the United and American Web sites. It took a few hours to get back to my office and by then United already had a statement on its Web site providing the company's concern for the victims and an explanation of how to get information. American Airlines was inaccessible for some time, then provided a convoluted method of getting at information. It wasn't until well into the afternoon before a similar statement of concern showed up on its site.

It can certainly be argued that no one responsible for planning online resources for these news organizations, government organizations, or involved companies could be blamed for not anticipating an event of the scope of September 11. Yet the warning signs were there. On January 31, 2000, Alaska Airlines Flight 261 went down off the coast of California and 1.2 million people accessed the company Web site in just 13 hours. When the *USS Cole* was bombed in August 2000, more than five million visitors logged onto the U.S. Navy Web site. According to Keynote, the Bridgestone/Firestone Web site crashed when the company's tire recall was announced on August 9, 2000. The same thing occurred when more than 200,000 people per hour tried to keep up with the 2000 presidential voting action by visiting the Florida State Department of Elections Web site.

In the global village a company's Web site is a front door. If big news occurs, the residents of the global village do not wait for the newspaper to be printed. They do not even turn on their car radios and wait for the news, or get the latest from the six o'clock evening news. When news hits about your company or organization, those in the village will come knocking on your front door—by the millions, potentially. Will there be anyone there to answer, or will they find the door closed and inaccessible with a sign saying, "We don't want to talk"?

The Personalization of Media

The television audience on September 11, 2001 was enormous, certainly in the hundreds of millions and probably in the billions. Television delivered on its promise like at few other times in history. All the technology, planning, and investment made by news organizations around the world proved its value in delivering the vital information demanded by millions of viewers and readers. The global village was very much alive and sharing, for the most part, the emotions of shock, grief, fear, and anger. However, in this grand moment of traditional media triumph, the newcomer was demonstrating that the future just might belong to instant, personal, digital communication.

The Internet was not used just to get the latest generalized information about the attacks. The other primary uses of the Internet on September 11 most clearly demonstrate the unique qualities of this new medium and its advantages over traditional media. An analogy could be made between the rail system and the automobile. At the turn of the 20th century, the railroads were the undisputed master of transportation on the continent. An upstart alternative, the automobile was in its infancy. The automobile and its variants (e.g., the truck) in the early 1900s could hardly be envisioned to replace the well-established rail system. Cars and trucks couldn't carry virtually unlimited numbers of passengers and freight over long distances at the cost that rail could offer. However, automotive transportation offered some important advantages that proved to be significant enough to overcome the great economic advantages of rail. It was personal, flexible, and available in an almost infinite variety of packages: buses, pickup trucks, long-haul trucks, motorcycles, limousines, sports cars, and so forth.

The clear advantages of the Internet as a means of highly personalized communication can also be seen in the use of this new tool on September 11. The Internet is a remarkably flexible and diverse tool. Although 50 percent of Internet users on September 11 used the Internet to get news about the attacks, 69 percent used the Internet to obtain information related to the attacks. For example, one third of Internet users sought financial information that day, and almost one quarter did some research on Osama bin Laden and Afghanistan. Among other popular uses, 19 percent used the Internet to download pictures of the American flag, 15 percent sought information about victims or survivors, 13 percent checked on flight status of their flight or someone else's, and 12 percent visited commemorative Web sites while online.

Because we are looking at Internet use on that fateful day as a way of predicting how people will use it in the future, perhaps the most telling uses were more personal. These included receiving comfort, participating in discussions, and making direct contact or finding information on what happened to their loved ones. Nearly one third of American Internet users, or about 30 million people, used the Internet as a sort of coffee house, bar, or family room. They participated in chat rooms, used bulletin boards, or signed on for a listserv. Only about 5 million posted comments or observations; most simply observed discussions about what the United States should do in retaliation, expressions of sadness and comfort for those directly affected, and suggestions for how individuals could deal with their emotions after the attacks.

The telephone was the second most used medium of communication on that day. Whereas most Americans phoned family members or friends that day, the use of email was down corresponding to the number of people on the Internet and the focus on news. However, for a surprisingly high number of people, the Internet was crucial to finding relatives. About one third of the people in the United States that day who tried to reach friends or relatives by phone had difficulty because of the extreme traffic on the phone networks. Four to five million Internet users reported that they used the Internet to contact loved ones specifically because of difficulty with the phone. Even though individual site performance was degraded that day because of heavy traffic, Keynote reported that there was essentially no negative impact on the Internet infrastructure. Unlike other events, such as an accident in a railroad tunnel that cut some critical fiber lines, September 11 showed the Internet infrastructure was not affected by the dramatic increase in page views and downloads.

In February 2001, residents of the greater Seattle area experienced an earthquake that caused some significant damage in downtown Seattle. In the minutes after the quake, phone lines were largely inaccessible because of heavy traffic. Similarly, cell phones were largely unusable. Email became a critical link for a number of people, including a client in Houston calling to answer media questions about impacts on their refinery located in the area. The crisis management technology described in a later chapter, which is used to aid public communication, became an important means of internal communication when the phone lines were unusable. The Internet is both a mass medium and a highly personalized medium: It is the power and intimacy of personal conversation melded with the accessibility and wide distribution of television. It can have the dramatic impact of stunning visual images and sounds combined with the most personal and individualized messages. Here is where the automobile analogy starts to break down. The railroads did one thing very well after they were well established: moving people and goods en masse, very efficiently along a very specific route according to a very specific timetable. Automobiles eliminated the specificity of routes and timetables and emphasized flexibility, but could not come close to railroads for mass transportation. You might have a vehicle like a bus or truck that could come closer to replicating some of the railroads' advantages, but you would lose some of the personal, individual, and flexible characteristics of the car. The Internet can be both train and car simultaneously. One moment the viewer can receive the latest possible information in audio and video form, placing his or her eyes at the very spot of the action. The next moment, the user can send a prayer request (one third of Internet users used it for prayer on September 11) to a loved one or share highly personal messages that would otherwise be done only by telephone or in person.

It is this quality of the Internet as a public information medium—mass personalization we might call it—that promises to change the way news and public information are handled. News in the traditional media is largely linear, particularly television. In other words, you get what they want to give you on their schedule: News at Ten! There is a totally predictable and uniform stream of information: the top local story, a few major national or international headlines, a more in-depth local story, then weather, then sports, and a wrap-up, all interspersed with commercials at totally predictable intervals. As a viewer, you sit and take what is dished out—highly efficient, completely impersonalized, and totally outside of your control.

Newspapers and magazines are also linear but in a different sense. At least they can be scanned. The creators of *USA*

Today recognized the significant change in how people gained information when they designed the paper and maximized the opportunities for scanning. With a newspaper, the reader can at least control which stories he or she wants to read and to what degree. It is this flexibility, combined with printed material's portability, that has kept broadcast media from becoming even more dominant in our world. However, printed material is linear in the sense that the information it provides is made available to the user on the publisher's timetable.

Certainly, there's the "Extra" edition. The terrorist attack also revealed the anachronism of immediate print, at least in our community. *The Bellingham Herald*, our local Gannett daily, which publishes a morning edition, published a midafternoon "extra." Certainly the cries of "Extra! Extra! Read all about it!" on the streets of major U.S. cities in the 1930s and 1940s made all the sense in the world. People just didn't have universal, immediate access to their radios or TVs. On September 11, 2001 I saw a *Bellingham Herald* employee on the street corner waving down busy traffic trying to sell those extra editions. I reached down to my text pager that kept me updated on what was going on as the world was changing almost minute by minute, and chuckled. Printed material by its very nature is required to be linear in terms of publishing. It simply can't meet the immediacy of broadcast or the Internet or text pagers or telephone or personal conversations. When it tries, it is both humorous and sad.

A Multitude of Broadcasters and Publishers

Publishers and broadcasters have had great power and influence and that will continue for some time. The mass media are a symbol of a capitalist world because there is a strong relationship between capital and control. The person who had the capital to build a water-driven sawmill or a steel mill was the one who had control of the vital resource. When totalitarian states wanted to control the economies of their nations, they nationalized property and capital. When dictators wanted to control the minds of their citizens, they grabbed control of the means of information distribution: the printing presses and transmitters. Control those few things and you can control information. However, as Peter Drucker pointed out in his book *Post-Capitalist Society*,[4] these fundamental underpinnings of our world can and do change. Knowledge, Drucker said, is the new basis for wealth creation. It is the new wedge between the haves and have-nots and the new underpinning of society: knowledge and the Internet versus capital and mass media. The synchronicity spells a fundamental change in our world.

The public relations industry exists, in part, because companies and organizations that depend on public perception and understanding do not and cannot control the means to gain those perceptions. It is a source of high frustration for a great many leaders. One leading business owner in a Western state became so frustrated with the media promoting ideas contrary to his understanding of the world that he used his considerable wealth to buy one of the daily newspapers in his city. In that way, he could control what appeared on the editorial pages. He found that owning the second daily paper in a midsized city was not a very economical proposition and he ended up selling out to the leading daily. However, part of the deal was that he or someone he designated had access to that paper's editorial page on a scheduled basis. Although not every executive will take his or her desire for control of the media to that degree, most at one time or another could relate to the frustration that led to those expensive decisions.

A new response is emerging: If you do not like what the media are reporting about you or your organization, you can be your own publisher. In the postmedia world, everyone can be a broadcaster or publisher. The control the mass media have held over the distribution of information to millions is eroding. Certainly, the major media are leading the way in the use of the Internet for public information distribution. However, they do not control it, own it, or make the rules. Individuals or organizations with computers, or even just simple Internet appliances, can create audiences, distribute information, and facilitate interchange. The executive who was led by frustration to invest millions in a daily paper could have published his views and built his audience for much less with this new medium.

The instant-publishing potential of the Internet gained momentum in early 2002. *Blogger* is a new term that describes a new form of Internet publisher. The term comes from *Web logger*, a frequent Web surfer who created logs of the information and links found on the Web that interested him or her. The Web site *www.blogger.com* has become a central focal point for these Web publishers, many of whom have become well known for their commentary on contemporary politics and social issues. The postmedia world potential of these bloggers was noticed by John Ellis, himself a blogger, writing in the April 2002 issue of *Fast Company*:[5]

> Major news organizations breathed a huge sigh of relief when dotcom mania came crashing down. That meant that the barriers to entry in their markets were reerected and that their (mostly) monopoly positions were resecured. Now the bloggers are at the gates, eating into the media's value-added proposition. It's no small threat, because the peer-to-peer technology that underlies it is what the military calls a "force multiplier."

However, if the media-frustrated executive can assume the role of publisher and broadcaster, the instant news world of the Internet also means that the executive's opponents can do the same. In fact, the early days of the Internet are showing that organizations and individuals who can be described as accusers, activists, or attackers are leading corporations and organizations in their understanding of this important new opportunity. This is one of the major trends that makes this new instant news era an exceptionally risky one for those concerned with protecting reputations.

If the perception about you, your company or organization, your products or services, and your brand or brands is important to you, then it is vital that you understand how the means of creating those perceptions has changed and is changing. More is at stake here than the best way of getting people and packages from one part of the country to the other. The new era of instant news means that the risks to brand value and reputations are higher than ever. Where there are risks, however, there are also opportunities. Those who choose to understand, prepare, and proactively communicate swiftly and directly will see that the new era offers access and information distribution opportunities not otherwise available.

Marshall McLuhan might have somehow been envisioning the Internet when he wrote nearly 40 years ago:[6]

> Rapidly we approach the final phase of the extensions of man—the technological simulation of consciousness, when the creative process of knowing will be collectively and corporately extended to the whole of human society.

The process of knowing is what communication strategy is all about: What do others who matter know about you, your business, your character, or your activities? Many people "know" more about Enron and Andersen and their activities and character than they did before the stock crash occurred.

What they know is due to the media, the extensions of humankind. The Internet promises to bring that process of collective knowing to a new and different level. With the Internet, consciousness can and is being technologically simulated and much of human society around the globe can now participate as one in this process of knowing. Communication strategists and those leaders responsible for building and protecting reputations need to carefully consider the implications.

Endnotes

1. ComScore Networks, Pew Internet and American Life Project, Washington, DC, Oct. 10, 2001, p.8.
2. "Public Relations Tactics," Public Relations Society of America, New York, NY, April 2002, p.1.
3. Keynote Systems, Inc. Web site, *www.keynote.com*, Sept. 12, 2002.

4. Drucker, Peter, *Post-Capitalist Society*, New York: Harper-Collins, 1993.
5. Ellis, John, "All the News That's Fit to Blog," *Fast Company*, U.S. News and World Report, Inc., April 2002, p. 113.
6. McLuhan, Marshall, *Understanding Media: The Extensions of Man*, New York: Signet/New American Library, 1964. Used by permission.

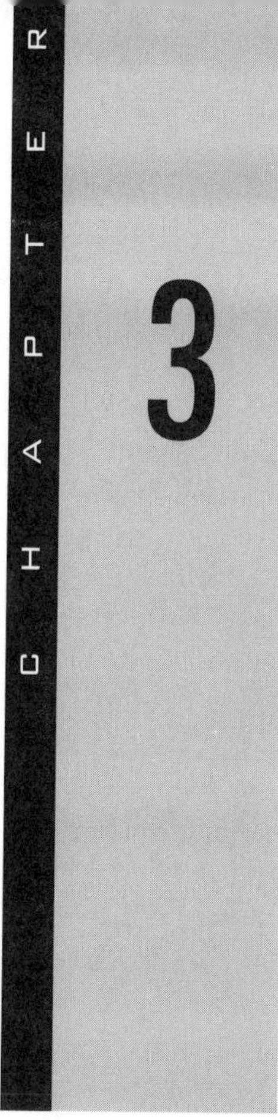

3 The New Audience

On Saturday, August 12, 2000, the Russian submarine *Kursk* experienced a devastating explosion in the Barents Sea. The explosion was heard by an American submarine on maneuvers and registered on a Norwegian-based Richter scale. The event started a tragedy of errors in public communication that demonstrated the Russian government was clearly not prepared for the openness and speed of the instant news world. Perhaps more surprising, it showed that the Russian population was prepared for this openness and speed—just a decade after the collapse of the Soviet Union with its totalitarian control over news media and public information.

The Russian Navy first reported on Monday, August 14 that the submarine was experiencing difficulties with flooded torpedo compartments after firing a torpedo. A little later a top Navy admiral reported that the submarine had been in a "serious collision." The Navy further reported that rescue efforts were "well underway." Russian President Vladimir Putin was vacationing near the Black Sea and the growing public outcry finally forced him to cut his vacation short—five days after the explosion occurred. In the meantime, the newly freed Russian press were scrambling to find answers and discovering for perhaps the first time since *glasnost* what it meant to be expected to deliver information to a nation demanding answers. Because real information was not forthcoming from those in the know, reporters followed the pattern of Western media by writing lengthy speculative articles and putting talking heads on television screens who argued about what might be going on and why it happened. And ironically, American news outlets noted their counterparts in Russia were lacking in real information and in place of that were featuring endless speculation. Some of it was coming from their own reporters, and much of it from an endless parade of "experts" offering their theories about what might have caused the accident and how they thought the rescue effort might have been progressing.

While on vacation, Putin had remained quiet and out of sight. Perhaps he decided the situation was something he should deal with when a local television station showed a meeting between Deputy Prime Minister Ilya Klebanov and family members of the sailors who many hoped were still alive. The meeting had barely begun when the angry crowd began to heckle him. It was left to Putin to tell the Russian people when he did finally return to Moscow that he had been informed very early after the accident that the chances for a rescue were remote.

A *Wall Street Journal* article summed up the instant news world lessons. The anger of the families was focused on the extremely poor communication, and they were complaining primarily that they needed to find out what was going on from the media. Meanwhile, the news media were complaining, with great justification, that the information they received was sparse, conflicting and inaccurate.

What makes this an interesting case study for the "now is too late" world is that the families—people with a very strong stake in this incident— had an expectation of information that was not realized. They expected and demanded that their government talk to them directly, give them the straight story no matter how painful, and not leave them with ill-informed speculators via the media. This was Russia in the year 2000! This was a people who have not had much of a concept of a free press in most of their history. The whole idea of *glasnost* or "openness" was a brand new and daring concept just 15 years earlier. Yet, in that short time, and due in large part to their exposure to the freedom and openness of information in the West, these people had built expectations that the Russian government and even their very enlightened new leader were not prepared to meet.

The damage to the young and dynamic new president serves as an object lesson for every executive and organizational leader who is not prepared for the new information demands of the instant news world. For many people in the world, this was Putin's introduction to the stage of public opinion. What opinion did they gain of this man? Was he someone unwilling to interrupt a vacation while his sailors were dying under the ocean and his people were clamoring for information and answers? He was, in crisis management terms, perceived as unresponsive. Unresponsiveness equals incompetence and irresponsibility in the heightened information expectations of this new world. The Soviet leader who had opened this Pandora's box of openness and who had learned his own painful lessons about the consequences of this reflected the opinion of the world when he publicly criticized the new president. U.S.-based cable channels noted this criticism and quoted Gorbachev, who called Putin's response inadequate.

RELEVANCE AND DEMAND

When events and facts matter to people, it has always been important to get information to them as quickly as possible. Expectations are what have changed. The new instant news world audience, largely because of digital technology and worldwide high-speed networks, has a radically different set of expectations about information than previous audiences.

This certainly is not the only time in history when technology has changed expectations—it is an absolutely predictable response to the introduction of innovations. We never used to expect packages to be delivered across country overnight. Federal Express changed our expectations, and as a result changed how everyone else in the package delivery business operates, including the U.S. Post Office and United Parcel Service. The Pony Express was a significant improvement in mail delivery—much faster than sending letters around the horn. However, the telegraph changed expectations about getting information, and it was only a short time later that the Pony Express, so recently seen as exceptionally fast, was viewed as slow and outdated.

The introduction of the telegraph, coming before the Civil War, provides an excellent illustration of the dramatic changes currently underway in the news business. Prior to the telegraph, news reporting was highly subjective, and unabashedly so, with most newspapers aligned with a political party or a point of view. Because the telegraph was a scarce commodity, the idea of pooling reports emerged and the Associated Press (AP) was created. The idea was that the basic facts would be sent to the various papers, where writers would then interpret those facts along party lines as was common in the newspapers of that day. However, some papers printed the AP reports with their bare-bones, information-only style. This led to a "just the facts" style of presentation that proved highly popular and quickly dominated news reporting. Civil War news coverage demonstrated the degree to which content and delivery mechanisms are strongly linked, and we see this same linkage now in the new world of instant news driven by technological change.

The demand for information can be extremely intense. It can overwhelm, for a period of time, the basic human needs, including food, sleep, and virtually all other pressing physical demands. Witness the families and friends of those lost in the World Trade Center and Pentagon attacks—many spent days wandering, asking, begging, and pleading for the slightest bit of information about what happened to their loved ones.

There is a relationship between the relevance of information, the demand for that information, and the expectation of being able to supply it in a timely fashion that can be simplistically charted, as shown in Figure 3.1. When information is highly relevant there is high demand—the higher the relevance the higher the demand. When this demand is combined with the belief or knowledge that the person or organization has the information and has the means of supplying it but does not, the frustration level escalates.

Relevance is directly related to what is important in the lives of the individuals desiring the information. Their personal security and well-being and the security and well-being of those closest to them are of the utmost importance. Relevance and demand for information is very high whenever security is at stake. Security, of course, can mean concern for physical safety, but it can also mean financial security and hopes and plans for the future. The families and friends of those people trapped in the World Trade Center had an extremely high demand for information, as evidenced by their unstoppable efforts to gain whatever bits and pieces of information they could find. The families and friends of the

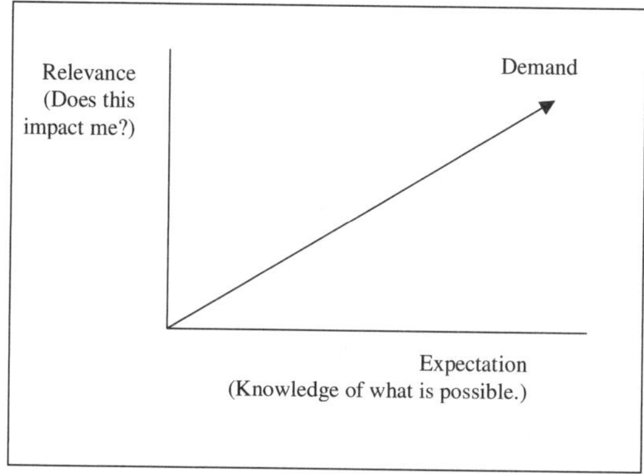

FIGURE 3.1 Relationship Between Relevance, Demand, and Expectations.

victims of the *Kursk* disaster, likewise, had a very high demand for information, particularly when there was still hope for rescue.

However, relevance and corresponding demand does not necessarily lead to frustration and anger. That reaction has everything to do with expectations. For example, suppose you hear that there is an accident in your community. You give it a passing thought, but there is little relevance based on that information because there are a number of accidents that occur and very few affect your security and sense of well-being. But, then you get some more information that indicates that this accident was in your neighborhood. Now you become a little more concerned because the chances that someone you know or care about was involved have increased. Next you find out that the accident involved a red Mustang. Your teenage son drives a red Mustang. Now the presumed relevance of the information is high and so is the demand. In fact, the demand is so high that, victims, like those relatives and friends of the World Trade Center and Pentagon attack, you will probably not rest, or eat, or even think of anything else until you get the information that you desperately need.

When you hear of the accident in your community, you do not turn on the national network news or CNN, because you have no expectation that they will cover some local traffic accident. You also probably do not expect your local television news broadcast, radio station, or newspaper to carry the information—most of them are far too slow for your information demands anyway. Where do you turn for information? Assuming no one is home, you might call your local police department or your local hospital. Should you discover they have the information you are seeking but don't provide it to you, your frustration level will go very high. There could be a host of reasons:

- "I'm sorry, we don't have the staff or budget to answer all requests for information about accidents."
- "I'm sorry but until our officers return from the field and fill out all their paperwork we simply can't release that information. Policy, you know."

- "I'm sorry, but we haven't installed radios or cell phones in our police cars, so at this point we just can't know what is going on."
- "I'm sorry, but until we can thoroughly investigate the accident and have all the information verified by our attorneys we can't tell you anything. It's important for us to be accurate and not cause anyone undue alarm, you know."
- "I'm sorry, but it is our policy to provide information about accidents to the media and they will probably have a report on this in about four hours."
- "Yes, we have that information, but the person who is assigned to provide it has gone home for the day. Could you call again tomorrow?"
- "Hold on just a second, OK, as soon as the person gets off the phone answering a call about a cat up a tree we should be able to get that for you. No wait, there's another call waiting about a stolen hubcap. Man, we're really busy. Sorry about that but we should be able to get back to you in a couple of hours."

When the demand for information is high, because the information being sought is of critical importance to the security and well-being of the person seeking it, and the expectation is that the person, company, or agency has the information needed and the capability of supplying it, but can't or won't, the resulting frustration is high. How would a parent confronted with technological, policy, or staff excuses perceive the police department? Uncaring? Incompetent? Bureaucratic? Would such perceptions extend to other areas of the department? When a newspaper article was written about the department's difficulty in capturing a local bank robber, isn't it more likely that the parent who had experienced frustration regarding information would determine that this was one more example of a poorly run organization?

When a company or organization is involved in an event that has a direct and immediate bearing on the safety, security, and well-being of anyone, there is now an expectation of information that is unprecedented. Even a few years ago, a company involved in an industrial accident, for example, was expected to provide information to the media according to their news cycles and directly to the family members involved. There was no technological capability and, therefore, no expectation to immediately communicate to employees, shareholders, an extended list of friends and families of those involved, community leaders, government officials, regulators, or even the media.

In the days before Gorbachev, the people of the Soviet Union had low expectations for information from their government even when events directly involved them or their loved ones. By the time Putin was president, their expectations were close to matching those in the West and they could be considered instant news world expectations. Key stakeholders, those individuals whose relevance is high, in the *Kursk* incident expected direct, immediate, top-level communication. Not hearing from Putin was a problem. They could have cared less that his holiday on the Black Sea was interrupted. Not hearing from him immediately was a problem, and not hearing directly from him was a huge problem.

Those are some of the key expectations of the postmedia world audience and one of the main reasons why it can be called the postmedia world. Stakeholders expect the following:

- *Communication from the top people involved.* They do not expect communication about things that affect their lives to be relegated to lower level staff or even communication professionals.
- *Immediate information.* If you have information now, they want that information now. Excuses about waiting until there is better information simply don't fly. They will understand the caveats, but they will not understand not being told what you understand to be true at that point in time.
- *Credible information.* The audience's demand for accuracy is primarily a demand that the source for the information be trustworthy. Understanding this helps deal with the potential conflict between speed and accuracy. They want to be told what you know now and they want assurance that you can be a trusted source of information. You will be trusted if you provide the information

you have, if you demonstrate that you are doing your utmost to meet their information needs, and that you will correct inaccurate or incomplete information as soon as you have better information. Primarily, you will be trusted when the audience knows that you take their need for fast, accurate information seriously and providing that is a higher priority to you than protecting yourself from negative consequences of that information.

- *Direct information.* Stakeholders do not want to be forced to get the information they need in the same way as everyone else who does not share their level of relevance. If relevance is high, so is the demand for direct information. One thing is certain: Expectations will increase. These expectations exist largely without factoring in the presence of the Internet and the widespread understanding that the Internet can facilitate speed, accuracy, and directness. Events such as the September 11 attacks and the widespread use of the Internet on an informal basis to connect, find information about missing relatives, and pass on information about what was going on during the attacks and the response will no doubt heighten expectations of the new audience.

Instant News Case Studies

The coast of Oregon was the scene of an international news story in 1998: the *New Carissa* incident. A freighter lost power, eventually becoming beached on the pristine coast of Oregon not far from Portland. The oceanside communities there are heavily dependent on the tourist trade, so the thousands of gallons of fuel oil on board threatened an environmental and economic catastrophe. In the postevent public information debriefing that I was able to attend, I learned about one growing expectation that is certain to increase in the instant news world.

Public information team members working for the Coast Guard and as representatives for the company that owned the freighter were inundated for weeks with reporters. The national media arrived in force and demanded a great deal of time and attention. The Coast Guard, which must deal with significant news events on a frequent basis and which has a generally excellent reputation for providing timely, accurate, and forthright information, was particularly inundated with requests for interviews, tours, and additional background information on topics such as "in situ" burning. After the event was over, an important issue was discovered. The local reporters, elected officials, and community leaders had felt shunned during the days of national and international media attention. As Lt. Chris Haley, Public Information Officer for the U.S. Coast Guard during the incident said afterwards, "After the Connie Chungs had left, we still had to deal with the local reporters and officials. And we needed to deal with them for a long time afterward. We discovered that they felt they had not been properly attended to while the national media were on the scene."[1]

The reality is that local reporters and stakeholders have a stronger vested interest in the events than the national audience, and they are going to be there for the long term. It is natural and understandable that communication officials on scene during an event might give priority to those media whose audiences are vast and whose impact on the reputations of those involved may be enormous. Combine this situation with increasing expectations based on the awareness of new technological capability and this demand for attention at all levels will only increase. It will be unacceptable to a local publisher when you try to explain unequal access by telling her that Tom Brokaw is more important. The good that might have been accomplished on the fleeting national level will be lost in the much less fleeting coverage at the local level.

Early in 2001, an accident occurred in a refinery in the United Kingdom. A prominent national newspaper there wrote: "[The company] had no information on the blast beyond that available from local police and fire brigade sources." What were these media folks expecting? That the company would communicate with them directly? That they should provide them more information than what they were getting from the local police and fire departments? Obviously they believed this was the case.

It was not the only information problem this company faced. Major industrial facilities have "fenceline neighbors," people who live near enough to the facility to be potentially impacted by accidents or other unpleasant events. They are definitely stakeholders when you define stakeholders as those people whose safety, security, and well-being are potentially affected by the organization. In talking with the company involved, it was their perception that they were quite busy after the incident providing information to the large number of media who were inquiring about it. When they finally got around to opening emails two weeks after the event, they discovered emails from fenceline neighbors asking whether or not they should evacuate their homes. Imagine the response of one of those stakeholders if they had gotten one of these messages in return: "Thank you for your inquiry. Your ideas, comments, and questions are very important to us. We will respond to this message when we are able." Or, two weeks after the event: "Thank you for your email. We hope that you were able to get the information you needed about evacuating from the local police. We apologize for not being able to provide this for you, but I'm sure you can understand that we were far too busy answering important calls from reporters to be bothered with your personal safety and well-being. Have a nice day."

These neighbors were using instant news world communications and expected a huge, multinational company to do the same. They were expecting direct, immediate, accurate information that affected their safety and well-being. What kind of success will the company have now in their community relations efforts in trying to convince these very important neighbors that the company is doing everything possible to ensure their safety and security? Who will be on the front lines of any activist activities aimed at driving this facility out of the area? Who will have a powerful story of corporate irresponsibility to tell?

Another major industrial accident involved the deaths of several people enjoying a recreational area. The two people within the company designated to handle the public information were inundated with calls. As they reported later, "We spent 24 hours a day responding to the media. That's all we were doing was responding!" This was a plaintive cry after newspaper reports came out claiming the company was "unresponsive." Why were they unresponsive? Because the reporters from those particular media outlets were not able to get through to these two beleaguered staff people, and as a result concluded that they were "unresponsive." And they were. If a reporter cannot get his or her question answered, no excuse in the world carries any weight. A question not answered in the time required by the media makes the nonresponder unresponsive.

The Role of the Internet in Changing Expectations

In 2000, members of Congress received more than 80 million email messages. That's almost 150,000 emails for each member. Most of those writing emails discovered, as I did, that the only response you can expect from your Congressional representative or Senator when you send an email is a totally oblivious automated reply making some promises that it is clear he or she has no intention of keeping. However, this is somewhat understandable, given the volume.

In mid-2001 more than 50 million Americans were sending emails each and every day. They sent messages to friends, families, coworkers, customers, pastors, teachers, and others; messages to their doctors' offices, fellow researchers, and someone in Turkey that they just bought an antique lamp from over eBay. Every imaginable kind of human relationship is represented every day in the bits and bytes flying through the fiber and wireless connections. They use this form because it is incredibly fast, inexpensive, and increasingly accessible. Although those opposed to computers and their role in our world view the use of electronic or digital communication as "impersonal," users of it see it as just the opposite. It is very personal, highly individualistic, and infinitely flexible as the incredibly wide variety of types of messages display.

The problem is that when we use this technology we expect a response that reflects the nature of the medium: personal, individualized, flexible, direct, immediate, fast, nonintrusive, and so on—mostly fast and personal. That's why getting an automated message three days after you sent an email to a senator's office is simply not acceptable. It might be all they think they can do, but it leaves the impression that either the senator has no concern for your communication, is technologically behind, or is simply incompetent and unable to adequately represent you.

There was a time when an American president invited his constituents to write to him directly and he sat down and replied personally to the hundreds of people who took him up on his offer. However, President Jefferson has been gone for some time. By offering email addresses to constituents, there is an implied invitation to write in, and with that implied invitation there is an implied promise of a personal, direct, and speedy response. That expectation is a long way from being fulfilled.

It is quite natural to assume that companies or organizations much larger and more powerful than you would have access to technology and systems at least equal to those you use from your home every day. That's why those people in England who used email to find out if their homes were safe to spend the night in must have been so disheartened to receive a message (presumably a form one at that) two weeks after the event.

The Web is billed as an instantaneous method of publishing information to potentially millions of users. That's why when a company Web site shows absolutely no recognition of earth-shattering events involving that company, it is quite understandable when those who go to that site for information come away with the impression that the company doesn't care or is incompetent. The impact of technology on expectations is all around us. We might create a reverse of Moore's Law, which described the exponential growth of computer performance. The dissatisfaction with outdated technology and methods will increase exponentially every 18 months, corresponding to the introduction of better, faster, cheaper technologies and methods. Once people understand that technology makes it possible for newsmakers to provide them direct, accurate, up-to-the-minute information about what is important to them, they will demand it. The more than 140 million Americans who are Internet users are very aware of the capability of this technology to deliver direct, personalized information, and they are demanding it.

Characteristics of the New Audience

The new digitally savvy audience has high expectations about information caused by their awareness of what the Internet makes possible. These expectations are explored in the following sections.

Speed

The first requirement is speed: Internet speed, light speed. The new audience has little or no tolerance for the fact that it might take time for those responsible for collecting, packaging, and distributing information to do their jobs. The major news media are coming to understand this. TV news programs and newspapers alike tout their Web sites as places to go to get more up-to-date and complete information. As we will discuss further, this has destroyed news cycles, which now occur every minute, 24/7. A *news cycle* is how long it takes to get information and post it up on a Web site. Once that is done, the process of using the slower methods of distribution can begin.

Most major media have come to understand this new demand and have responded to it, but newsmakers have only begun to comprehend what this demand for speed means for them. Crisis communications plans written for the media world are simply out of date. Instant news world crisis communications plans require virtually instantaneous communication of even the smallest amount of information available. This violates all the old rules, but such is the nature of change.

CREDIBILITY

The new audiences also demand that those providing information to them be completely believable. There is no tolerance for "spin" in the sense of selectively providing information or twisting the facts to leave impressions that are not truly reflective of reality. It certainly appears at first glance that there is a gross contradiction between the demand for speed and the demand for credibility. If credibility were truly equated with accuracy, that would be true. Accuracy, however, is only part of the picture. Credibility is the whole picture.

In the early reports of the September 11 attacks, there were a great many stories reported on national news outlets that were highly inaccurate. The presidential election crisis of 2000 was caused in part because of national news reporters making significant errors in calling the election for Bush, then Gore, then Bush, and so forth. However, these inaccuracies are for the most part quickly forgotten—if the party making the error owns up to it. We are remarkably forgiving of mistakes, but we are much less forgiving of the hubris that seeks to convince us that mistakes are impossible.

A case in point: Who is probably the least credible person on the 10 o'clock news team? I would suggest it is the weather reporter, because I have never seen a weather reporter stand up and say, "You know, on last night's news I predicted a winter storm with 70 mile-per-hour winds and, frankly folks, I was dead wrong. I apologize and I'm going to work even harder to take this maze of data that I get and give you a forecast that will be more reliable." Similarly, one of the greatest criticisms of newspapers is that they make an error on the front page that causes people or organizations a great deal of problems, but the correction is buried someplace on the inside and in such small type that only the most bored newspaper reader would ever come across it.

In an age of extremely high-speed expectations, those providing information need to understand that there is considerable tolerance for error, providing the errors are acknowledged and explained, and it is clear that there is a strong desire and intention to provide the best and most accurate information then available.

Priority on Communication

The new audience also has little tolerance for the many pressures on company or organizational leaders during a crisis event. When it is their family or loved one involved, when their personal security is at risk, there should be no higher priority for the top people in the company to deal with than the need for information. A company executive might disagree with this perception, but the problem is, as the saying goes, perception is reality. When a perception grows that the executive involved is too busy to tend to the priorities of those whose perceptions really matter, it can be a career-ending priority mistake. President Putin learned that lesson the hard way. Fortunately, he didn't make that mistake during a presidential election. New York City Mayor Giuliani might have understood this concept better than anyone in the last few years. The demands on him were overwhelming in the hours and weeks following the attacks on his city, but he made communicating with the citizens of his city—from individuals to the masses—his absolute top priority. As a result, he was not only *Time* magazine's Person of the Year, but has been used as a model for effective leadership in a crisis in the hundreds of crisis communications seminars and presentations offered after September 11.

One of the greatest challenges for communication professionals today is to convince the leaders of their organization that their own long-term viability and the ability of the organization to operate could very well depend on the priority they place on public communication during a time of crisis.

Direct

Perhaps the most significant and challenging expectation of the new audience is the demand for direct communication. When a voter who has supported an elected representative in the past election with financial contributions sends an email to that representative, he or she usually does so expecting a direct response that indicates that the elected representative has paid attention to them. It really doesn't matter to the voter that his or her message is one of 300 emails the representative received that day.

When a person in a house near a plant containing hazardous chemicals finds smoke from the plant billowing in her direction, she does not expect to wait to hear from the media about whether or not she and her family should evacuate, shelter in place, or not be concerned. She doesn't expect to have to wait to hear about it on the evening news or until she opens her newspaper in the morning. Family members of those in a plane reported down expect to be able to get information immediately and directly. Employees of a company that finds itself the target of a Securities and Exchange Commission probe expect answers on their desktops, now.

The new audience is well aware that the technology to provide direct and immediate information to those seeking it is readily available. Should a company, organization, or elected representative choose not to use that technology, it sends a signal that communication is not important. It is no longer a viable excuse to say, "We communicate to the public through the media." That is like saying, "We prefer to use a town crier, if you don't mind."

With the growing use of the Internet for public information, there is a very rapidly growing audience that expects information directly. An airline experiencing a tragic crash is certainly expected to communicate directly with family members of those on the plane involved, but passengers flying to that destination on tomorrow's flight also expect and demand direct information. Company leaders around the world expect it; shareholders large and small expect it. Members of the public with fear of flying and experts with special knowledge of a potential problem involved all expect direct communication. The fact is, everyone who knows that direct communication is possible because they are Internet users and because they have at least some level of interest in the event expects direction communication. This reality, perhaps more than any other, makes the instant news world a postmedia world.

Personalized

Like Federal Express in the package delivery business, *Amazon.com* and other e-tailers created an expectation for direct communication that extends to everyone in the public information business. Amazon tailors its offerings to me. When I sign on, the company shows they know my name, they know what I like, and presumably they know what I don't like. They make suggestions about products I might be interested in based on my previous purchases. They give me helpful hints about products based on other people's purchases. It is, in effect, intelligent technology that creates the benefits of personalized service. No one is fooled for a minute into thinking this is really personalized service—and a great many prefer the personalized service over the superefficient replica. However, for those who want the advantages of efficiency with at least some degree of pseudopersonalization, this is a huge step forward. This creates a huge problem for providers of public information because when it is known that technology can provide this kind of personalized, customized information, it will be expected and demanded.

The demand for personalization is expressed on several levels. One is the growing understanding that technology can make providing very specific, very relevant information possible. This eliminates the need to wade through a lot of extraneous material that might be of interest to someone else. With an understanding of the capabilities of technology, there will be no patience for that. Information must be custom tailored—if not to individuals then at least to groups and subgroups. Investors have a need for different information than fenceline neighbors. Employees have a different need than national reporters. However, personalization also means the information is personal. As mentioned earlier regarding the *New Carissa* incident, local reporters and dignitaries expect to be treated with at least as much respect, deference, and time as national reporters or the state governor. A communication plan that does not take into consideration these very high expectations is almost certain to result in reputation damage, even though every other aspect of the communication plan might work to perfection.

The News at My Hip

When I think of the instant news world and the rapidly expanding expectations of hundreds of millions of people around the globe, the picture that comes into my head is not the millions hunched over their computers in spare bedrooms and office cubicles around the world. It is the commuter in her car or riding on his train carrying a text pager that first comes to mind.

On September 11, 2001, like everyone else, I can remember exactly where I was when I heard the news. I had just received my boarding pass at an Alaska Airlines electronic kiosk. I was at SeaTac airport bound for Los Angeles. I checked the boarding time: 6:45 a.m. Pacific Daylight Time. I made a quick trip to the restroom, expecting that by the time I returned to the boarding area, the flight would already be boarding. Instead, when I returned I heard the tail end of an announcement from the service counter saying that all flights were temporarily on hold because of terrorist activity. I remembered a very brief announcement on the radio just as I was parking the car about some early reports of an airplane hitting the World Trade Center. Automatically I turned to the CNN Airport Network News monitors hanging from the ceiling in the boarding area. The screen was blank. I reached for my text pager. That's where I learned the news.

While others waited further word from the service desk, I followed the breaking news on my text pager. From that I deduced that it was not likely that we would be flying soon. Not long after, the announcement came that all flights were canceled indefinitely. Planes that had already pushed back from the gate were being called back and passengers were being deplaned.

When someone has a text pager with instant news service, not only is the newspaper a ridiculously slow way of receiving news, but even the instantaneous world of broadcasting begins to look outdated. People simply don't have a radio or television with them all the time and it is frequently not convenient to park in front of a tube—either computer or television.

As information technologies further combine so that a wireless phone is indistinguishable from a PDA, which is indistinguishable from a Internet device allowing two-way text or voice communication, expectations for information delivery will be significantly greater than they are now. This means that the challenge of getting the right information to the right people right now will be all that much greater.

Endnotes

1. Used by permission.

CHAPTER

4 How News Is Changing

In the media world it has always been clear who is in the news business and who is not. News businesses provided news, whereas non-news businesses did not. News businesses get paid, usually by advertisers, to collect, package, and distribute information of interest to news audiences. Non-news businesses or organizations exist for other purposes—perhaps to deliver a public service such as environmental protection, or to produce commercial goods such as fertilizer. Providing news is simply not the reason for existence for these businesses. In an instant news world, that distinction is getting increasingly fuzzy.

In the instant news world, companies and organizations that find themselves at the center of public interest will be expected to collect, package, and distribute the news because the Internet user with high relevance and demand requires it. The U.S. Navy is in the business of protecting our nation. They do not get paid for providing news. However, for the five million people who went to the U.S. Navy Web site after the *USS Cole* was bombed on October 12, 2000, the fact the Navy is not in the news business was of little interest. Those five million people expected the Navy to provide them with the information they were seeking about who, what, when, why, and how. Some might say that this is just information and not news. The distinction is lost on the stakeholder or news viewer who simply wants to know what happened. Similarly, when an airliner goes down, the airline is expected to provide the news even though there are hundreds of reporters and news agencies fighting hard to provide the fastest, most accurate information needed to build and keep the audiences needed to keep advertisers happy.

Government agencies are increasingly finding themselves to be news packagers and distributors. September 11 certainly demonstrated the high degree of interest shown in government Web sites relating to the attacks. Government news sites such as the FBI slowed to a crawl under the burden of increased traffic. The U.S. Postal Service suddenly found itself a primary news source for information about the anthrax attacks. In less than a month the Postal Service saw its Web traffic burst from a few hundred visits a week to nearly 300,000. During Operation Enduring Freedom, the antiterror campaign in Afghanistan, viewers could go to their television news programs or the Web sites of commercial news organizations such as *CNN.com*, *Foxnews.com*, or *MSNBC.com*, or they could go directly to *www.defenselink.mil/news*. There viewers could get the press releases issued by the Department of Defense and see videos of press conferences. Information there was available as it was presented, which can be substantially different from what is conveyed after the information goes through the packaging process. If anyone has seen an actual press conference, or even watched an entire press conference on C-SPAN, the difference in meaning between what actually is said and what is used in the few-second sound bite that ends up in the packaged news can be astonishing.

Competition among news providers is expanding. Most companies, organizations, agencies, and individuals—those I am referring to as newsmakers—would much prefer the news businesses do the job of providing the news. They don't want to get into the business of supplying public information in the sense of profiting from it by attracting advertisers, nor do they want the requirement of providing information to detract from their reason for existence. However, the new audience will not allow them that option. When the information is relevant and demand is high, the burden is put on those people or organizations in a position to provide the fastest, most accurate, most up-to-the-second information. We instinctively understand that the news media are rarely, if ever, the first to know and they do not necessarily have the most complete knowledge. They are intermediaries; they go in between; they mediate the news; they are media.

There are executives and perhaps even communication leaders for newsmaker organizations who are thinking right now, "We don't have to accept this situation. We have a choice about whether to provide the information directly or go through the news media." The problem with that thinking is the impact on reputation. We have seen the impact on the reputation of the Russian government and President Putin in particular when he failed to meet expectations about providing direct and accurate information. We have repeated examples in corporate communication history of the devastating impact on brands when companies do not communicate with the speed, directness, credibility, or humanity that today's audiences expect. This is in the very early stages of the postmedia world when it is still commonplace to get news from the news packagers. When more news consumers become Internet veterans, when the Internet is freed from the prison of spare bedroom PCs, and when universal, full-time, wireless access is commonplace, those companies or organizations that choose to communicate through intermediaries will be viewed as heartless, oblivious, backward, or all three.

For those willing to allow the news media to do the communication job for them, Enron and particularly Arthur

Andersen provide uncomfortable object lessons. Andersen's situation was a reputation crisis that became a financial crisis, unlike Enron's, which was a financial crisis that became a reputation crisis. The reputation crisis for Andersen was precipitated primarily by decisions made by some to destroy documents needed in the Enron investigation, but it was greatly exacerbated by a slow, uncertain, inconsistent, and indirect communication response.

There is another aspect to this growing competition among news sources that will cause many newsmakers to rethink a strategy of simply allowing the news businesses to be the source of information about the organization: opponents. The competition for news audiences is not just among news businesses, and not just among news distributors and newsmakers. Add opponents to the picture, including activists, competitors, disgruntled former or present employees, busybodies, or anyone with an agenda that conflicts with yours. All these are now potentially equipped with technology that levels the playing field for gathering and distributing information in a way that wouldn't have happened two decades ago. As you will see in the next chapter, opponents are becoming very aware of the instant news world reality that everyone is a broadcaster. They are grabbing the microphone, building audiences, and communicating directly. They are not content, for the most part, to allow the media to do their speaking for them.

News audiences in the instant news world have a dizzying array of options for information about an event relevant to them. Information or news about the event can come from traditional news media, traditional media using nontraditional channels such as Internet news sites, the company or organization involved in the incident, opponents, politicians weighing in, bloggers (the new form of instant news journalists), activist groups, disgruntled employees, and so on. All are competing for the fleeting attention and fickle perceptions of the news audience. The outcome of the competition could have significant consequences.

Understanding the News Business

The purpose of this chapter is to better understand how news businesses compete with each other to provide today's audiences with what they want. Understanding the news packagers and distributors better accomplishes two important purposes for newsmakers: It enables the communication team to provide the journalists with what they need to do their jobs, and it helps newsmakers cum news packagers properly package the news in ways today's audiences expect.

It is a strange but powerful testament to the American democratic and market system to have one of its most important democratic institutions be a resounding market success. Imagine if the military or regulatory agencies such as the EPA found a way to effectively do their job and make a profit without taking any tax dollars. Yet, few would argue that the news media, the fifth estate as it is sometimes called, is an essential pillar of our open, democratic system. Aside from the minor exception of public broadcasting, it is not supported by tax dollars but instead generates huge profits and represents a sizable portion of the national and local economies. That freedom from taxation, and therefore from government ownership, is central to the news media's ability to do its job.

The news media's diversity, ubiquity, and competitive instincts have, for the most part, served America exceedingly well, and not only America, because CNN and other major news outlets have become world brands, delivering news and information around the clock to audiences around the globe. This sharing of information and vicarious experience, through television in particular, has created the global village predicted by Marshall McLuhan. However, he would likely be amazed at the depth of change created by this universal information sharing that we now refer to as *globalism*—quite possibly the most important trend of our generation.

The news business as it stands today is considerably different from the news business of the past. That is obvious; what is not so obvious is the continual change that occurs in how people charged with delivering public information do their jobs. As consumers of their product, we take things pretty much as they come, and go about our lives and work without giving too much thought to the ongoing struggle to attract us as an audience. We take it as a given that automobile and computer manufacturers are continually designing new products and innovations to sell us and gain a competitive edge; we don't usually view the news business as competing in similar ways.

A fundamental factor driving change is competition. This will continue as the driving force as long as the news media are free from government support and control—a long, long time, we hope. Understanding this competition will help newsmakers in the instant news world respond more effectively to the demands of both traditional media and news consumers.

News executives have a clear-cut task: Assemble an audience that advertisers will be willing to pay good money to reach with their commercial messages. The audience must have qualities that the advertisers desire (money to spend above all) and must be in sufficient quantity to make buying advertising reaching that audience a reasonable investment for the advertisers. Accomplish this task and the news executive will have the resources available to continue to build the audience. Fail at it, or succeed less well than competitors, and the resources to gather the news and effectively package and distribute it via printing presses and transmitters will be very limited.

There are a great many options available to news executives trying to squeeze out a few more viewers or readers for their products. A few years ago, one regional television station clearly was in some ratings difficulties and decided it needed to make some changes to recapture lost viewers. The employees must have conducted a brainstorming session to do some "out of the box" thinking, for when the changes were presented to the local audience the advertising proclaimed: "On March 10 [name of station] comes out of the box." The "out of the box" message was hyped well beyond curiosity, almost to the point of nausea. When the great day arrived, they had taken away the desk from their news anchors, who were now "free" to roam the set and stand and deliver the news. In no time audiences found all the random movement distracting and uncomfortable and clearly the anchors were more comfortable sitting behind a desk where they could rest their papers and focus on delivering the news rather than figure out where they were going next. The "box" came back and the television station went on to competing for local viewers on the same basis as it always had.

Competition for news audiences within each audience segment is focused on four key attributes: speed, depth, credibility, and entertainment values. This has probably not changed since the days when two different people in the same town put out a regular town newspaper, but the emphasis has changed considerably. As you will see, entertainment values are at a premium in this day of intense audience competition.

Speed

There are some old hands in the public relations business who continue to hold on to the belief (or is it vain hope?) that the media operate around news cycles. For younger readers, I feel compelled to explain what a news cycle is. News cycles operate around deadlines when publications or broadcast news shows operate on a regular schedule. If a newspaper comes out at 5 a.m., a reporter's normal deadline might be 8 p.m. that evening. Unless it is a huge story, anything coming in after the deadline is going into the next news cycle. In broadcast, where news cycles really drive timing of releases, to make it on the 6 p.m. news, reporters needed to have the information a couple of hours in advance.

News professionals and communication professionals reading this will say that the couple of hours aren't reality any more, and this is exactly right. Competition, cable television, satellite broadcasting, and the Internet have combined to make news an instantaneous business. Virtually every local television news program features live feeds with satellite trucks and news helicopters flitting about the territory, setting up in just minutes, interviewing just about anyone they can get their hands on and running a "breaking news" story. Virtually every newspaper, local TV station and local radio station has its own news Web site where the latest news is uploaded regardless of the schedule for printing or broadcasting.

The national news competition in the past used to exist among the three major networks at the 6 p.m. news hour. That audience has shifted to a considerable degree to the all-news channels on cable television. CNN pioneered the concept and came of age in the 1990–1991 Gulf War, and now the competition is fierce among the 24-hour cable news channels, which now include two CNN channels, MSNBC, Fox News Channel, and CNBC.

The primary focus of this competition is speed. There is a sense of urgency and immediacy surrounding all the coverage. The quality of the image doesn't matter nearly as much as the image being live or as close to live as possible and as close to the scene of the action as possible. In the ultimate picture of this new style of immediacy, reporters sometimes put just about anyone on camera that they can who might have even a remote connection to the event, until finally they resort to interviewing each other while waiting for real news to show up on the scene. In another somewhat silly attempt to convey immediacy, television stations will show a reporter amidst lots of equipment in their "satellite center" to show they are providing the news even as it comes off the satellite. Local reporters turn back to one of the monitors in the "satellite center" to view what is coming off the satellite feed. What makes this silly is any of the information coming in to the news channel can just as well be fed to the anchor desk, but putting a live reporter in the "satellite center" somehow replicates some of the immediacy of being on location. Of course, it also provides an alternate set to add to the entertainment value.

Broadcast's strength has always been speed and immediacy. Print journalism suffered in comparison. Occasionally there are ludicrous examples of how even daily print publications attempt to compete on a speed basis, such as the example of our local daily hawking an "extra edition" on the streets following the September 11 attacks. Most newspapers understand that readers probably have already heard or seen the basics via radio or television by the time they pick up the morning or evening paper. When readers pick up the paper, they usually have a few minutes or even longer to relax, enjoy the process of reading, and get information that the broadcasters can't fit into their 30-second sound bite reporting style. Print publications almost always compete on the basis of depth rather than speed.

Depth

Years ago I went into the publishing business. I bought a monthly business publication that covered our local area with a population of about 150,000. The only daily newspaper in town showed a strong distaste for competition of any size. I knew they would come after me with everything they had. How would I compete for the precious minutes the people in the business community spent reading? If I couldn't deliver an audience, I wouldn't be able to attract and keep advertisers. I knew I couldn't compete on real news stories—the newspaper would beat me there every time. I couldn't compete on in-depth business trends, helpful advice, economic news, or anything like that because the other national and regional business publications had far more editorial resources than I ever would. I concluded the only thing I could compete on was depth: depth of information about what was going on with local companies, depth of analysis about local business trends and conditions, and mostly, depth of information about the community. Based on my training in college as a drama major, I was and still am convinced that we are mostly interested in people: first, ourselves; second, people we know; third, people like us, or people we can relate to. I focused the business publication on the people involved in the local business community and dedicated the magazine to building a real community of business people. Even though the local daily soon launched their own "business magazine," they couldn't match mine for depth and soon gave it up.

The New York Times' famous slogan shows perfectly the commitment to depth: "All the news that's fit to print." *The Wall Street Journal* likewise competes on depth of business-specific coverage. National news magazines compete against other print publications such as daily newspapers by going one step further in depth. Each week, *Time*, *U.S. News & World Report*, and *Newsweek* dig deeper than the newspapers into the major stories of the day.

Here's the rub with the Internet: It has the capability of providing information at speeds considerably greater than the most efficient cable news organization and in unlimited depth. The cost of publishing a few extra pages of *The New York Times* is considerable. The cost of adding 200 extra pages to *CNN.com* is virtually nothing once the story is written. News organizations are demonstrating that they clearly understand this by using their traditional media print pages and broadcast minutes to direct readers and viewers to more in-depth information contained on their Web sites.

Credibility

"Don't cry wolf!" should be the first lesson taught in journalism and public relations schools. The ancient wisdom of Aesop very much applies to those who would provide public information in our day as much as Aesop's. As the little shepherd boy discovered, an audience quickly turns a deaf ear to the purveyor of information who proves to be less than credible. As another saying goes, "Fool me once, shame on you; fool me twice, shame on me."

To that degree, all media compete on the basis of credibility. As newsmakers evolve into news packagers and distributors in the postmedia world, credibility will be a primary concern. A corporation or organization that proves less than respectful of the truth will quickly cede its right and ability to communicate directly to the public to others who have no interest in protecting the organization's reputation. The role of credibility in communication was clearly understood almost 2,500 years ago and articulated by Aristotle with clarity that has never been improved. He said there were essentially three modes of persuasion: *logos*, or appeal to logic; *pathos*, or appeal to emotion; and *ethos*, or appeal to the credibility of the speaker. Of these three, there was no question in his mind about which was the most effective: The perception the audience has of the credibility of the speaker outweighs every argument of logic or emotion. That credibility can never be compromised.

However, credibility is much more than being trustworthy with the truth. You don't see news businesses competing with each other by saying, "You can believe us, not like the other guys," or "We tell the truth, they don't." They do, however, compete for credibility in other ways. One of those is by the particular slant that they take, because credibility, after all, is subjective. Senator Ted Kennedy would not be the most credible speaker to a Rush Limbaugh audience and vice versa. Credibility, therefore, has a lot to do with the particular biases of the audience.

Most major news organizations do their best to be credible to the widest possible audience in various ways. One is to be cautious about taking positions and to try to be completely objective, even though they understand that complete objectivity is impossible. Another is to intentionally balance the biases of their audience by including competing voices. On television today you see frequent examples of a conservative and liberal cohosting a commentary program, or a radio station featuring a conservative talk show host one hour and a liberal host during the next hour. Other news outlets simply state the philosophical basis they operate from and do not try to maintain credibility with all groups. Publications put out by radical environmental groups would not have much credibility with development- or resource-oriented business readers, and neither would *Oil Exploration Today* have a lot of credibility with members of Greenpeace.

Another important aspect of competition based on credibility is accuracy. As mentioned before, accuracy and credibility are not exactly the same thing. Certainly, no one providing public information will be believed if they consistently provide inaccurate information. The Russians certainly found that out in the *Kursk* incident. However, there is a head-on battle between speed and accuracy, and today's audiences put a premium on speed. Many communication professionals who have been at this business for a long time have not noticed this very significant change. Getting it right is always more important. I am very aware that I am breaking every existing rule by suggesting that speed comes before accuracy. It does, with this condition: To maintain credibility when accuracy fails, a news provider must show that every possible effort was made to get the correct information and must be willing to admit that inaccurate information was provided.

Serious anger was expressed by news viewers during the 2000 Bush–Gore election when the major news organizations first called the Florida vote for Bush, then Gore, and then determined it was undecided. Undecided, indeed—it was for weeks. This was relevant information at nearly the highest level when it comes to national stories, and essentially every major news organization blew it. Calling an election before all the votes are in is a response to the demand for news speed. The only way the news organizations recovered any credibility was by explaining, in some detail and with a significant amount of repetition, that all news organizations contracted with the same organization to provide exit polls and these exit polls proved to be somewhat inaccurate. Although not entirely satisfactory, this explanation covered some things that were otherwise incomprehensible, placed the blame to some degree somewhere else, and showed that the news organizations were doing their best to provide accurate information. I use this relatively extreme example to make a point: Would any news organization today, given this situation, refuse to report what they know until they are absolutely sure of the accuracy of the information while all their competitors go forward? I doubt it. Speed comes first. To use another saying, "It is better to ask forgiveness for being wrong than ask permission to be late."

Even though the problems in news coverage accuracy were so severe that congressional hearings were held on the subject, the September 11 attacks showed that those same news organizations remained committed to speed versus accuracy. Early reports were consistently wrong, and in some cases seriously wrong. This can be easily understood given the confusion of the events, but news organizations demonstrated that they will go on the air with what they have, clearly explaining that it is incomplete, unverified, and potentially wrong, rather than risk being perceived as too late with the news.

This is a critical point, and a difficult one, for many of today's communication practitioners, who have long operated under the entirely reasonable assumption that accuracy is the heart of credibility and therefore always takes precedence over speed. The message in plain terms to organizational executives and leaders is this: If your public information officer is pressing you to get the information out now, in spite of the fact that not everything is buttoned up the way you want it to be, consider the consequences. Between a rock and a hard place hardly describes this dilemma, but at least you know how the professional news businesses are dealing with this same dilemma.

Infotainment

In 1984, communications professor and critic Neil Postman wrote a book called *Amusing Ourselves to Death.*[1] Subtitled "Public Discourse in the Age of Show Business," the book railed against the intrusion of entertainment values into how we deal with important issues. No doubt, Postman would be amazed at how the news business has been overwhelmed by the entertainment business 15 years later. Where there were once relatively clear lines between information and entertainment, now no lines can be drawn. This is the most important and influential trend in public information and of even greater consequence to the potential newsmaker, packager, and distributor than the accelerating speed caused by the Internet and the unremitting demand for credibility.

There are a number of trends that have converged to create the current situation. Some of these are driven by culture and others by the competitive nature of the news business. Activism, the politics of attack, and growing negativity toward big business and globalization are important contributors. Add these important cultural factors to the reality of media and news competition, and it is not surprising that what has emerged is a blending of information and entertainment that I refer to as *infotainment*. Infotainment in its various forms is by far the dominant mode of public communication today, and as a result it must be clearly understood by executives and communications professionals who must deal with contemporary journalists as well as today's news audiences.

THE END OF THE NEWS EXECUTIVE

The news executive has always been in a tight spot. He or she has two masters to serve: the news audience, which is the "customer" for the news product, and the advertiser, who is the customer for the audience the news product delivers. Serving two masters, as ancient wisdom tells us, is impossible. However, the old-style news executive, who had either complete control of the business or at least a great deal of influence, made compromises based on a firm commitment to the value of legitimate journalism. In major network and cable broadcasting, true news executives no longer have that position. Ownership and control, for the most part, has transitioned to executives who control corporations with many different business elements and who live by the quarterly report dictum of today's stockholders. General Electric now owns NBC, AOL Time Warner owns CNN, Viacom owns CBS, Disney owns ABC, and News Corp. owns Fox. A former chief executive for one of these new network owners commented that none of the new leaders of the major networks had a news legacy.

Kim Masters, author of a January 2002 *Esquire* magazine article, stated, "The news divisions are now little pieces of big machines and the people who run those big machines are hardly news junkies." Larry Grossman, a former president of NBC News who tangled with Jack Welch, the famed chairman of NBC owner GE, complained, "All these companies have fallen into the hands of guys who couldn't care less about [news] and are dealing with it because it's a hangover from things past." Jack Welch, who fired Grossman, countered, "He operated under the theory that networks should lose money while covering news in the name of journalistic integrity."[2]

This battle is at the heart of the infotainment trend that drives much of the news business today. From a corporate performance standpoint, executives can hardly be faulted for presenting programming that delivers the best audiences for advertisers, but what happens to serious journalism in the process? The question was played out on the national news when in February and March 2002 a public battle ensued between CBS and ABC over replacing the highly respected *Nightline,* hosted by Ted Koppel, with the late-night comedy program *Late Show* with David Letterman. In fighting to keep his job and his program, Koppel resorted to the unusual step of requesting and receiving guest editorial positions in major newspapers. The op-ed piece was titled "Network News Is Still Serious Business."[3] Koppel spent a good deal of his limited space explaining how profitable his show has been for ABC, but conceding that *Late Show* would generate more profits. He stated, "It is perfectly understandable that Disney would jump at the opportunity to increase earnings by replacing '*Nightline*' with the more profitable David Letterman show." What clearly got under Koppel's skin was the comment by a corporate executive that his news program was no longer "relevant." Koppel wrote, "When, in short, the regular and thoughtful analysis of national and foreign policy is more essential than ever—it is simply wrong to describe what my colleagues and I are doing as lacking relevance."

Relevance wasn't really the appropriate word. What the executive probably meant to say was that *Nightline* was not entertaining enough, at least not enough to compete financially with Letterman. As it turned out, the negotiations failed and Koppel continues with his "irrelevant" program.

The Prime-Time News Magazine

We have seen, in the past few years, that news can compete very effectively with other forms of television entertainment. To do so, however, it has adopted many of the methods and techniques of entertainment, creating infotainment.

Prime-time television is now dominated by news programming. CBS's *60 Minutes* created the *news magazine* format, and a host of imitators followed. This new programming format proved to be very successful for CBS and *60 Minutes* is one of the most successful, longest running television programs in history. ABC's *20/20* and *Primetime Live*, NBC's *Dateline*, and a number of cable television imitators noted the success and came up with their own versions. In the process there was a convergence of news and entertainment: Prime-time news programs merged with entertainment to create the news magazine formula and sitcoms merged with real-time stories to create a new genre (imported from Europe) in the form of so-called *reality shows*. CBS's *Survivor* and *Big Brother* led to extreme and outrageous "reality" programming on Fox, such as *Temptation Island*. Viewers are hard pressed to tell what is real and what is not real, and for the most part, they don't seem to care. They do care, however, that they are entertained.

Another form of infotainment emerged in radio broadcasting. Clearly it emerged from the competitive realities of radio broadcasting, for this trend, talk radio, virtually saved an entire broadcast band. Since the late 1960s and early 1970s, AM radio had been on the decline, giving way to the higher quality audio and stereo capabilities of the FM band. Because music emerged as the dominant means of gathering a radio audience, and FM could outperform AM in delivering music quality, it seemed a matter of time before AM would go the way of the plastic 45 rpm record and the eight-track tape. However, Rush Limbaugh, with his "Excellence in Broadcasting" network and his ability to create a rabidly loyal if distinctly niche audience, almost single-handedly saved AM radio. Sound quality didn't matter as much for talk. Broadcasters discovered that people liked to talk back to the radio. Now talk shows of all kinds with every stripe of expert and every viewpoint across the political spectrum are represented. AM radio has new life and the instant news world has yet another segment of frequently loud and boisterous voices clamoring to be heard.

Print media is not at all immune from the infotainment trend. When now retired Gannett chief Al Neuharth decided to launch *USA Today,* he was accused of creating a fast-food version of a newspaper where all news products would have the same dull presentation and where the news was all happiness and fluff, all marketing and hype, all entertainment values, and no real substance. Neuharth was on the money, however, and his venture has developed into the second-most circulated daily in the United States. He was right in assuming that the American reader wanted a publication that was exceptionally readable, highly scannable, full of color and splash, and light on details or in-depth coverage. As it turns out, there is an audience for both *The New York Times* and *USA Today*.

Infotainment is the natural consequence of aggressive competition for news audiences. The simple reality is that news producers need to give audiences what they want: speed, depth, and credibility. However, news audiences also want to be entertained. They look in their news coverage for the same elements that grab and hold them in the movies, or in television programming, or in the books and magazines that they choose to read in their limited spare time. We are not entertained today, as we have been in the past, with social interaction, with lengthy discussions over coffee and beer, and with hours of shared family activities. Social activities frequently involve going to the movies or watching a game on the big screen. We need color, action, high-impact visuals, and most of all, a good story.

The fact that infotainment has come to dominate specific publications and programming is fairly clear cut and obvious. Where it becomes more insidious and therefore, dangerous to both viewers and newsmakers alike, is when those same infotainment values dominate the "hard news"—those traditional news programs or vehicles where the lines were more clearly drawn. There can be no doubt that those lines have been crossed. The evidence for this is not so much in the color, splash, and compelling visuals that characterize much of news, but in the entertainment formula that is used to present the news. I call this the *melodrama formula*.

The Black Hats and White Hats

The melodrama has been a popular form of entertainment for perhaps as long as humans have entertained each other. The conventions of the melodrama formula can be seen in early forms of drama such as the *commedia del' arte* of the early middle ages. The word *melodrama* in our culture brings to mind images of bewhiskered villains in large dark hats tying white-skinned, flowing-clothed virgins onto railroad tracks as the roaring train approaches in the distance. A battle ensues between the dark villain and the white-hatted cowboy who rides into the scene to defeat evil and release the petrified maiden at the last possible instant.

The intriguing thing about melodrama is that in spite of the fact that it is strictly formulaic and entirely predictable, it almost never fails to please. It is a handy and convenient device for the writer because he or she simply needs to follow the formula with only minor modifications to sustain interest and audience satisfaction. It is pleasing to the audience because the audience is spared the discomfort of the unknown and is offered instead the satisfaction of knowing that right, truth, and justice always win in the end.

The most pervasive entertainment value that has emerged in the last 15 years in our contemporary news media is the melodrama formula, and this is seen in our daily newspapers as much, if not more, as in our prime-time television news programming. The reason that it has become popular is that it responds directly to our need for story, for compelling narrative, and for a suspenseful tale of good versus evil.

In a melodrama there are only a few basic requirements, but they are essential: the good character, the bad character, and something or someone to fight over. The bad character almost always looks like they are winning, but then the good character arrives to rescue the "maiden" from evil. Today, this formula can be seen most clearly in those news programs that compete head-to-head for primetime entertainment, the television news magazines. However, the same formula can also be seen at work in local television "investigative" reporting and many print reports. The "maiden" is always the public good, as seen by the reporter or news media. It might be public health, safety, protection of the environment, and in some cases, financial well-being or quality of life issues. There is always a "black hat" and a "white hat." What makes it particularly formulaic is that seldom are shades of gray revealed: the white hat is purely white and the black hat is purely black. The black hat is placed securely on the head of a person or group who is putting the public good at risk by what they are doing, usually by selfish pursuit of corporate profits or pure evil. The distinction between those two seems increasingly lost on a great many of today's news viewers.

With the melodrama formula in mind, the pattern becomes more obvious in many news stories. A company stands accused. Investigative reporters, activists, disgruntled former employees, or even competitors have raised the issue to the media or the media have uncovered the accusation. The company has been marketing defective equipment, spilling chemicals, hiring dangerous workers, selling untested products, and so on. A cover-up is usually detected. In these situations, the accused automatically has the black hat. The accuser has the white hat, regardless of credibility or motive. The maiden—the well-being of the reader and, sometimes, of all society—is at risk.

One might think that journalistic responsibility and integrity would require some verification of the accusations before putting a hard-earned reputation at risk. However, when I have pointed out to reporters that the person making an accusation against a client was not credible and was not speaking the truth, the answer I have received is, in effect, "That is not our concern. Our job is to report accurately what they say."

In some egregious cases of journalistic irresponsibility, the reporters, producers, or editors themselves cross the line of dishonesty that is frequently the strategy of accusers. The situations in television news magazines involving a news crew sabotaging a Volvo so that the roof would collapse on cue and rigging a gas tank with an explosive to demonstrate how tanks can explode in a collision are outrageous examples of a common trend. The primary difference between investigative reporting and straight news reporting is that the reporter plays the role of accuser instead of having an activist or opponent play this role. Now it is the media not only serving as the story teller, as in the author of the melodrama, but also stepping in to be the white-hatted cowboy.

Although some of the more notable cases of reportorial excess have been in television news, print reporters are far from immune. In some of the situations described in later chapters, print reporters have obstinately stuck to the white hat/black hat formula even when the private or organizational agendas of those carrying the white hats were clearly demonstrated to them, and the lack of honesty in the information they provided was clearly revealed. It is difficult to abandon the direction of a story when it plays well, fits the formula, and provides the reader interest the publishers and editors want.

Clearly, investigative reporting has benefited our society greatly, as has quality news reporting that brings to light failings in companies, government agencies, celebrities, and other newsmakers. However, there are two fundamental problems with the melodrama formula absorbing our news coverage: It is fundamentally false at its premise and it is easily abused.

Melodrama is not considered among the more elevated forms of art because the very formula that makes it popular also makes it fundamentally false. Life, as we know, is not as clear cut as the good guys and the bad guys. The maiden is usually not as pure, beautiful, and helpless as pictured in the standard melodrama. The good guys sometimes do bad things and the bad guys might turn out to have redeeming qualities. In other words, life is not black and white, but is instead filled with shades of gray. Great storytelling art avoids the melodrama charge by reflecting at least some of this complexity of life. Great journalism also reflects that the accuser is not always purely good nor the accused always purely evil—even though the accused might have been surprised getting into his or her car and the only thing he or she knew to do in the face of those lights and cameras was hide behind the briefcase he or she was carrying.

Alaska Airlines' well-deserved reputation for safety and quality was undermined in the aftermath of the Flight 261 disaster by relentless news reports calling into question its safety record and performance. Much of this information came from a single disgruntled former employee who made some very strong accusations against the company's maintenance policies. When companies are engaged in activities involving regulatory inspections, it is highly unusual to not have at least some reports that can be construed as damaging. Maintenance records involving Alaska Airlines were brought forth in the week-long series of articles in the Seattle papers that supported the clear conclusion of the editors that the company was irresponsible. A once stellar reputation was very much damaged, but fortunately, not entirely destroyed, despite the apparent intentions of a disgruntled employee and complicit reporters. More responsible and less formulaic reporting would have included some perspective or context about the airline's safety performance in relation to the entire industry, and would probably also have more closely evaluated the credibility and potential motives of the person making the accusations.

This pattern is very much part of the formula. Once an event has occurred that has captured public interest, news media have an interest in stretching the story over days and weeks to capture and sustain the continuing interest. When an industrial facility had a dramatic explosion and fire killing some workers, it was of high interest to the community. For at least two years after the event, every time this particular facility was mentioned in any regional television newscast, still or video images of the fire were broadcast, regardless of any relationship of those events to the story being presented. What was imprinted into the public consciousness was the image of this facility and burning equipment. The attorney representing the families, who was always more than eager to talk to the media about his case, clearly wore the white hat and willingly aided the television stations in their desire to stretch this story to its limit.

Thus, one problem with the melodrama formula when applied to news is that it is false on its premise because it overly simplifies the truth. The other problem is that reporters with agendas operating within a melodrama formula are too easily tempted to abuse the truth.

A newspaper in the Northwest has taken a strong editorial position against a proposed energy facility on environmental grounds. There is no pretense of objectivity in the editorial stance, and surprisingly, when the idea of fair reporting is still subscribed to by most readers, neither is there much of a pretense of objectivity in the news pages. As a relatively small paper, there is not much degree of separation between the editorial page and the news pages. In all but the largest papers, editorial page writers depend primarily on the reporters working on the story for information, so often the bias of the reporter is then magnified by the bias of the editorial writer. One of the reporters contacted a member of a government environmental agency repeatedly asking a whole series of questions. The calls came over a period of weeks and it was clear that the reporter was looking for this regulator to say something negative about another facility operated by the company proposing the new facility. Finally, the regulator said something that could be vaguely construed as negative. The next issue of the newspaper contained glaring headlines claiming that the agency was critical of the company. The outraged regulator, who saw how she had been manipulated, wrote a detailed complaint to the publisher. The reporter was temporarily taken off the story, but no retraction or correction was offered even though the regulator stated that in her frequent interviews with the reporter she had clearly communicated the opposite of what had been reported. In a final irony, this reporter won several journalism awards for these stories, which were entertaining, but fundamentally untruthful.

Another extreme example that I personally experienced involved an Argentine newspaper at the tip of South America. My client was proposing a forestry operation in the area. Environmental activists were strongly opposed to this, and gave the small local newspaper "information" about the project, including company plans to clear-cut the forest (absolutely false), chip the wood (absolutely false), and then send the chips to Japan to be processed into fax paper (absolutely false). The newspaper dutifully reported the accusations, and when representatives from the company arrived to make a presentation at a town council meeting, they felt physically threatened by the anger of the townspeople. We needed to get our story out, so we approached the newspaper about purchasing some advertising. "Certainly," they said, once a budget figure was agreed on. "Would you like that in the form of advertising or a news story?" I immediately accepted the offer of a news story, which we wrote and had printed as "news."

Because the previous example of the power plant involved a Canadian newspaper, American readers might assume such abuses of journalistic integrity are limited to foreign news businesses. However, anyone in media and public communication in the United States would most likely be able to come up with his or her own "war stories." Another example involved a U.S. daily. Engaged in a pitched battle involving medical waste, my client had come under unrelenting attack from a local legislator. The newspaper delighted in the story because the legislator, in the tradition of Joseph McCarthy, provided colorful accusations and good copy. It fit the formula perfectly: Heroic public servant accuses big company of putting the entire community's health at risk for the sake of big profits. The reporter and editor clearly liked the story, so when information emerged that made the situation gray instead of black and white, it was fiercely resisted. Accusations made about the company's regulatory record and the health and safety record of its own employees were presented in a way that disregarded the truth. When we attempted to correct the misinformation, the guest editorial was rejected because the editorial page editor couldn't "verify it as being true." When we pointed out that no attempt had been made to verify the truth of the accusations, and should that attempt be made, the accusations would be found to be false, the conversation ended.

When the formula must be followed, the truth is too easily sacrificed. That is the real risk of the melodrama mode of public information.

Infotainment represents a significant challenge for newsmakers in the instant news world. It is the cultural and media environment that communication professionals and executives must live and work in. It is not a matter of choice, but a reality. To continue to pretend, as so many do, that news reporting is anything other than a business of gaining and maintaining audiences is self-deception. The key to those audiences is speed, depth, credibility, and infotainment. As newsmakers enter this world—willingly or unwillingly—they must learn what the audiences expect and what their competitors can be counted on to do. From that, they must formulate policies and strategies to help them compete effectively in this increasingly strange world of public communication.

Endnotes

1. Postman, Neil, *Amusing Ourselves to Death: Public Discourse in the Age of Show Business*, New York: Viking Penguin, Inc., 1985, p. 87. Used by permission.
2. Masters, Kim, "No News Is Bad News," *Esquire* magazine, January 2002, p.42. Reprinted by permission of International Creative Management, Inc. Copyright 2002 by Kim Masters. First appeared in *Esquire* magazine.
3. Koppel, Ted, "Network News Is Still Serious Business," originally published in *The New York Times*, March 5, 2002.

CHAPTER

5 When Opponents Grab the Microphone

Internet use in the United States reached a milestone in early 2002. It was reported that over half of U.S. residents were now Internet users. Well over half of Internet users, perhaps 70 million, use it daily. A few of them might not like you or your organization. In fact, if you present a significant target, they might make it their hobby, or even their career, to make life as miserable for you as possible. Their reasons might be pure, in that they might think they are performing a public service, or they might be less than pure, seeing the opportunity to damage or destroy your reputation as a means of building their own. Having opponents is probably not anything new, because opponents have been around for a long time. The difference now is they own the most powerful transmitters and printing presses the world has ever created.

Suppose along the way in your business career you did some unintentional damage to the career of a co-worker who has since gone on to bigger and better things. The anger seethes. It happens. Suddenly he or she is hired as an executive producer for CNN. This individual is the kind of person incapable of forgiving or forgetting and doesn't mind stretching the truth to get even. Does this make you nervous? All of your opponents with computers and Internet connections have in their hands the power to create an audience and communicate their idea or version of the truth. They no longer need to buy out a broadcast channel or purchase a newspaper to get public attention. They can do so for essentially no cost, working in their bedroom in their underwear.

In late 2001, the energy trading giant Enron crashed. In a matter of weeks the company's stock went from a high of $90 to as low as 28 cents per share. Shortly after this, stories emerged in national newspapers reporting that while employees and ordinary investors were losing their life savings and retirement accounts, Enron executives were handing out multimillion dollar bonuses to each other. A story as large as this, enhanced by the Andersen shredding scandal, stayed on the front page and on the television newscast schedule for some time. Most stories erupt very quickly and then almost as quickly go away, replaced by a new breaking story. What doesn't go away so easily is the anger and despair of those who feel they were burned by executive incompetence, deception, or worse. Shortly after the Enron news broke, a number of new Web sites were launched by the victims of the disaster, dedicated to continuing the story, communicating in excruciating detail all the information they could find and publish. One of those sites offered assistance to former employees interested in telling their stories to the media by helping them contact reporters who had expressed interest in talking to unhappy former employees.

Five public information trends have emerged that, when combined, pose an unprecedented risk to the reputations of high-profile people, companies, and organizations:

- The growing cynicism and negativity in our public discourse
- The movement of the media away from traditional news reporting to infotainment

- The emergence of the powerful activist and opponent
- The ability of these powerful opponents to create and effectively use their own means of information distribution
- The eager involvement of politicians

Although we can identify them as independent elements, as you will see, these trends weave together in a complex tapestry of dependence so that the impact of all five together becomes much more significant than if each were to develop and operate independently.

A Time of Cynicism

Few will contest the idea that we live in a deeply cynical time. The real-life tragedy of September 11, 2001 probably did more to relieve us of some of this cynicism and return to a more realistic view of life than anything else could have. Nevertheless, as has been pointed out by numerous commentators, Americans have become increasingly cynical of the political process and the economic forces that deeply affect them, over which they have apparently little control. This can be seen in voter turnouts, in the frequent "throw the bastards out" votes, in the continually degraded political discourse (e.g., highly negative and effective "attack ads") and perhaps most vividly, in the growing antiglobalism backlash seen in the World Trade Organization protests in Seattle and other host cities.

There is a chicken-and-egg question about whether the media created this trend or contributed to it. Most communication historians point to Watergate as a critical point in our history when, in conjunction with the Vietnam debacle, the American people lost trust and faith in politicians and the political process. At the same time that our elected leaders and their associates shamed themselves and us, investigative reporters emerged as heroes. It was a role they accepted with a little less humility than might be appropriate. A turning point in the respect shown by the media toward those in elected office might have been the interchange between President Nixon and ABC's aggressive reporter, Sam Donaldson. When Donaldson was asking questions of the president, Nixon asked,

"Sam, are you running for office?" Donaldson quickly retorted, "No sir, are you?" The fact that this does not seem disrespectful today demonstrates the degree of change in the relationship between the media and those involved in the political process. A new king has been crowned and, in effect, every elected official is required at one time or another to bow before this new leader. Those who do not show the proper deference or respect to the powerful in the media soon learn that there is a significant price to pay.

Similarly, the decline in respect for business institutions, businesses, and individual business leaders is also due in significant part to the incredibly poor behavior and low moral standards of so many in the business community. The numerous stories of scandal, corruption, moral failures, and greed that demonstrate this problem in the business community are matched by the same kind of character and value disappointments in every walk of life. Business leaders have no monopoly on greed, lust, dishonesty, or corruption. The same behavior can be found in the professions, church leadership, education, organized labor, agriculture, and every other occupation. Many prominent news stories from early 2002 demonstrate this, ranging from child-molesting priests to highly respected historians who plagiarize. That's what makes the current situation somewhat unique and interesting. Moral and character failure in the business and political realms is not unique—it just has become the focus of reporting as well as popular entertainment. Clear evidence for this decline is provided by a study conducted by Media Research Center in 1997.[1]

This study examined nearly 900 television entertainment shows. It showed that businessmen commit more crimes on television than anyone; in fact, three times more than career criminals! Most murders on TV are committed by businessmen, again by a factor of three. Businessmen are more likely to cheat than contribute positively to society (28.7% vs. 25%). Let me emphasize that this isn't reality; this is television's picture of reality. However, as is frequently stated in advertising and public relations, perception *is* reality.

Because the public in general holds the view that most in business are corrupt and evil, it plays extremely well when the media present businesspeople in this light. In fact, portraying characters that go against the grain of public opinion is a risk that most media are not willing to take—particularly when the melodrama formula is working quite well. As one network executive stated, as quoted by Eric Dezenhall in his book titled *Nail 'Em*,[2] "We need villains. And if we portray businessmen as not caring about society or their employees, would we be all wrong?"

Public discourse is where we have most dramatically seen the slide into negativity and cynicism. In 1978, when I became involved in managing a state legislative campaign, I attended a campaign school in Olympia taught by a grizzled veteran of political wars. (At least because I was a 20-something political newcomer, he seemed old and grizzled to me.) During the course of his seminar he stated that voters do not vote for candidates. By a strong margin, they usually vote against candidates. Although not explicitly stated at this time, the meaning was clear: Your campaign should be about why the voters should *not* vote for the other candidate more than about why they should vote for your candidate. That view might surprise many in the public today, especially when they are now used to hearing candidates at the beginning of a campaign talking about how they want to run a clean campaign and simply talk about their record or their plans. However, most who have been on the inside of a campaign instinctively know that this is what most campaigns, particularly hotly contested ones, have been about for some time.

Negativity reached new heights (or lows, depending on your point of view) during the Clinton campaigns. Bill Clinton was simultaneously one of the most vigorously and perhaps viciously attacked candidates ever, and at the same time he and his political teams virtually perfected the only response that has proven effective against vigorous and vicious attacks: attack. His remarkable saga as "the comeback kid," well chronicled in campaign advisor George Stephanopoulos's book *All Too Human*,[3] demonstrated the truth of the adage, that the best defense is a good offense. The story of Clinton and his personal failures is sad primarily because he had to go to that well so often against others. Ultimately, his greatest challenge—protecting his presidency from collapse—was won by his remarkably effective attack on Special Prosecutor Ken Starr and the "right-wing conspiracy" behind the investigation. All he needed to do, like a great defense attorney, was create sufficient doubt in the minds of Americans of the fairness of his accusers and the political battle was essentially won.

The James Carville–Stephanopoulos "war room" strategy developed in the first campaign has proven remarkably effective and has been repeated by most campaigns since then. It consisted of two basic principles: Stay on message regardless of attack ("It's the economy, stupid!") and attack the attacker; the sooner the better. The Dole campaign, although not a stellar example of effectiveness, nevertheless adopted a similar approach in trying to beat any criticism from gaining momentum by countering it before the attack had an opportunity to really develop in the media.

Media Infotainment

Speaking of presidents, the media have had much to work with in the past few years. There are the tales that include a sitting president caught in serious criminal activity and paying to keep it quiet, a front-running political candidate with a mistress on his lap on a luxury yacht, and the one about another sitting president groping White House staffers and taking sexual advantage of young interns. All these played into the hands of media business executives charged with the responsibility of filling more and more airtime with "news" that would lure television audiences away from competing networks' sitcoms. It raises this question again: Did the media create infotainment to compete, or did it fall into it by simply reporting the unfortunately all-too-entertaining shenanigans of our nation's leaders? When it ran out of politicians misbehaving, was it simply forced to turn to other powerful people and expose their frequent frailties and failings?

That question, although interesting, is hardly the point here. What is the point, as discussed in the previous chapter, is that infotainment is the style of news du jour. As a result, it is what newsmakers in the instant news world must contend with. It is pointless and counterproductive to pretend that we still live in an era of "just the facts" reporting. In those days the concerns about bias and objectivity related more to getting the quotes straight rather than forcing every story into a tight, predictable melodramatic formula of white hats and black hats.

The interweaving of these two trends now becomes clear: The public holds a perception of misbehavior on the part of our political and business leaders and is quite interested in stories that demonstrate this perspective. News business executives need to deliver the audiences that would normally turn to evening drama or sitcoms, or the readers who would pick up Danielle Steele, Dean Koontz, or Tom Clancy novels. Some of the greatest moments of success for the media, if you leave aside great drama of good versus evil (e.g., the Gulf War), came during the Watergate and Lewinsky scandals. The public's temporarily insatiable desire for all the tidbits, historic or not, have fed the development of the all news channels initiated by Ted Turner with CNN and Headline News. These cable "all news, all talk" media are now joined by the Internet and cable teams of CNBC, MSNBC, and Fox News. Such good versus evil stories have also fed the development of other important trends in public information including talk radio and the almost endless pundit shows such as *The Capital Gang*, *Hannity and Colmes*, *Hardball with Chris Matthews*, and so on.

Now we need to add one more important element to this tapestry: the accuser. Without the accuser, the media is left to be the prosecution as well as judge and jury. Even though the investigative styles evidenced today show little concern about the impression left by this mishmash, most hard news outlets prefer to have a person or group other than an investigative reporter make the accusations against the black hats, particularly because the accuser need not respect the same level of honesty and integrity or adherence to the truth that most investigative reporters need to preserve credibility.

Activists and Other Opponents

Grassroots political activism has a rich and storied history in the American democratic system. Some of our most revered national heroes were activists of the first order, going back to the American Revolution. Activists are frequently colorful characters who have had a profound impact on the course of history. Cary Nation of the temperance movement, Susan B. Anthony of the women's suffrage movement, and Harriet Beecher Stowe of the antislavery effort are a few of the remarkable female activists who contributed to our American story and traditions. Martin Luther King, Jr. is deservedly a national hero on the level of our most respected leaders and presidents. Certainly there are a number of others who also had a profound impact, but live more in infamy than in fame. Senator Joseph McCarthy and John Brown come to mind, as does the activism of Eldridge Cleaver, Tom Hayden, and others from the cultural revolution of the 1960s.

Activists have always been an important part of our democratic process, but it is quite certain that at no other time in history have so many made a career out of it. Nor have activists been so instantly successful at gaining fame, or been so ingrained as an accepted, everyday part of our lives and culture. We have become, in some respects, a democracy that depends on activists and our news media have become information and entertainment vehicles that depend on activism.

The career of one activist, of which I am perhaps too painfully aware, is instructive of some of the trends. This person, whom I will call Jean, began her activist career more than 15 years ago. One of her children became ill with a serious disease and she became convinced that the cause was an industrial facility located within a few miles of her home. She took her accusation of disease-causing emissions to anyone who would listen, including those at the state capitol. In meetings with local representatives, she demanded that this company be put out of business to prevent other children from dying, weeping hysterically during her tirades. When her demands did not result in the action she desired, she literally camped on the lawn in front of the capitol building. There she made a great discovery that would serve her well during the next 15 years of her efforts at bringing this company down: The media loved it. Her accusations were widely reported without regard for whether they were true. Photos of her attempting to get the ears of the governor and state legislators were printed in local and regional newspapers. She gained instant fame in her local community, and this celebrity status was elevated when she received a national award for activists. Another result was that the state launched an epidemiological study to test her theory at a cost of tens of thousands of taxpayer dollars. The ironic thing is that the officials knew her claim was medically impossible because the particular disease her child suffered from was not transmitted via airborne contaminants. Nevertheless, the study went forward and resulted in a very predictable report, showing that not only was there not an increased incidence of this disease as she claimed, but that it was medically impossible to contract the disease through the method studied. The newspapers ran an inside-page story on the study but it never stopped her from repeating the now-discredited accusation. Fifteen years later, she still boldly states the accusation as if it is truth and as if the state study has verified her claim.

If that were the end of the story it would not be so instructive. Because state and local health department action would not shut this company down, she would find other means. She ran for county council member and won.

By this time, she had a well-established, mutually beneficial relationship with the local newspaper: She provided exceptionally colorful copy and was bold and relentless in her accusations against this locally owned company. She tried a few other targets, but only against this company could she create the vitriol needed to gain attention, supporters, and media attention—at least on a sustained basis.

The battleground shifted from the emissions to the very existence of the business. She worked closely with a competitor, leveraging her position as an elected official to help them gain legal standing that otherwise would not have been possible. She then helped them sue the county to change laws that affected the operation of the company. Despite the fact that a community-wide survey showed that well over 80% of the populace supported the environmentally positive activity of the company, the 200 angry citizens who believed her accusations of the death-dealing activities of this company persuaded the other council members to support her efforts. As a result, the company's primary business activity was halted and only by astute business moves was it able to salvage its business and sell out most of its operations to a larger company.

It is important to understand that her method of doing business was intimidation, temper tantrums, wild accusations against anyone who stood in her way, and the perfection of the 90% lie, taking 10% of the truth and distorting and exaggerating it so that the net result is completely untrue information. However, when pinned down, the accuser can always go back to the 10% and blame the listener for going beyond that kernel of truth. This technique is a specialty of many of today's activists and can make even the most harmless records look vile. The tenor of public debate with this person on the county council became so negative and intimidating that by a vote of six to one (she voted against it, obviously) every other member of the council voted to censure her for her behavior on the council. Astoundingly, the local paper criticized all the other council members and commended her for her bold protection of the public interest. They were not about to have such a convenient marriage of accuser and reporter put at risk by the reality of her horrible public behavior and serious disruption of the democratic process.

There was yet another part of this company that was still operational, so it became the next subject of attack. She had attempted to put this portion of the operation out of business a few years earlier by successfully passing a citizen's initiative that would ban the import of materials used by the company, knowing that most came across the border from Canada. The initiative was a clear violation of the interstate commerce clause of the U.S. Constitution and, because this came up before she was elected to office, the county refused to pay to defend it in court. She formed a citizens' committee to defend it but the initiative was summarily dismissed as illegal. Undaunted after her success in destroying the company's main business, she attacked with another initiative after failing to get the necessary council votes to put the company under. The company foolishly refused to fight the ordinance publicly and it passed overwhelmingly. When it became clear that this was also illegal for a number of reasons, including constitutional ones, and the county would not defend it, she put the initiative in the form of an ordinance and, based on the supposed overwhelming public support, secured a unanimous council vote.

The battle waged over several years with many court appearances. Although the company has won every step and will no doubt prevail in the court of law, both parties have spent hundreds of thousands of dollars on the legal fight, and the battle goes on. Although the company's legal position is absolutely solid, its name is so tainted in the community that it is virtually impossible to gain any support for any efforts it might make that would involve getting permits—even to change processes that might be positive for the public. It might win in the court of law, but it has already lost in the court of public opinion. Perhaps sooner than later, the continued cost of defending itself in court will outweigh the company's future profits and the activist and politician will win.

The question, of course, is why. Why did the company allow it to get to this, as there has never been one shred of evidence that the business activity the company is engaged in has been the least bit harmful to any member of the public? Why did this person dedicate 15 years of her life to a cause that she knows is based on personal motivation and not any realities of public risk? Perhaps, most important, why does the newspaper continue to keep from the public the outrageous and newsworthy excesses of this public figure while continuing to treat her information as credible—even when it is clearly demonstrated that it is not?

If this were an isolated instance, it would not be worthy of consideration. The reality is that, it happens all the time in almost every community in one form or another. This was an ongoing story on a very local level. This same story is playing out right now at the national and international level and in virtually every town, community, city, and state. There's a very good chance if your company or organization has a significant profile, you are currently contending with activists in situations fundamentally similar to what has been described.

The Alar scare, in which unfounded accusations were made against a substance used to improve the market appearance of apples, is one of the most notorious examples of activist excesses. Actress Meryl Streep lent star quality and high credibility to claims that proved to be totally unfounded. However, by the time the media got around to reporting the pseudoscience behind the claims, the damage to the apple industry was immense and the public had lost interest in the story. The limited amount of backtrack reporting by the media went largely unnoticed and did little to restore public confidence in an important food and industry. Virtually every industry that manufactures products for public use or consumption can point to similar national and regional situations in which bogus science put forward by activists has been accepted without scrutiny by the media and caused significant damage to safe products or industries.

The most instructive and common situations involving activists involve environmental issues. Environmentalism has become one of the most significant forces in our consciousness and our economy in the last 20 years, and for very good reason. Human existence has a profound impact on our world and in general we have not been good stewards of the resources we use. As I write these words I find myself in the Mexican city of Mazatlan where clearly visible from the harbor is an oil-fired power plant that apparently has little to no environmental controls. All day long it spews an endless cloud of dirty smoke into the otherwise clear, sun-filled sky. It adds dusky, rose-gray color to the morning and evening skies, and hangs like a shroud over the entire city and mountain region throughout the day. Seeing that ominous cloud reminded me of the benefits we enjoy in our prosperous America where we have been able to afford the revolution in pollution control. I have yet to meet a person who did not consider himself or herself an environmentalist. All of us with a stake on this earth and concern for future generations cannot avoid favoring any effort made to protect and preserve resources, most particularly those resources such as air, water, and food on which we all depend.

I am profoundly grateful for the many accomplishments of the environmental movement, and respect the daring leadership that many in this movement have provided, but I am also too painfully aware of the excesses and the damage that the marriage of convenience of activists and media can cause. Today's corporate leaders and communication professionals need to be very aware of the risk of activism, particularly if a business or organization has global reach, because one result of the globalization of communication is that activists and opponents now operate in a global community, as the next example illustrates.

My client was a smallish company with huge ambitions, and it launched the largest private forestry operation in South America. The company acquired vast tracts of forestland on the southern tip of South America, mostly on the island of Tierra del Fuego. The forest there consisted largely of a hardwood tree that provided excellent furniture-grade lumber. The company set about the project with high hopes and a lofty aspiration of setting a new global standard for environmentally sound forestry. There would be no clear-cutting, and scientific studies of an ecosystem that was poorly documented to date would be provided. The company would set aside huge areas as permanent forest preserves, establish local lumber processing to support a much-diminished local economy, and so on. One of the most respected experts in environmental forestry was named as land steward and given unprecedented control over the company's plans. The land the company purchased included permits that would allow it to begin harvest virtually immediately. However, in its efforts to do things right and gain adherents in the environmental community, the company opted not to make use of those existing permits, choosing instead to go through an exceptionally lengthy and expensive planning process.

The effort proved to be disastrous. Nearly 10 years later, no significant forestry activities are taking place. Although the company did succeed in gaining the support of many in the environmental community, those who did understand what they were trying to do wanted to keep their support quiet so as to not confuse and undermine their more extreme supporters. The primary story is told in the methods of a very few—fewer than five—extreme environmentalists with as much persistence in keeping the company from cutting trees as the company had persistence in carrying out its effort to gain approvals.

In earlier days, the company had been the target of some members of Earth First, an ecoterrorism organization that threatened the company owner's children and vandalized company offices. Although there were only two people involved in criticizing the company's activities, their protests were covered extensively in the local newspapers, creating a "track record" of environmental ire. Years later, this negative press record came back to bite them, when the Northwest island that was the focus of these protests became almost a household word in the national newspapers of Argentina and Chile. This, in itself, is a significant lesson for companies who face opponent accusations. A permanent record is created that, if not balanced by complete reporting and a significant number of other positive stories, represents a long-term risk in the hands of those who wish to damage reputations.

How did the company's relatively minor problems in the Pacific Northwest become international news? The activists in the Northwest quickly made common cause with the activists in the southern tip of South America. A few of the more vocal activists from the Northwest traveled to South America and were paraded in front of rallies and held meetings with government officials. The leading activist in South America traveled to the Northwest and became the star attraction at the protest rallies held in the company's hometown. It was almost a situation of one-plus-one equals millions, or at least that was the perception that was created. The story that emerged wasn't one of a small company attempting to set a new standard for environmental forestry; it was a demon corporate giant that, having ravaged the forests of the Northwest out of existence, was now turning to do the same in South America.

In talking with one of the executives about lessons learned from this disappointing effort, one was that the original permit should have been implemented immediately. The company's efforts to "do it right" would likely have been easier if it had proceeded on the original basis and negotiated changes in those plans in exchange for the opportunity to expand its operation. Another lesson was that the mainstream environmental community, fearful of alienating the more extreme elements, is virtually powerless to support companies or individuals who attempt to conduct industrial activity in a positive manner. Although they received tacit support, that could not be translated into a moderate environmental consensus for obviously economic reasons. The environmental groups did not want to put their fundraising efforts at risk to support something they believed in because of concern about alienating their more extreme supporters. Finally, a key lesson was the power of a very few people to undermine the best intentions and tens of millions of dollars of persistent effort. That power is based in part on their persistence and dedication to a cause they deeply believe in, but mostly by their willingness to do and say anything, regardless of the truth. This willingness, combined with the eagerness of the media to promote controversy and strong accusations—to put white hats and black hats on the usual suspects—means that gaining political support for even an unusually enlightened project is tenuous at best.

The power of the few was clearly demonstrated in the battle over a natural-gas-fired power plant planned for development just on the U.S. side of the Canadian border. The local paper carried the headline: "Ten Opponents Successful in Stopping Power Plant." This headline enraged those 10 because they claimed the support of more than 80,000 citizens opposing the project. The truth is fewer than 10—two or three, really—combined with the power of the media on both sides of the border intent on sticking to their infotainment melodrama script. This potent combination resulted in the first-ever state permit denial of a power plant in the midst of the worst power shortage in the region's history.

The assumption might be that the proposed plant did indeed represent environmental risk. The truth is the opposite: At that time there was no cleaner gas-fired plant planned, permitted or operating. The permit was denied not because the plant violated any environmental regulation on either side of the border, but simply because a very few people were very successful in creating the perception of public concern. I say the perception of public concern because in the county where the plant was to be located, polling showed that between 60 percent and 75 percent of the people supported the project.

If the plant was exceptionally clean and if there was strong local support, and the state panel was established to permit such facilities without being unduly influenced by nimbyism—the “not in my backyard” phenomenon—how could such a thing happen? The simple, true answer lies in the combination of activist and politician and media infotainment. In this case, the two key opponents were both elected officials: one, a county council member in the U.S. county where the plant was to be located, and another in a similar position in the small British Columbia city across the border in Canada. Both were bright, articulate women with pleasant demeanors that masked the anger and bitterness that characterized their efforts.

Eric Dezenhall pointed out some of the consistencies in these kinds of activists, although in his experience most were not elected officials. He said; “I don’t like attackers, but my job has taught me they are not all evil. They can be the people next door who complain about chemicals in food and fat in popcorn and muffins. Once I strip away the rage, I find a desperate person looking for credit, recognition or celebrity. I find an exile from an exciting world that has passed him by.”[4]

The combination activist and politician is not a new phenomenon, but it might be far more widespread than in the days of Joseph McCarthy. Their success, despite their frequently narrow appeal, can be attributed in part to the remarkable treatment they often receive from the media. As mentioned before, the activist and politician and the media enjoy a marriage of convenience when one provides the colorful copy, frequently outrageous accusations, and bitter controversy that the other happily transforms into the melodrama formula. This was certainly true in the situation mentioned earlier of an activist and politician dedicated to destroying an industrial facility, and it also was the case of the two activists who fought the power plant.

The convenience in this marriage is about money. As Dezenhall pointed out in discussing the Alar situation, all parties involved in the accusation stood to gain financially, whereas the defendant, the apple industry, had much to lose:

> The NRDC [National Resources Defense Council—the accuser] is an agenda-driven entity that relies on fundraising and a high profile to prosper. Fenton Communications [NRDC's PR agency] is a for-profit PR group, and *60 Minutes* is the most profitable franchise in the multibillion-dollar CBS empire. They all benefited from the controversy. NRDC raised its profile, Fenton pleased its client, and *60 Minutes* got high ratings. If they were motivated exclusively by public welfare they might have waited for evidence before making accusations. As it was, they shut down an industry—the definitive conclusion required of all witch hunts.[5]

A common characteristic of the successful attacker is the unabashed use of the dramatic statement or hyperbole. Providing attention-getting quotes is another reason why the entertainment-oriented press goes to great lengths to report on and defend these activists. Someone who provides the kind of copy and headlines needed to sell papers, attract an audience, and get people talking around the water cooler is of significant economic value to news publishers.

One of the most stunning claims offered by the elected official involved in the power plant siting controversy was that the company was intentionally setting out to kill people. This outrageous accusation was based on the fact that emissions are an unavoidable result of burning fossil fuels and scientific evidence that shows air quality has an impact on mortality. The logic was that if you add to emissions in the air you are no better than a person caught in attempted murder. Of course, the same logic could be applied to the person who gets in his car in the morning knowing that the exhaust emissions are adding to an already burdened environment. Such hyperbole and emotionally charged accusations are characteristic of virtually every melodrama in which there is strong public interest.

A visual example of this kind of statement is the coffee table book published in the mid-1980s during the outcries about loss of forest land that contained nothing but pictures of clear cuts. It is true that there are enough clear cuts in the United States to create a sizable coffee table book, but the impression left was that there are few if any trees left standing—an impression contradicted by the fact that since the 1950s the United States has been *gaining* forestland.

In the industrial facility melodrama discussed earlier, the elected official and activist in public hearings made dramatic claims about trucks involved in the operation, including doors falling off and tales of dripping horrible contents onto public roads. She also claimed repeatedly, in the press and in public hearings, that a worker at the industrial facility contracted a life-threatening disease. She did this knowing full well that the state agency had repeatedly denied this worker's claim because he was not in the company's employ long enough for it to be medically possible for him to have contracted the disease there.

True Believers

Truly effective attackers and activists make full use of the media's strong interest in headline-grabbing accusations, but the characteristic of most activists that I find that most company executives and communication professionals are least prepared to deal with is what I call the "true believer" mentality. Modern democratic society has developed a deep fear of fundamentalists of all stripes. Extreme fundamentalists have demonstrated their willingness to commit outrageous acts of terrorism or murder, feeling fully justified by the righteousness of their cause. This is as true of al-Qaeda coming from the Islamic religion as it is of White supremacists coming from the Christian religion. Extremist anti-abortionists have demonstrated that in their understanding of God and morality they are fully justified in bombing clinics and killing doctors in cold blood. What characterizes these true believers is their view that the end justifies the means. This is what makes the anti-abortionists so dangerous, the Islamic terrorists so hard to comprehend, and the radical White supremacist an object of fear. We know that these people do not conform to what most of us believe about right or wrong. They believe that the justice of their cause qualifies them to do anything and everything to those who oppose them.

This true believer mentality is not reserved for the most extreme religious or political fundamentalists. In a much more moderate form, it is a characteristic of many activists, and it is the reason that combating their attacks is a difficult game. They simply don't play by the same rules. Although most would never sink to commit illegal or violent activities, many of the true believer variety of activists do believe that the justice of their cause gives them great latitude in the tactics they employ and with the way they deal with the truth.

The ironic thing about this is that the activist comes to the public eye through the media and invariably has the white hat on. The company dragged into the spotlight starts with two strikes against it. First, because the accusation has been made, it already has the black hat on. Second, even before the accusation was made, it is presumed that the company's leaders are bad people chasing profits at the expense of the public good. Whenever company officials speak in their defense or tout their record, from the jaded news media's standpoint, they are just "spinning."

Activists come into the public perception battle with several advantages. We have already discussed one: the predisposition of the media to award them the white hat. Another is that they see such battles as largely emotional and effectively appeal to the fears and anger of the audience. Another is the simplicity with which they approach what are often complex issues; this simplicity plays well with how the media are able to treat the news. Finally, they seem to understand better than their corporate opponents that the real battle is over credibility.

This seems to be particularly true when the activist or opponent is of the true believer mentality. As a result, there tends to be a very disjointed debate as both sides spar. The company or organization under attack focuses on the "facts" (e.g., the extent and nature of emissions) and to carry on this discussion in a fairly formal, somewhat friendly, very professional tone. The activist, on the other hand, tends to focus on whether or not the company can be believed or trusted. The nature of the discourse is frequently much more personal, informal, passionate, and unambiguous. Whereas companies clearly want to be careful in what they are saying for legal as well as accuracy reasons, and they want to be dignified and professional, opponents are not equally hampered by these niceties. They clearly understand that ultimately the battle will be won or lost on the public perception of credibility or who is to be believed.

The reason this is such a powerful advantage is that credibility is the most powerful of all means of persuasion. As pointed out earlier, the ancient Greeks clearly understood that credibility (ethos)—the believability of the speaker—was a more important factor in persuasion than the best logical arguments or the most powerful emotional appeals.

This all-important issue of credibility is discussed later, but it is important to note the strategic advantage most activist opponents enjoy in this. The contemporary rules of public debate are that they can wholeheartedly and without too much regard for the truth attack the credibility of their targets, whereas the company responding needs to maintain the high road and focus only on the merits of the logical argument.

The two elected officials who have served as our models of activists and opponents have both perfected the techniques of undermining the credibility of the companies they oppose. In the power plant issue, the early debate focused on greatly exaggerated claims about environmental risk and damage. When those claims had largely been discredited, the focus shifted much more toward attempting to undermine the record of the company and the methods used to gain approval. For example, in a public hearing, the opponents focused an inordinate amount of time on the "discovery" they made shortly before the hearing began that, according to them, the company had paid to have their supporters show up at the hearing. It was one of the first times that the number of supporters had nearly equalled the number of opponents and that was of clear concern to the opponents. The accusation of the company paying its supporters to attend was a shock and a surprise to those of us who had worked hard to get community members supportive of the proposed facility to attend. The truth, as we discovered later, was that one local union strongly supportive of the project had offered to pay a small amount to cover the cost of fuel to its members who attended the meeting. The union members there were a minority of the supporters, and those who accepted the small payment were even fewer. The critical point was that the company knew nothing about those arrangements and would not have supported them had they been asked. However, the truth, as usual, was irrelevant. The opponents who made much of this in the public hearing accomplished their goal. The news media and perhaps the state panel listening to those speaking in favor of the facility became skeptical of the authenticity of the support.

The county council member opposing the plant pulled a similar stunt that almost proved physically dangerous. A public rally held by opponents on the steps of the county courthouse had attracted a crowd of a couple hundred opponents. At the last minute, to create a bit of balance, we had recruited a few supporters to hold up signs in support of the project. These few received strong abuse from the opponents, to the point where one decided he had had enough and left in disgust. One of our staff members grabbed his sign and was holding it when the county council member took the microphone. She focused the crowd's attention on the three plant supporters holding signs and announced that they were paid representatives of the company. She got the reaction she wanted. The crowd of opponents was incited and became physically threatening. Rather than risk injury or further incite an ugly crowd, we took the signs down and left the rally.

Companies engaged in these sorts of public issue battles might wish to keep the debate focused on the merits of their proposals or on the facts of the incidents causing concern. However, they need to be prepared for the very strong likelihood that the activists will shift the debate to whether or not their company is evil and whether they as leaders are evil. The starting point for those arguments will be that the company is big and has earning profits as its sole purpose. However, that is only the starting point. Next will come an exposé of the company's regulatory compliance record. Then, any negative news reports about the company or its leaders that can be accessed through today's Internet research tools will be rehashed with the most negative spin imaginable. Company leaders should also expect that if they or their company has ever been sued, the accusations of the legal opponents will be quoted at length and treated as if the accusations are the final judgment and truth. Finally, if the personal or professional ethics or behavior of the company leadership, any employees, or even friends and associates are less than squeaky clean, these failings may be trotted out as if they were core to the issue at hand. In a very real sense they are, no matter how unrelated to the subject, because the opponents understand that this is about which party is to be believed. They trust that you will stick to the facts and issues of the controversy and not counter with questions about their credibility.

Now They Have the Microphone

Understanding opponents and their tactics should give organizational leaders and communications professionals pause. They have some cultural advantages, some advantages in rules of engagement and, in many cases, they have the passion and freedom of true believers. Add to that the ability to communicate freely, quickly, and powerfully with a rapidly growing Internet community around the globe.

As a general rule, activists, opponents, and their organizations have been far more eager, skillful, and willing to employ the communication potential of the Internet than the companies and organizations they attack. It's not because the companies don't have a lot at stake—they have millions or billions of dollars of brand equity at stake. It's not because they don't have the resources. Of course, most have far more communication resources—including Internet access and tools—than their opponents. The reality is that it is precisely because of the strength of the company that makes the activists' use of these tools so effective. It might be called the *judo effect*, where the very strength and advantages of a company are used against it.

Look at what the Internet offers someone with the dedication and commitment to attack you. A Web site containing all the accusations and evidence or pseudoevidence supporting the attackers' claims can be launched in minutes at essentially no cost. The billions of pages of information on the Internet provide a rich source of information for those looking to damage your reputation. Communication between others who share concerns is accomplished at no cost and at the speed of light. Coalitions can be built not in months or weeks, but in hours. An audience can be attracted with relatively little time or effort, particularly when attackers make use of rapidly growing databases of like-minded people and organizations around the world. Momentum is created easily by mass emailing every bit of progress in the battle against the company to the growing audience around the world. By the time the savvy attackers bring the media into the picture by simply directing them to their Web site, a compelling case for widely supported public outrage has been built. The reporter's job is now much, much easier. There is no need to dig for angry people to interview or for the facts of the situation—it is all conveniently provided in instantaneous form. In fact, reporters who choose can simply go to the Web site to find names and contact information for people who would love to be quoted or go on camera. Then, when the report comes out in the media and the Web site address is announced, the attackers' efforts immediately become magnified.

Yesterday, at the office, we received an angry note via a client's Web site from a young person opposed to the power plant project we represent. She was angry because she did a search online to gather information for a school report about why this plant is so awful. Instead of finding the opponent's Web site, she found the proponent's—ours. She didn't like the information she found there at all. It explained why this plant was environmentally clean and responsible. What was most interesting was the tone that suggested we had somehow tricked her by having a Web site that was in favor of the project when she clearly only expected a site opposed to it. Might this attitude also be somewhat common in the general public? Certainly, consumers expect a manufacturer or even an industrial facility to have a Web site extolling the virtues of their product. Do they expect them to have one that counters arguments against them, or defends their environmental record, or touts the positive things they provide for their communities?

The two main uses of the Internet in public issues are to communicate information (or the organization's version of relevant information), and to build and activate a common interest group. Before looking at this second activity, we'll review how activists are making use of the Internet to communicate their version of a public issue or incident.

A Platform for Attacking Credibility

The tactics used by many activists identified earlier are clearly evident in a review of activist Web sites. We identified the 90 percent lie, in which a miniscule amount of truth is used to leave an impression that is fundamentally untrue. We talked about the activists' typical strategy of attacking the credibility of the company or its leaders, particularly when their factual or logical argument for opposition has been weakened. We also talked about the powerful, informal, emotional style of discourse and their use of overstatement and hyperbole.

An opponent's Web site about a proposed power plant in California is instructive. In this situation (in which I had no involvement), the opponents had strong support from the city's mayor and unanimous support from the city council in opposing the plant. Then the energy crisis happened, and despite strong local opposition to the facility, the California Energy Commission approved the plant. A review of the opponent's Web site subsequent to this approval clearly demonstrates that their primary objective was and is to damage the reputation of the company involved. There was no discussion of their perceived problems with the plant. Instead, it was all about the company's, in this case Calpine's, falling fortunes in the aftermath of the Enron debacle. Every negative article about stockholder concerns and slumping stock prices is rehashed on the opponent's Web site, along with the opponent's own take on the bad news the company is facing. Although this has virtually nothing to do with the proposed power plant that the organization opposes (their Web site identifies two area women as the founders of this organization), it does contribute to their effort to undermine company confidence and credibility.

A more blatant effort to undermine credibility is the next section of their site that purports to expose the companies lying about the proposed plant's steam plume. The Web site states,

> It takes the District Attorney to get Calpine to tell the truth. Throughout the two-year approval process Calpine maintained, despite plenty of evidence to the contrary, that the Metcalf Energy Center would not emit a visible plume. Recently a concerned neighbor contacted the District Attorney's office to see anything could be done to get Calpine to tell the truth. Unfortunately there are no laws against lying in such a manner but the District Attorney did meet with Calpine to discuss this issue. Here is the before and after of Calpine's web site:
>
> [Before]
>
> Will there be a steam plume?
>
> No. The Metcalf Energy Center will include "plume abatement" technologies in the project design. This means that the water vapor that is released from the facility will not be visible, even on cold days. Calpine and Bechtel are investing several million dollars in this design feature in order to meet the high visual standards proposed for North Coyote Valley.
>
> [After]
>
> Will there be a steam plume?
>
> In modern power plant construction, the water vapor normally rising above the cooling towers or stacks is called a "plume." The Metcalf Energy Center will include "plume

> **abatement" technology in the project design in order to meet the high visual standards proposed for North Coyote Valley. The system is designed to prevent prominent plumes during normal weather conditions year-round when equipment is in normal operation.**

A careful reading of the two statements shows the nature of the "lie" that Calpine is accused of. The second statement states that the plume abatement technology employed "is designed to prevent prominent plumes during normal weather conditions year-round when equipment is in normal operation." Apparently there is the possibility of abnormal weather conditions and abnormal operating conditions that could result in plumes that the abatement technology cannot effectively manage. Therefore, the straightforward "no" offered by the company is seen as a lie.

The conclusion to this clarification offered by the company in response to the District Attorney's inquiry is, according to the opponents, "One more reason why Calpine should not be trusted."

If this is the primary basis for undermining the company's credibility, it shows how far the opponents need to stretch. What it most clearly demonstrates is that the issue is not really about plume or no plume, it is about who is to be believed. Because opponents and companies are in effect forced to operate by different sets of rules, the opponents have a strong advantage in the credibility claim and blame game.

Building Audiences

The use of Web sites by activists to present their version of the controversy is important; however, the far more significant use of the Internet in these battles is the ability to create audiences and to efficiently communicate to large groups of people. This is what brings this kind of battle into the postmedia world, because previously anyone wishing to communicate quickly to large groups of people was forced to use the media. Paid advertising, large-scale direct mail, or news stories favorably presenting your point of view were the communication options.

Today, the Internet, much more than a means of publicly presenting information that audiences can "pull," has the ability to proactively "push" information and in the process build audiences or communities around shared interests. It is this ability that activist groups have used to great effect and this represents the true power of the microphone in their hands.

The fact that activists and others using the Internet as a communication tool can relatively quickly build audiences is demonstrated by the blogger phenomenon discussed earlier. Andrew Sullivan, one of the most successful of this new breed of Internet publishers, started Internet publishing in fall of 2000 and now routinely has 30,000 or more readers per day. Writing in the April 2002 issue of *Fast Company*, John Ellis stated, "What amazes the mainstream media community about the bloggers is how quickly they've established themselves. Sullivan is without question the most influential print journalist in Washington today."[6]

Using the Net to Network

One key to the success of Internet publishers is the way in which they link to existing groups, communities, or networks to quickly build audiences. In the pipeline accident discussed in Chapter 1, a small group of local activists took up the cause of pipeline safety immediately following the accident. Thanks to the Internet, it probably took them all of 10 minutes to link up with small but powerful groups of activists in other parts of the country already dedicated to the cause. The power plant opposition Web site contains numerous Web links—including links to organizations fighting causes completely unrelated to the concerns of this group. A "we'll scratch your back if you scratch ours" strategy is in place that enables one group to tap into the resources of another and create a much greater impression of political clout.

A quick review of activist Web sites demonstrates that two of the most commonly used words are *network* and *networking*. The ability to forge alliances and to tap into resources of other groups is one of the reasons why activists, who usually represent an extreme political position, have been effective far beyond their numbers to secure legislative and opinion change. It is current Internet technology that gives this basic and wise strategy wings. All the many advantages of the Internet from research, individual and mass email, shared information resources, compelling presentation, and no-cost instant publishing all make the task of an activist easier and less expensive.

The Web site for the Video Activist Network, *www.videoactivist.org*, is instructive and gives a hint into the future of activism. This organization promotes the use of video technology in the hands of amateurs to enhance the effectiveness of their causes. A particularly popular application of this strategy targets police brutality. Certainly, the disgusting images of police officers in the World Trade Organization riots in Seattle did much to turn public opinion against the Seattle police, with one result being the political defeat of the one-term mayor in office during the riots. The Video Activist Network Web site provides a variety of services, including the opportunity to present your activist video on their site in either downloadable or streaming video formats. The section providing advice on how to get maximum impact out of the video catching the bad guys in action illustrates the point being made here. The first two suggestions are to use email and a Web site. Advice is given about asking for Web links so that "viral marketing" techniques can be used to facilitate distribution and exposure of the video.

The emphasis on the Internet as a means of inexpensively reaching audiences is clear. Those savvy enough to build audiences, capture email lists and contact data, and network with ever more powerful cohort groups have the power of the media in the laptop in their back bedroom.

When the Politicians Get Involved

It has become a virtual certainty that when an accident or issue hits the public consciousness with enough force, political activity will ensue. We have become so accustomed to this that we might have to look back in our history as a nation to realize that not every industrial accident or large-scale business failure in the past resulted in congressional hearings and sweeping new laws. Today, however, it is assumed that outraged citizens will call for and get the attention of elected officials to the problem covered in the news today. Politicians react instinctively to the opportunity to address a pressing and current problem while getting much-needed publicity. I have yet to hear a politician respond to a problem without suggesting that there is some legislative cure for which he or she will take personal responsibility for making happen. New laws and regulations are the inevitable result.

The Oil Pollution Act of 1990 stands out as a primary example. This sweeping act, which monitors and controls the environmental behavior of the nation's oil companies, was created out of the *Exxon Valdez* disaster. One effect of this and similar laws has been subjecting people engaged in activities that result in damage to the environment to severe criminal penalties. I heard a state environmental official tell a group of oil industry managers that any oil spill will involve criminal investigation. This, no doubt, was an overstatement. Within the oil industry, for one, there is a new type of job. They are called "go-to-jail-jobs," which simply means that the role includes supervising processes in which there is a risk of going to jail should something bad happen. Clearly, in this world, there are no more accidents. Behind every unfortunate event, the immediate assumption is of negligence, evil intent, or profit-driven apathy, but nothing is ever an accident.

The issue is not whether this is good or bad or whether the legislation and regulations that result from these high-profile situations are positive or negative. From a public issue management standpoint, it is vital that today's leaders and communication professionals understand that when the politicians get involved, the incident takes on a whole new dimension.

In the pipeline accident mentioned earlier, the activists, strongly supported by the grieving family members, immediately attacked the regulatory body responsible for pipeline safety. They effectively pitted one federal agency against another and put the head of the pipeline regulatory agency in a very difficult spot. Her natural and reasonable reaction was to play it as tough as possible against the company involved.

Imagine for a moment that you have an outstanding regulatory record. In dozens of years of operation you have had no major citations and you have one of the best safety, health, and environmental track records in the industry. Then something bad happens. It is to be expected that the activists will attack whatever they can find in your record that can make you look bad. It is also to be expected that the news media will report those accusations and consider that your efforts to put them in context are "spin" and "defensiveness." Now, the very people in high places that you had worked hard to develop positive relationships with based on your excellent performance turn on you. Just when you need them to state the truth—that you are a careful and responsible operator—they treat you as if you are a pariah. They really don't have a choice: It is you or them—your business or their career. If it appears you are too cozy or they are not being sufficiently harsh, the pressure mounts, not just from the press and the activists, but from state representatives or senators and members of Congress. Once the black hat has firmly settled onto your head, even your closest friends in high places will appear strangely distant.

However, things can get worse when the momentum is built for real political action. All that is necessary for momentum to build is for one or two elected officials to determine that the situation in which you are involved is the political horse they are going to ride. At that point, it doesn't really matter if they are tilting at windmills and real, toothy legislation will never result. From a reputation management standpoint, the incident has suddenly turned from a sprint into a marathon. Now you have more than one player who wants to keep the story front and center. The political opportunity dies when the public focuses on another subject—and then the horse dies. So, now the news media have one more force intent on keeping the story hot. We can no longer talk about the marriage of convenience between media and activist. When politicians join the fray, a mutually beneficial relationship grows among all three parties, so the black hat becomes even more firmly fixed and the battle is guaranteed to last a long time.

Three years after the pipeline incident in my hometown, legislative activity at the federal level was still ongoing, so the news story continues. Reporters doing their job need to assume that readers need background. If your company is involved in such an event, as long as the legislative process drags on, your name will continue to appear in the background of these stories. It is very difficult in these circumstances to be very effective in public efforts at rebuilding confidence when there are continual reminders of the events in question and your role in them.

Here, then are the problems: Activists with the power of the media. Politicians eager to jump on emotionally charged public outrage bandwagons. News reporters needing to tell a gripping story to compete effectively against other entertainment opportunities. A public audience tired of all this—jaded, cynical, and angry. It is no wonder that few corporate leaders feel adequately prepared to deal with reputation crises of large magnitude. The instant news era of the Internet does indeed magnify the risks, but it also magnifies the opportunities of dealing with those risks.

It's time to turn from the problems posed by this instant news world to the solutions and opportunities it also represents.

Endnotes

1. Lamer, Timothy and O'Steen, Alice Lynn, "Businessmen Behaving Badly: Primetime's World of Commerce," Media Research Center, *www.mediaresearch.org*, June 16, 1997.
2. Dezenhall, Eric, *Nail 'Em: Confronting High Profile Attacks on Celebrities and Business*, Amherst, NY: Prometheus Books, 1999, p. 108. Used by permission.
3. Stephanopolous, George, *All Too Human: A Political Education*, Boston, New York, London: Back Bay/Little Brown & Company, 1999, p. 87.

4. Dezenhall, p.55.
5. Dezenhall, p. 55.
6. Ellis, John, “All the News That’s Fit to Blog,” *Fast Company*, U.S. News and World Report, Inc., April 2002, p. 112.

CHAPTER 6

How the Rules Have Changed

Today, a significant number of companies conduct incident drills. Some of these companies, particularly in the fuel industry, do so in part to meet federal requirements. Although the primary purpose of these is to exercise the operational response, or the work done to contain the incident and clean up the mess, practicing the public communication function is also an important part of these drills. In one drill I observed, as a provider of the communication technology used, the issue of old rules versus new rules became very clear. The person who assumed the role of public information officer (PIO) was from the "old school." Others on the communication team, younger and less experienced, were working hard to get out an initial press release, but the veteran PIO advised them, "There's no reason to get this out before 2 p.m. because we'll have plenty of time for the evening news cycle."

Someone forgot to tell him in the era of instant global news, of multiple 24-hour news channels, of satellite trucks and the hunger for breaking news, of intense competition, and mostly of the widespread use of the Internet to gain public information, every minute is a news cycle. Scheduling releases made sense when everyone would wait. Now the news is distributed all the time. It's just one example of how understanding some of the fundamental changes occurring in the preparation and distribution of public information forces a reassessment of the traditional way of doing things.

We have identified three streams of change in public information: the coming of the Internet with its demands for speed and directness, the development of infotainment as a popular style of news reporting and presentation, and the enhanced power of the activist, whose ability to influence opinions is based in part on the other two streams. These converge to create a new public information environment.

When the environment changes, the old ways of doing things don't produce the same results. Someone has described insanity as doing the same thing over and over but expecting a different result. Well, if the environment has changed, if the rules have changed, and if the way the game is played has changed, doing the same thing over and over again will indeed produce a different result. If the temperature drops, wearing the same coat you wore yesterday will no longer keep you warm. Conducting the business of corporate communications, crisis management, or issue management in the same old way when the public information environment has changed will not produce the expected results.

Although there is no possibility of fundamental agreement on rules for such a subject as complex as public communication, these "old" and "new" rules are suggested as a means of stimulating thinking about how things change in response to changing conditions.

Rule 1:

- Old: Meet demands of the media.
- New: Meet demands of a wide variety of stakeholders who expect immediate and direct information.

There are a couple of good reasons why the old rule was written and continues to be practiced today. First, in the media-dominated world, the way to quickly get the news to all stakeholders was through the media. That was how they were going to get the information anyway, so the best strategy was to concentrate your efforts on telling your story the way you wanted it told. Second, public relations was a neat corporate division that defined boundaries of activities. Advertising people dealt with the public in selling the product or service, human resource people dealt with employee communication, financial communication to stockholders was handled by the finance department, and the public relations people dealt with the media. Although this has been changing and more companies and organizations have communications executives that manage external communication with all audiences, the vast majority of public relations professionals who I have dealt with continue to view their primary task as managing media relations.

In the instant news environment, these nice neat divisions lose their relevance. Key customers need to know what is happening and the impact on the company when they read about their supplier in the news and it is wearing the black hat. The most pressing financial news information suddenly isn't about the upcoming quarterly report; it is about efforts underway to rebound after the terrorist attack that hit the headquarters. Fenceline neighbors need, for their very health and safety, to find out what is happening in the facility, and if they should evacuate. Agencies responding to a major incident need to be informed continually of the unfolding response, even if they are in another part of the state or country. If the event is in the news, elected officials will have a great many people asking them what they know about it and what they are doing about it. As a result, they will be pressing hard to be "on the inside" of the response. One huge lesson that came out of September 11, 2001 was the critical need for multiple communication methods for employees and their families. There is no higher urgency of information than when the lives and livelihoods of friends and family are at stake.

In this new information environment, leaders and communicators need to think through various scenarios with these questions: Who will have high relevance and high demand for information? Given today's instant news expectations, how will they expect to get the information from us and when will they expect it?

Rule 2:

- Old: Follow news cycles.
- New: There is a new cycle every minute.

We discussed this rule briefly at the beginning of the chapter. When talking with public relations professionals, this is usually my first clue about whether someone is operating in the instant news world. It tells me whether or not they realize how profoundly the news environment has changed.

News deadlines are becoming extinct. Certainly there are media outlets that have regular deadlines, particularly print media. However, those deadlines now apply more to the in-depth, follow-up stories, not the major announcements that inform the public of what is going on. The news magazine coverage is extremely important, but it provides the context, background, and details after the public has gained interest in the story that they got via broadcast, off the street, or from the electronic news service on their desk. Even this important service is threatened by the virtually unlimited detail and background that can be inexpensively published on the Web and provided to audiences on their terms.

In several drills I have observed or participated in recently, the public information expectation was that the first release of information would be somewhere between one and eight hours after the incident began. When asked about what his expectation was regarding the initial release of information, Scott Miller, a respected environmental reporter for KING5, the NBC affiliate in Seattle, replied, "Immediately. It may not be realistic but that's what we have to deal with." The expectations have clearly changed. As we discuss later, the consequence of not meeting expectations is the very real risk of being viewed as unresponsive and therefore irresponsible.

Rule 3:

- Old: Bad news usually goes away quickly.
- New: Bad news can be controlled by opponents and politicians and frequently has a long life.

There's good news and bad news about today's news environment. The fast pace and priority on the instant news channels of broadcast and Internet tend to make stories come and go quicker than ever. Breaking news, after all, can only last so long. The depth of coverage is limited, as is the time a story stays on the top of the news editor's priority list. The bad news is that the story can hang around a lot longer than it used to because the story is no longer controlled only by the media.

Two factors can result in the lingering of stories that would otherwise disappear into the ether of old news. One is that opponents have the tools to keep a story alive; the other is that many stories result in political interest and this inevitably results in stories becoming protracted.

If your situation results in activist or opponent activity, you can count on the story being around a lot longer than you would like. With a person or group with a vested interest in keeping the story in the headlines, it will normally have a much longer shelf life. Any new information, problems with previous statements, or new developments such as legal actions are fair game for the activists to reactivate the story with the media. It is not the reporter who won't let go that is the concern here; it is the activist, who for various reasons has a personal stake in making certain the story doesn't die. Not only does he or she have the opportunity to keep it in the media's radar scopes, he or she has the broadcast tools to keep delivering information or misinformation personally. The audience might be smaller, but it can be troublesome and demands ongoing company resources for a surprisingly long time.

Similarly, when elected officials get involved in the story, their involvement inevitably creates an entirely new dimension: Now it is not just the story about the controversy or the event. The story evolves into what the people or the government are going to do to make certain such behavior doesn't occur again or go unpunished. From the media standpoint, each new development on the political front requires at least a brief rehash of the event or controversy that led to the action, so your company or organization will be featured again, and not in a way you would choose.

The old rule, very much in place in most organizations, is to muddle through the story while it is in the headlines, then get back to business as quickly as possible. That strategy must change because in many situations, the story could last months and potentially years. Ongoing damage to the organization's reputation must be anticipated. A recovery strategy must include the possibility or likelihood that the company or organization will not take just the main hit of the breaking news or headlines, but the pain of a thousand cuts. Strategic considerations include how strongly to communicate directly with the public and key stakeholders, for how long, and what resources are needed to focus on this issue even long after the public furor has receded.

Rule 4:

- Old: Accuracy above all.
- New: Speed above all.

The old rule is a very good one, and many communication professionals are going to roll their eyes when I suggest that this rule has changed. After all, there is nothing more damaging to an effort to build public confidence than providing false information. Indeed, credibility is everything. This vital topic is explored in much greater depth later. The problem in the world of instant news is that credibility is not just being accurate with the information: It is also based on providing that information very quickly. In fact, speed might be more important than accuracy when it comes to credibility now.

When the competition for fickle news audiences depends to a great extent on who is first with the information, the media frenzy can be overwhelming. In this environment, it matters less to reporters, editors, and producers what the information is and who it comes from than it does that they have real information to convey. At the scene of an accident, it is usually considerably more valuable to get an on-camera interview with an eyewitness who says he thinks he saw four people taken away by ambulance than to wait and get official word from someone in a position to more accurately determine the number of people injured. After all, the reporter could be faulted for providing inaccurate information if he or she speculated, but reporting on someone else's speculation is just reporting.

I do not mean to suggest for a moment that responsible reporters have little regard for the truth. Certainly they do, because they also know that their future as a reporter is dependent on their own credibility and the credibility of the stories they present. However, no self-respecting reporter will wait patiently while the right company official checks and rechecks the facts when those "facts" or presumed facts are available from other sources.

The question for the leaders responsible for protecting the reputation of the company or organization comes down to whether or not they wish to be the source of information about the issue or incident; if not, they must be willing to allow others to provide the facts and the perspective for them. It is well-established public relations doctrine that to have any real influence on the course of story, the company involved must be the source for as much information as possible. What many have not realized is that the pace of reporting has increased such that if they are not able to respond very quickly, they give away this important opportunity to impact the story.

The accuracy versus speed dilemma is at the heart of needed changes in communications planning for most organizations. Crisis communication plans normally identify in some detail the organization structure appropriate for various types of crises and who is to approve what information when. These very reasonable measures are put in place to make certain that the organization speaks with a single voice and that the leadership has the opportunity to maintain control of the message at very critical times. These plans now need to be re-evaluated. If the approval process in place cannot deliver the information with the speed required in the "now is too late" world of instant news, those plans must change.

There are three basic reasons most companies and organizations today will fail to meet the speed and accuracy demands of the instant news world: people, policies, and technology. To respond effectively, the communication team—which includes the communication professionals, the executive leadership, lawyers, consultants, response managers, and so on—needs to clearly understand the speed and accuracy demands and must have a well-honed command, control, and communication system in place to meet those demands. Crisis response policies need to place a very high priority on the public information function, providing responders and executives with specific speed and accuracy response guidelines. Finally, the technology needs to be in place that will allow these frequently far-flung team members to implement the policies and work efficiently together to meet this difficult demand.

It must always be remembered that credibility is what is at stake and credibility depends on speed and accuracy, although it is not equated with either. Scott Miller, the environmental reporter quoted earlier, pointed the way out of this dilemma: "Tell us what you know, when you know it."[1] In other words, if you have clearly established facts, don't wait to accumulate a complete story to provide them. Give them to the press now. If you don't have all the information, give them what you have and tell them what you don't have and when you might be able to provide it. Never, ever speculate and never provide information that you are not certain is accurate.

Rule 5:

- Old: Legal review optional.
- New: Legal review required.

Every situation is different, and certainly there are going to be public issues and news events in which the role of attorneys is minimal or nonexistent. However, attorneys are increasingly involved in situations involving public interest, the news, and the reputation of the company. This is true for a few reasons. One is that the overwhelming majority of crises that affect companies have a direct legal component. Most corporate crises involve legal action or are caused by legal action. The company or individual executives are being sued, are suing, or are being investigated for regulatory or criminal violations. The second reason is that there is a much higher risk of legal action coming from an accident, environmental event, or product or service issue. Finally, and perhaps most significantly, there has been a strong trend toward criminalizing corporate behavior, particularly as it relates to environmental damage.

What this means is that communications professionals, either working as consultants or operating in communication departments within companies or organizations, need to consider that attorneys are going to be part of the response team in most situations of high public interest. Let's be honest here—the working relationship between the professionals dealing in the court of law and the professionals dealing in the court of public opinion is often uncomfortable. This difficult topic is addressed in more detail in a later chapter. What is important here is to understand that at the very time there is a premium on speed of response, there is a significant addition to the communication team—a group of attorneys—who march to the beat of an entirely different drummer. If court cases were handled like news stories, the evidence would be collected in an hour or two and the case would seldom extend past a couple of days.

Because speed of response is as critical as getting legal approval on statements, there is no way out of this dilemma other than to get everyone who will be part of the communication response on the same page as it relates to the public information requirements. Only executives with strong leadership who are aware of the new instant news demands can truly make this happen. In both preparing for and responding to a news event, few public information professionals have the power to overrule attorneys (nor should they). Executives have the responsibility to look out for the best interests of the company and therefore need to weigh the frequently competing requirements of the court of law and the court of public opinion. It is only the executives who can pull these two forces together to make certain that the public information demands are understood and the preparation is in place to enable a speedy and accurate response.

Rule 6:

- Old: Provide the minimum needed.
- New: Provide what the most detail-hungry audience requires.

The media are no longer the only audience of today's communicator. Reporters are just one of many groups of stakeholders who expect and demand information from you. Meeting the very different information needs of the very different audiences represents a new challenge for most in corporate communications.

Although I continue to be surprised by it, it is clear that many seasoned public relations professionals subscribe to the "less is better" theory of providing information to the media. There is some justification for the idea that the company should provide only the minimum amount of information needed: Don't tell more than what they ask for, never volunteer anything, and if you know something bad might come out, wait until it is out before providing any information on the subject. That is a matter of communication strategy and although in general I don't subscribe to the thinking behind it, in the instant news world, it is largely a moot point because communicators are not dealing with just the news media anymore.

Leaving the media aside for a moment, those responsible for providing public information about the company need to take into consideration a variety of stakeholders, starting with employees. Employees whose livelihoods depend on the success of the company and whose social life may well revolve around many other people employed in the company have a high relevance/demand quotient. Their view of management will depend to some degree on how vital information about important public events is conveyed to them. Large customers, stockholders, government officials, bankers, neighbors, and community leaders are some of the other groups that might have a high relevance/demand quotient. In this instant news world, they simply cannot be brushed off. They demand and expect information and if they are important to the future of the company, their demands need to be met.

In terms of quantity of information, the media's demands vary greatly. Reporters for national news outlets can only deal with minimal information, whereas local and regional reporters and those representing specific interest groups such as trade publications have a much higher demand for detail. Reporters for major news organizations have exceptionally high relevance/demand in the very early stages of a major story. After all, their reputations and the reputations of the news organizations they represent are at stake in getting information to their audiences as quickly as possible. However, for most stories, this relevance/demand dissipates relatively quickly. The relevance of California Congressman Gary Condit, for months the subject of numerous news reports about a missing intern, disappeared in the dust of the World Trade Center disaster. Although news media relevance can disappear quickly, the relevance to other key stakeholders is not likely to disappear. Voters in Condit's congressional district continued to have a strong interest in his actions, even after the September 11 attacks.

To meet the demands of these other groups, today's communicator needs to be prepared to provide in-depth, ongoing information about the issue or event for a considerable time. Because that is the situation, they also need to be prepared to continue to provide it to the news media during the entire time because the public information provided to stakeholders is, after all, public information. It would take a very small company to be able to provide relevant details to its employees without fear of those details finding their way to the media. The case is similar with stockholders, neighbors, and others. Although the news media may have lost interest, the continuing flow of information might result in renewed interest or at the very least, a continuing source of information indirectly provided to the media. If it is going to find its way indirectly to the media and your interest is in protecting your credibility with the media, it makes sense to provide the complete details directly.

RULE 7:

- Old: Assume some level of news balance.
- New: Someone is going to be wearing the black hat.

It is very difficult to devise an effective response strategy if there are fundamental differences in understanding of the news business. Most executives believe that within today's news business there still exists the underlying philosophy of fairness, objectivity, and telling the whole story as carefully and truthfully as possible. At the risk of being cynical, that is not my observation. I am not saying that today's reporters are bad people or that they have evil intent. It's just not how they see the game being played. They know their bosses have their eyes continually on the ratings meter. Ratings are determined largely by how the news story they are covering or how they are covering it grips the audience. Compelling visuals, heart-wrenching human reactions, clear-cut good versus evil, ironic twists, and surprise endings are the elements they look for in telling the everyday stories that might involve your company or organization.

Anger and frustration were clearly written on the face of the executive responsible for a large industrial facility. Another news story had come out about an ongoing serious legal issue. There had been no attempt to understand the underlying meaning of the legal action the company had taken. There had not even been any call or conversation. The facts were gathered from the court record and the headline in the local paper made the company look rotten. There was nothing untrue about what was written, it was the interpretation, the subtle nuances of writing, or the "spin" the reporter had put on the story that was troublesome to the executive.

This was a very mild-mannered executive, so the depth of his anger was surprising and it was clear he expected me to do something about it. I couldn't explain it at the time, but there was little to do. No retraction could be requested—the facts were there. The headline is almost always written by someone other than the reporter and is usually taken from the first paragraph or two of the story and in this case (as in so many others) the headline writer caught the reporter's spin and spun it further. The later parts of the story provided more balance but the headline writer clearly didn't get that far or didn't care given his or her orientation to the story.

Primarily what I needed to explain to the executive was that in this particular situation, in the greater controversy of which the legal action was a small part, the media had placed the black hats on our heads. Given that context, the story wasn't overtly bad. What we needed to do, rather than react to a particular story, was remove the black hat. That was a bigger challenge and a more important one than reacting to one day's reporting.

Communication strategy is greatly affected by the anticipation of how the news media will perceive and present a story. That's why gaining a gut-level understanding of the new media environment and the instant news world is fundamental. It's vital not just to communication professionals who need to develop the strategic recommendations and implement them, but to the organizational leaders who need to approve and participate in them.

Fortunately, because the news media often adopt the same approach to attracting and keeping audiences and their attention as the entertainment industry, the new rules are quite predictable: Does the subject in question have anything to do with the health, safety, or well-being of the public or of individuals in the community? Is there a hint of crime, corruption, conspiracy, or scandal involved? Is there any heart-wrenching human impact that can be visually recorded or powerfully presented? Are there antagonists involved who are willing to make bold, outlandish statements or accusations? Are there powerful people in trouble? If the answer to any of these questions is yes, the media believe that the story has some compelling interest and will drive the story in a way that takes advantage of that. The urgent question that communicators need to consider in that early response time is who is going to be wearing the black hat and who will be wearing the white hat.

Rule 8:

- Old: Wait for them to call.
- New: Credibility depends on getting to them first.

I remember the conversation well, especially the patronizing smile on the face of the senior public relations manager in this situation. Yes, important new facts had come out in an accident investigation; facts that the reporters would gather soon. No, we would not contact the reporters and proactively give them the information. Hell, they hadn't been treating us all that nicely, why should we do them any favors? Besides, it's better if they ask us the questions and we can respond. Who knows, maybe they don't even have the information yet or something else will come along and it won't be such a big deal. Why try to make it something bigger than it is?

I pushed. After all, this was in my community and I had worked hard to gain the respect and trust of these reporters. I wanted them to know that if I had information of importance to them that I could release, they would get it. Trust, respect, and credibility were the most important tools of the trade.

In a different situation, a client had a small-scale incident. Given extensive coverage of not much larger incidents, it was likely that even a minor situation would get coverage. In this case, it was my call to make and I had the trust of the facility management. I released the information as soon as I had it. One lower level manager went semiballistic: How stupid of us to draw the attention of the media to something that they might not even find out about. Certainly, emergency agency notifications had been made and all the local media were tapped into those notifications, but it didn't mean we had to bring it to their attention, too. The senior manager was now in a position to settle the argument. What was at stake was how we would handle proactive release of information for future events. I explained that I was brought into the situation because of extensive negative media coverage. My primary concern in working with the media was for them to trust me and the company. I would not necessarily tell everything they wanted me to or give them "inside" information, but the reporters should trust that if I was able to give them information that they needed, they could count on me to provide it. They should also count on me to help get management to understand what information they needed and when. I wanted their trust and respect and I wanted the company to have the trust and respect of the local reporters and editors. I explained to the manager that to gain that, we needed to be forthcoming. He agreed. There was no coverage of the minor incident.

One of the changing circumstances of the instant news world makes this situation easier to resolve. As we will see in the next rule, proactive and direct communication is becoming the required strategy. If you are going to proactively tell your story to employees, stakeholders, and members of the public, you should tell the media directly. In this open, instant information world, telling one is telling all. Even bad news is taken much better if it comes directly from the source.

Rule 9:

- Old: Let the media tell your story.
- New: Tell the story yourself.

A recent discussion with an executive responsible for crisis management for one of the world's largest companies illustrates the philosophical divide between the media and the postmedia world. We were discussing use of the Internet in a major crisis. Whereas he and I were proponents of the idea of "push," the consensus of the management team was "pull." The managers decided that if the company experienced a major crisis, they would supply information on the corporate Web site but would not proactively distribute that information to those interested. If somebody wanted information, he or she could come to the company and ask for it. This included the decision not to prepare server infrastructure that could withstand the potentially millions of hits their servers would take should a number of people decide they wanted to "pull" the information from the site. The managers decided their best strategy was to be information reactive, and not worry about whether or not they could actually react.

An instant news world strategy provides the capability of instantly "pushing" information to predetermined audiences and the ability to accumulate audiences on the fly. It means thinking in advance about whose opinion of you is vitally important, and making certain they have the story correct and straight from the horse's mouth. It means being instantly responsive to those who are interested enough to inquire and making certain that they are proactively given information as updates become available. Fundamentally, it means building credibility by meeting or exceeding information expectations.

What the managers of this large company apparently did not yet understand is that information expectations have changed and are continuing to change rapidly. As more people have access to the instant information technology of the Internet and as they gain an understanding of the potential this represents for a company to communicate directly and personally with them, they will not be satisfied with "pull." If my daughter is in an accident and my best friend knows how she is doing and knows that I don't know, but doesn't pick up the phone to call me, will that friendship be damaged or destroyed? Absolutely. Friends don't let friends remain ignorant, especially about something that is vitally important to them.

What those managers were indeed saying was that those people who invested their pensions and life savings in our stock don't deserve to be informed of events that could deeply affect their futures. Those employees who have dedicated their lives to making this company successful don't deserve to hear from us how a crisis might change their lives. Those neighbors and community members whose health, safety, and sense of security might be threatened by our actions can just check our Web site or read in the newspaper what we are doing to protect them. They don't deserve or need to hear from us directly.

That attitude is fine if the stakeholders have no expectation of communication. Today, however, if they have no expectation of direct, personal, instantaneous communication it is either because they are in the ever-decreasing minority who do not understand the potential of current communication technology or because they have already lost faith and trust in the corporation. If they have the communication expectation and they are treated as these managers planned to treat them, it is a virtual certainty that they will lose whatever faith and trust they might currently have in the company.

Several months after I had the conversation with that executive, the company had an incident that was covered in the national news. In news stories taken from the AP wire and written in *The Wall Street Journal*, it was noted that no company spokesperson was available for comment and all the information about the event came from the government agencies responding to the incident. The "pull" theory was clearly not working to the advantage of the company's reputation.

What most surprises me is that this way of thinking can be so prevalent at the highest levels of some of the world's greatest companies, yet it is these same people who frequently sit around and talk about how poorly they are treated in the press. It is these same communicators and executives who authorize the spending of millions of dollars in paid advertising to get their message out. This can only be attributed to the fact that they do not understand that they too have become broadcasters. They have the power of the media in their own hands. They can tell their own story. However, they continue to allow others to tell their story for them, even while expressing complete distrust in those whose hands they have placed their brand value and their very future.

The rules of public communication are being rewritten almost daily. As our legal system is struggling to keep up with changes brought about by new technologies, such as the protection of artistic and intellectual property, so today's business leaders are struggling to keep up with the changing rules of public information. That challenge is not likely to go away anytime soon.

Endnotes

1. Personal communication. Used by permission.

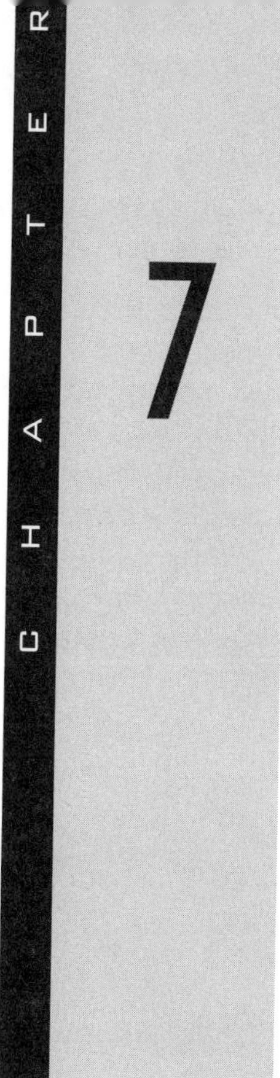

7 Communication Strategies for the Instant News World

What do you communicate and to whom in a world where now is almost always too late? That is the overriding question for communicators responsible for reputation and brand value management in the early years of the 21st century. Here's another way of putting it: How do I get the right information to the right people, right now?

Nearly every day in the international news, major companies are struggling mightily under the onslaught of accusations and revelations:

- A leading airline came under heavy fire for not allowing a Secret Service agent on a flight to join the president in Texas. When it became known that the agent was of Middle Eastern descent, the charges of racial profiling and even racism by Arab American groups were printed in papers and broadcast into homes across the nation.

- A national restaurant chain spends millions of dollars sponsoring and affiliating with every African American cause it can in the wake of national press coverage of one or more of the restaurant chain's disturbing racist practices.
- One of the most powerful oil companies with a potent consumer brand became absorbed into another major oil company and its famous brand was scheduled for phase-out after accusers demonstrated sexual and racial discrimination at the highest executive levels.
- Two giants in the automotive industry were sent reeling and one brand was potentially permanently damaged as a result of a slow response to a tire manufacturing problem. The auto manufacturer laid off nearly 30,000 employees in early 2002.
- The early months of 2002 found the national press focused on the actions of one of the world's most prestigious professional service companies in the aftermath of the collapse of Enron. In the wake of a criminal indictment for obstruction of justice, clients of the firm headed for the nearest exit, resulting in the company's demise a few months later.

No effective communication strategy can cover for people and their organizations who foolishly squander the public trust. When real and serious problems become known, those problems need to be addressed quickly. Alert management will root those problems out and solve them before they become an organization-destroying public embarrassment. Each and every day, executives of companies and organizations are discovering and responding to problems within the organization that could result in serious public perception problems: sexual harassment, safety lapses, environmental issues, illegal activities, and questionable ethical behavior. When positive actions are taken by alert and responsible managers, there is no news to report. It is when these things go on without being noticed or continue uncorrected after being discovered that a reputation crisis is possible.

There are two very different starting points in dealing with a reputation crisis. If the accusations are false, the response must address the negative perceptions caused by the false accusations. However, if the accusations are true or even partly true, the communication response is wholly dependent on the organization recognizing the wrong and very quickly communicating the recognition and the changes made. Only then can work begin on repairing damage to the company's public image. Unfortunately, too many perceive public relations as fundamentally dishonest because too often corporate or organizational communication has been disingenuous. It doesn't work. The truth will always come out. That's why the communication team can only do its work if the company is indeed innocent of the charges it faces or has moved quickly to rectify the real problems that have been identified.

It has become painfully clear in the past few years that companies and organizations depend on the good opinion of a great many people to operate. In some respects this is not new. The village cobbler would probably see his business suffer if his customers and fellow villagers believed him to be a lout and a crook. Now, however, we live in a global village with many people with the motivation and capability of accusing huge companies with valuable brands of being louts, crooks, and environmental destroyers. The role of public opinion in the ability of a company or organization to operate and grow might be called the *public franchise*. It is an unspoken agreement, an unofficial consensus of various groups. It is granted virtually automatically; in other words, when a company or organization comes to the attention of these groups that make up the "public," there is the presumption of innocence. However, this presumption is fragile and easily lost. When companies lose their public franchise, they cannot operate effectively. ValuJet lost it and became a new company. The industrial facility referred to earlier in the discussion on politicians and activists lost its public franchise and although it continues to try to operate, it is so boxed in and restricted that it has essentially no room to maneuver. Its ability to operate under its existing name and brand has been seriously compromised.

At the time of this writing, Firestone continues to do business while attempting to rebuild its brand and its public franchise, but the jury is very much out. Ford will almost certainly survive with its brand intact, but it is paying a high price and its CEO already paid with his job. The professional service giant Arthur Andersen lost its public franchise and with it, its corporate life. Exxon, now ExxonMobil, continues to operate but its name and public franchise have been damaged and that damage has cost the company and its stockholders billions of dollars.

Communicators cannot prevent the mistakes, misbehavior, and carelessness that often cause this loss of public esteem and subsequent loss of brand value, but communicators and executives are tasked with protecting that value whether the organization deserves the scorn and disrespect or not. One very sad reality of this instant news and infotainment-dominated world is that far too often the accusations are not justified or the consequences paid far outstrip the faults that caused the controversy in the first place. In these situations, it is most certainly a communication issue.

How does one go about devising a communication strategy that will protect that public franchise and brand value? Are there differences in that strategy required by the instant news environment?

Strategic thinking starts with a clear picture of what a happy result will look like. We've been repeatedly advised by management gurus to start with the end in mind. Another way of putting it is what is your picture of winning? It is very difficult to play a game if the members of the team do not understand or agree on the definition of winning. Far too many executives have a negative view of public relations expenditures, and it is almost always because the communication professionals have suggested solutions without clearly defining the desired end result of those tactics.

The goal or definition of winning might very well be different if the organization is in a precrisis mode, or in the middle of a reputation crisis, or recovering from one. If your organization has any risk for a reputation crisis at all, you are currently in one of those three modes. Regardless of the specifics, once there is an understanding of the public franchise and the fact that relationships with strategic individuals constitute the core of a business' value, the definition of winning will always revolve around creating maximum value in the minds of the right people. In other words, the ultimate goal of a communications effort is to create, strengthen, or recover relationships. It is to help the right people place a high value on what the organization does for them.

It seems to me that gaining the confidence and loyalty of the right people is or should be the bottom-line goal of virtually any organization whether it is articulated that way or not. From a communication strategy standpoint, it is very helpful to think of the goal of the communication effort as building relationships. Relationships, after all, depend on communication. Therefore, the starting point of communication strategy is some form of this statement: We want the right people to place a high value on our existence. Now, how do we do that?

It starts with determining who those right people are. The specifics of any communication strategy are going to deal with the questions that follow. Nothing in these questions is specific to the instant news world. However, the answers might vary somewhat from the more traditional views of public information and communication strategy. The key communications strategy questions are as follows:

1. Audience: Whom do we need to talk to?
2. Message: What message do we need to convey?
3. Listening: What do we need to hear from them?
4. Voice: Who needs to deliver the message?
5. Media: How should we communicate?

Audience: Whom Do We Need to Talk to?

The media world response is clear: reporters. However, in the instant news world, communicators need to look past the reporters to the recipients of the information. The key questions are who has a high degree of interest in the information about our company or this event and why? For which audiences is this information highly relevant and who has high demand for it? Certainly reporters have high relevance/demand because their jobs and futures as reporters depend on delivering the information that delivers ratings and readership.

The communication team needs to think like a CEO at this critical point. Companies and organizations exist only because certain people value their existence. If no one places a value on whether or not the organization is there, it will not be there for long. So who values the organization? If it is a government agency, the value is in the minds of the elected officials who authorize funding, and their willingness to fund is directly related to the value they perceive their constituents see in the agency. A police agency, for example, will suffer severe consequences if the public it serves perceives it as ineffective or—even worse—evil and corrupt. An environmental agency will lose prestige, funding, and perhaps its existence if the elected officials believe their voters see nothing good coming from the agency's efforts. For companies, the question of value extends to a whole number of people. Do the employees value the company? Hopefully, but only in relation to how easy it is to replace the company's contribution to their income and the fulfillment of meaning and purpose in their lives. Do stockholders value the company? Probably directly in proportion to the company's performance in meeting return expectations. Do customers value it? Yes, in direct proportion to how easy it is to replace the products or services with alternatives. Do members of the community where it is located value it? Only as it applies to their own hopes and aspirations for quality of life in their community. When the CEO and other top leaders have a clear understanding of the importance of meeting the expectations of these various audiences, the communicator's job is easier. If the entire focus is on operations with little to no regard for identifying and building high-value relationships, the communicator probably needs to start here, as challenging a task as that might be.

It becomes crystal clear when you look at the value question that everything centers around the old question central to marketing and sales: "What's in it for me?" That is what everyone wants to know. Thinking like a CEO at this point means thinking about who values the organization or on whom the company depends for its existence, and then having clearly in mind why they value it or what's in it for them. Analyzing potential audiences from that standpoint will quickly lead you to a list of groups with individual priorities, and that list is the first step in a communication strategy.

A simple chart, like that shown in Table 7.1, might help identify audiences and priorities in communicating with them.

TABLE 7.1 Identifying Audiences and Priorities

GROUP	VALUE	PRIORITY
Executives	Opportunity to build their careers while being well-compensated	
Employees and families	Same	
Stockholders	Competitive or better return on investment	
Fenceline neighbors	Minimal disturbance of their lives while contributing positively to the community	
Customers	Providing needed products or services in a way that is not easily replaced	
Lenders	Business performance that assures repayment	
Media	Source for speedy, reliable information that will facilitate fast, accurate reporting	
Suppliers	Reliable and secure source of revenue	
Contractors	Similar to suppliers or employees	
Analysts and industry consultants	A direct, trustworthy relationship that will contribute to their being "in the know"	
Elected officials	Positive perception in the minds of voters	
Regulators	Compliance and respect, confidence that their career will not be threatened by behavior of company executives	
Community leaders	Continuing contributions to their community in the form of taxes, resources, positive role of employees in community, and so on; do nothing to threaten the community's security and well-being	

In thinking about priority, this question needs to be: Whose poor opinion of the organization most puts the enterprise at risk?

A priority column is listed, but prioritization varies from organization to organization and even varies within an organization depending on the situation. What becomes clear when reviewing the list is that there are important people in nearly every category who need to have a positive opinion if the organization is to be successful in the long haul. That positive opinion needs to have some "stickiness" or some depth that will enable it to withstand some bumps and bruises along the way. When attacks come, you want those people whose opinion of you matters the most to give you some benefit of the doubt.

When your company or organization suddenly finds itself squarely in the public eye, all those various audiences will gain an impression about the organization. It is not really a question of whether or not to communicate, because should you choose to remain silent, a strong message will be sent. In fact, the only way you have any hope of managing perceptions is by communicating. To choose not to, or to communicate too slowly for today's instant news requirements, puts your message in the hands of others. Those others might have agendas very much contrary to your own.

It's helpful to look at various reputation crises experienced by different organizations and see what messages were communicated and what public perceptions resulted. In the aftermath of the September 11, 2001 attacks, the Red Cross faced one of its most serious reputation crises when it was revealed that plans were being made to use excess funds raised for victims for other purposes. The early message provided by the executive director was that this policy was reasonable given the outpouring of donations, the need to prepare for other emergencies, and the fact that they carefully worded their televised appeals to allow for this policy. It was the wrong message. Ultimately, after congressional hearings and much discussion on the cable TV pundit shows, the Red Cross admitted this was a mistake and the organization would use the funds only for what most people understood they were donating them for. By this time, the high-profile executive director had left, a board–executive rift was revealed, and the organization's reputation for compassion and integrity was significantly tarnished.

Can there be any doubt that Firestone sent the wrong messages in the weeks leading up to its massive tire recall? In a sense, it didn't really matter what the specifics of the messages were. After all, most news viewers didn't read their press releases. The most important day of their company's life, the day of the product recall, their Web site crashed under the weight of the hits, meaning their voice to communicate directly was silenced by poor preparation. It didn't matter, because whatever Firestone said came off as too little, too late. This is one of the strongest reinforcements for a central premise that in this postmedia, instant news world, speed is perhaps the most important message. It is dreadfully easy to get behind the news and accusation curve and extremely difficult to get in front of it. However, the consequences of getting behind can be dire. Not only did Firestone inadvertently send the message of "too little, too late," they also sent the message, "It's not really our fault."

There are two huge message mistakes that are made repeatedly when companies come under fire. The first is, "It's not our fault," and the second is, "We did something wrong but we tried to cover it up." The first one is a message that is frequently overtly conveyed and the second one is conveyed by others, based on information or misinformation about company actions. Even the hint of a cover-up almost immediately changes the nature of the story and the reporting. A cover-up to the news media is the equivalent of blood in the water for sharks. If there was any question about who should wear the black hat in an emerging story, the question is immediately resolved if there is any real evidence or even the appearance of a cover-up.

The executives at Arthur Andersen certainly experienced this. Until a partner in the Houston office led an effort to shred documents that investigators needed to evaluate the propriety of Enron's financial dealings, there was only uncertainty about what role, if any, Andersen might have played in the Enron financial disaster. After the shredding, however, the press, congressional investigators, and the public clearly placed the black hat on the formerly highly regarded company. From that point on, almost anything said by the company in its defense was looked on with a much higher degree of skepticism.

In one situation I was involved in, a company was notified that a criminal investigation had been launched almost immediately following a sizable environmental spill. State law required the company pay for but not provide an attorney for any employee accused of doing something criminal while in the normal exercise of his or her duties. The company therefore notified the individuals involved and they immediately hired their own attorneys with the company paying the bill. Government accident investigators, company attorneys, the U.S. District Attorney's Office attorneys, and of course, the media all wanted to talk to these employees immediately. Their attorneys, having just been dragged into what was obviously a very serious situation, immediately gave them the advice not to talk. They were told that no one could force them to discuss the situation because they could plead the Fifth Amendment. Now, the popular perception of the Fifth Amendment is something that guilty people use to avoid incriminating themselves. When the media heard from the federal investigators that the employees were not answering their questions about the accident but pleading the Fifth, a cover-up was scented. At that point, no cover-up was intended at all; attorneys just thrown into a highly charged situation needed to take a little time to find out for themselves what their clients had done or not done. However, because the company did not and would not clearly explain the situation involving employees' legal rights, it stood guilty as charged of directing its employees to not cooperate and hide the truth. Several years after the incident, if you ask a reporter or member of the community about the company, the first thing they will comment about is the company's refusal to allow its employees to cooperate with investigators. This is a false perception, but it stands and will stand for some time because no real effort was made to communicate the truth.

It might be easy, with the benefit of hindsight, to see message mistakes made by others in the heat of a crisis, but the question here is what the message should be. One thing should be clear from everything that has been presented thus far: Whatever it is, it had better be fast. A slow message is almost invariably a "too little, too late" message. Beyond speed, here are a few things to consider in developing your message.

What You Do Is More Important Than What You Say

There is nothing new in this truism. Actions have always spoken much louder than words. It is easy for the communication team to get focused on wordsmithing and crafting messages, but a good communicator must think like a CEO. If many of the key audiences place a value on the health of the enterprise, and the health of the enterprise is very dependent on the public trust, what specifically is being done in light of the circumstances to build public trust? The great temptation when the media lights go on and real problems have been revealed is to start thinking about the expensive legal battles to come. That's why communicators and the legal team so frequently tangle at this point. The lawyers are paid to think about protecting the company in court. However, if public trust is lost, there will be nothing of value to protect in court. Actions must be taken, sometimes even strong and painful actions, to protect the public trust and maintain the confidence of the key audiences.

Be Human: Show Compassion and Empathy

In any situation in which there are victims, the public sympathy will be with them. This is natural and good, but it is also how the infotainment game is played. Victims are critical to the story and effective communication of their pain and suffering is an essential element of telling a compelling story. From the company's perspective, that pain and suffering might be overstated or even completely false (unfortunately there are many people eager to claim victim status even when they have had nothing to do with the incident, as even September 11 demonstrated). However overstated or false it might be, public sympathy is going to be with the victims, so a company shows callousness to the victims at great peril. A company or organization with priorities that are focused from beginning to end on those who have been genuinely hurt by what has happened, whether or not the company is to blame, is a company that gains and deserves the respect of the public.

Accept Responsibility

Here's the really sticky one. Who do you respect? Do you respect someone who does whatever they can to push responsibility on someone else and look for the slightest excuses or flimsiest reasons to say, "It's not my fault?" Or do you respect someone who says, "I am taking responsibility for this mess." The problem is simply that the public wants someone with the character to stand up and say, "I accept the consequences of my actions." Attorneys, meanwhile, fully aware that everything said in public will show up in court, want the company to completely avoid saying anything that might cause a problem in court. The two positions cannot be easily reconciled.

One reason this is so difficult is that the word *responsibility* has multiple meanings. It can mean: "I'm accepting responsibility for cleaning this mess up while we find out who is at fault." It can also mean, "I am responsible, therefore I am stating that I am the sole cause of this disaster." The two are very different, but easily confused. In the oil industry, the law requires that the "responsible party"—that is the actual term used in the law—assume responsibility for the cleanup, regardless of fault. The responsible party is the one who owns the product at the time of the release. A common question of reporters in a spill is, "Who is responsible for this?" An appropriate response is, "Although the cause of this incident is not yet known and is under investigation, we are accepting full responsibility for the response and the cleanup." This separates at least to some degree the issue of fault, blame, and financial responsibility for the response.

There's a similar problem with saying, "I'm sorry." On more than one occasion I have witnessed attorneys, executives, and public relations professionals discuss at length while a horde of reporters are waiting whether or not the executive should say, "I'm sorry" or "I'm very sorry." "I'm sorry" could mean, "I understand and regret the pain and suffering those who have been affected by this situation have experienced." It could also mean, "I'm really sorry our negligence caused this suffering." The two are very different.

When difficult conflicts emerge relating to whether the court of public opinion takes precedence over the court of law, the answer must come from the executive level. It is the CEO or chairman of the board or executive director who is charged with the responsibility of looking after the best interests of the company. These people must understand that there is a strong possibility of conflict in crisis situations and they must be prepared to use their best judgment. It is not exercising fiduciary duty to stockholders, employees, and other key stakeholders to turn over executive decision making to attorneys (or communication professionals for that matter) and then hide behind the screen of doing what these professionals told them.

Be Straightforward About What You Know and Don't Know

Transparency, honesty, and openness are the qualities we look for in a person. At no time are these more important than when someone is trying to fit you with the black hat. However, the very natural reaction, particularly when lawyers are giving strong advice to keep quiet, is to hunker down, say the minimum necessary, and spin the information.

In the earliest stages of an incident or emerging issue it is critical to be open and direct with both the media and stakeholders. The problem is there is little information, but this provides no excuse to keep quiet. The information that is available needs to be carefully and completely disclosed, but perhaps even more important, there needs to be communication about what is being done to get the information that the audience wants but is not yet available.

Reporters and the public always want to know as quickly as possible the cause of an accident. If an airliner goes down in good weather, taking hundreds of lives, of course we want to know what caused it. However, unless a crowd of people was standing around while someone shot an antiaircraft missile at the plane, the cause will likely not be known for some time. The common rule when providing information about an accident or incident is to avoid speculation. This is sometimes easier said than done because reporters would love to get a direct quote or an on-camera statement from someone who provides some strong indication that supports a favorite theory of the reporter. The best method of dealing with this line of questioning is to state, "We simply cannot speculate on the cause right now. Our concern is for those who have been affected by this and dealing with the cleanup. We have experts already in place looking at what has happened and why and we want to know for ourselves as well as providing that information to the public. But it will take some time to investigate this and understand fully what happened and why."

A major reason companies and organizations do not appear to be forthcoming early on as a story breaks is the speed versus accuracy dilemma. The strong and reasonable desire to get it right causes a lot of closed-door scurrying, discussions, and delays. If the public could look behind the scenes they would see well-meaning people wanting to make certain that everything they say is correct and beyond question, people concerned about keeping their integrity intact. However, the public cannot see behind the closed doors and therefore what they observe is a company refusing to talk or so slow with their information and statements that the news of the minute or the hour has long left them in the dust.

If you ask reporters what they want and expect in this instant news world, they will say, "Tell us what you have right now. Tell us what you don't have. And tell us when you are going to get it." It's that simple. If you don't have confirmation on key facts, such as injuries, then the limited information you have cannot be presented as factual. The answer then is, "We do not currently have reliable information on any injuries but we will get that to you as soon as possible." Secretary of Defense Donald Rumsfeld has earned high praise from the press corps and high respect from many in the public for his simple, straightforward manner of providing public information during the war on terrorism. He tells what he knows, tells when he can't divulge something, and tells when he simply doesn't know or can't confirm the information.

The real difficulty emerges when it becomes known inside the organization that the company or organization has done something wrong: The smoking gun is found. Once the communication team gets over the shock of realizing that the black hat might indeed fit, the discussion turns to whether the media will find out, when, and who. The common practice for dealing with such a situation is to prepare a holding statement. This document contains the official company line about how to respond when asked difficult questions that have been anticipated. However, if we look at the basic principles we have already outlined, this difficult situation might call for a different response. Credibility is everything; if you lose that, the game is over. The public wants openness, honesty, and transparency. The best policy is to tell what you know when you know it. The word *cover-up* almost immediately changes the story to something more sinister, entertaining, and long-lasting. These principles lead inevitably to the conclusion that the best policy is to be the source of the information. Do not let the investigators uncover it for you. Do not allow some unhappy employee the enticing opportunity to make the claim that he or she brought you down. However, before telling what you know, there is one more important principle to remember that is especially critical in this kind of situation: What you do is much more important than what you say. If problems have been identified, confidence and credibility depend on the public and stakeholders knowing that you understand the depth and significance of the problem and are taking the appropriate measures to ensure that the problem is resolved and does not recur.

Message: What Message Do We Need to Convey?

It might appear that in talking about providing information in the early going of a crisis event there is no such thing as a message. As events unfold, it is the facts and specific information surrounding the event and what the company is doing about it that is conveyed. However, there is a difference between information and message. Ultimately, the only thing that really matters in communication is the perception of the audience. That's why there is such truth to the statement that perception *is* reality. The message, in this sense, is what the recipients of the information are understanding about the situation and the players involved: It is their perception.

News viewers or readers might gather information about a financial scandal, a massive legal battle, or an environmental disaster involving your company, but what are they thinking about the people involved and the quality and character of the company involved? The Chinese character for crisis has two meanings: danger and opportunity. In a previous book, *Friendship Marketing*,[1] I stated that trust is normally built in a relationship when there is a problem between the two parties. You certainly don't want to create a problem to create trust, but how you handle a difficult situation with potentially conflicting interests says a lot about your character and therefore whether you are to be trusted by the other party.

Understanding the distinction between information and message is helpful in understanding the role of presentation in the communication process. An effective response with all the right words can be greatly diminished or destroyed if presented by an officious-looking spokesperson with his or her head down reading a script. A smirky smile can create a damaging impression when the message is one of sorrow and regret.

One company's leaders decided to hand a written statement to waiting television crews instead of having a spokesperson on camera to deliver the message personally. The handing over of the message by a low-level communication staff member was the visual presented on the television reports. The words were strong and effective, but the message was clear and contradicted the words. The message was: "We are afraid to be seen on camera."

One of the most difficult jobs of the communication manager is helping executives who need to represent the company in the public to convey the right message with the right information. If personal characteristics or lack of ability in this regard prevent the effective communication of the right message, alternatives must be found.

It is very helpful to keep your relationship goal in mind during the most difficult and dark days. You want those people who are important to the present and future of your organization to place a high value on your existence. You want them to want you to be here. Evaluate every action of the company, every communication with the public and stakeholders, and everything visible in the response and recovery efforts with this question: Does this result in the people important to us wanting us to be here?

If we go back and review the list of potential audiences and their reasons for wanting your company to be alive and healthy, the connections between what you do and say and their interest in your company should start to become clear. The employees, for example, assuming they place a high value on their employment and the company's ability to continue to help them meet their needs, do not want to see the company trashed in the public eye. They do not want to be embarrassed when they meet someone new and tell them where they work. They want a company that is healthy and respected. Stockholders want a company with the leadership to get through difficult situations, that can right the ship, get it back on course with minimal financial and public franchise damage, and get back to the business of providing a healthy return on investment. What is critical to them at this stage is strong, dynamic leadership focused on rapid recovery while demonstrating true compassion for those affected by the events.

It is very important to evaluate the various audiences in thinking about a central or umbrella message, but the result needs to be creating that single message. To attempt to communicate too many divergent messages to too many audiences means that any and all messages will be lost. The brilliance of Bill Clinton's first campaign strategists was that they understood this clearly. There are many things to talk about in a presidential campaign, and opponents go after whatever relatively minor item is successful in undermining credibility. However, campaign strategist James Carville and his crew stuck to the basic message: "It's the economy, stupid." The basic message a company or organization must communicate during a crisis needs to have this kind of simplicity and strength. A single, overriding message is usually communicated; the question is whether the organization will control it and whether the message is the one the organization wants the world to hear. Exxon sent a loud message in the early days and even long following the *Valdez* disaster. It was communicated most loudly through the absence of the top leadership who communicated, in effect, even though they had the capability to travel the globe on corporate jets and that they could go anywhere they wanted, when they wanted, the situation was not significant enough for them to attend to it personally. The message needed to be that the company saw this as a disaster of the highest magnitude and was providing all its resources to contain it, clean it up, and find out what happened so it could be prevented in the future. That message was never conveyed.

LISTENING: WHAT DO WE NEED TO HEAR FROM THEM?

For communicators there is a natural tendency to forget one of the most basic tenets of communication: Communication is a two-way street. It involves interaction, give and take, and listening as much as talking. At no time is this more true than in situations in which the media are telling the world about you in the way they want to. Effective listening helps you understand how perceptions are evolving and drives the most critical strategic decisions.

I am convinced that one reason this is not commonly practiced is that corporate executives have accepted the accounting view of life that says the worth of a company is measured in the bottom line. In the *relationship value* model, the value of a company is found in the value placed in the company's existence and well-being by those people who benefit from it. The bottom line is merely a reflection of that relationship value and frequently is a lagging-indicator reflection. The real value then is in the perception of those people on whom the company's future depends: customers, bankers, stockholders, key suppliers, employees, and so on. Knowing what they think and how their perceptions are being altered by events is critical to the executive team and should be the purview of the communication team.

It is surprising that more communicators are not stronger champions of listening to key stakeholders. Knowledge, after all, is power, and the knowledge of the perceptions of people critical to the organization is very significant power. Being the one to suggest this and then deliver the vital information serves the executive leadership with information that is critical to effective decision making. More than just about anything else, it can put the communicators on the executive team. Even if communicators are not motivated by the opportunity to become more strategic in their role in the company, they should consider that listening is part of their responsibility. If communication teachers are right that communication involves speaking and listening, then speaking is not enough. The communicators need to be not just the mouthpiece for the organization, but its ears as well. When the future health or even existence of the enterprise is at stake in a public crisis, it is more critical than ever that communicators exercise both facets of their responsibility.

Perhaps one of the main reasons why communicators, and executives for that matter, are somewhat reluctant to consider listening is because of the presumed trouble and expense. Listening is generally understood to mean large-scale scientific opinion surveys with high degrees of statistical accuracy, relatively long lead times, and the review of endless charts and numbers. There is definitely a time and place for this kind of listening, but it is not the kind of listening we are talking about here. What is suggested here is much simpler and less costly.

The listening that should occur in the midst of a media event can be divided into two groups: informal and formal. Informal listening is just a habit. Every opportunity to find out what people are thinking should be exploited. Reporters are not just people who are seeking information from you, they are potentially excellent sources of information about any and all aspects of the situation. Because it is their job to get information from a variety of sources, they might know more about what is going on than you do. They also have opinions about how the public is perceiving the situation and their opinion about public opinion is critical. Reporters do not write in a vacuum, and they usually believe that the approach they are taking is consistent with how the public is perceiving the situation. If they think the public perceives you wearing the black hat, they will be fairly reluctant to put the black hat on someone else. Their sample size is usually related to a few friends, coworkers, or family members, but it nevertheless is sufficient for them to develop pretty firm opinions about public perception. It is one reason why when media coverage diverts significantly from public perception, as you might determine from your more formal listening, one of the most important things you can do to change the reporting is to show that their understanding of the public's response might be in error.

Informal listening applies not just to reporters, but to every stakeholder and audience group. Members of the communication team who have the opportunity for direct interaction by phone or face-to-face conversation should be strongly encouraged to ask how the people they are talking to are feeling about the situation, how the company is doing, what could be done differently, and how they think this situation will resolve itself. This information, anecdotal as it is, needs to be relayed back to the communication managers and, if trends emerge, needs to be conveyed to the executive leadership.

Formal listening is similar to informal listening in that members of the team are tasked specifically to identify people to talk to and then interview them. There is no need for statistically valid sampling at this point. There is a need to avoid bias in the questions asked, but this is usually done using common sense. Questionnaires that clearly appear to be used to gather numbers and enter them into a computer for processing should be avoided because, frankly, people don't care to give their time and opinions simply to become an anonymous number. People are very interested in sharing their opinions and recommendations if they perceive they are being listened to as unique individuals, that their opinions really matter, and that what they say might make a difference. Those items should all be realities in the way interviews are conducted.

How many interviews should be conducted? Common sense suggests enough to set a clear but not necessarily unmistakable direction. If you ask 20 people the same question and you get the same or a similar response from 18 of them, you have some degree of assurance that you have your answer. If you ask 20 people and you get 15 different answers, it is probably a good idea to keep asking.

The point here is that there is a place for formal, scientific, and expensive surveys, but they are not the only way to get vital information. When it is perceived that there needs to be a $30,000 survey that will take two weeks to complete, the response is usually that nothing gets done. It's a shame because the vital information needed for effective communication response can usually be gained in a few hours at very little cost.

In one major incident referred to earlier, we did the informal and formal listening, focusing on community influencers. We conducted fewer than 30 interviews and gained valuable information for the executive team on the perceptions within the community. A few weeks into the situation, we were joined by a much larger public relations company with a worldwide practice and we shared the results of our snapshot community listening with them. Predictably, they told the client that a $20,000-plus statistically accurate survey was required and they downplayed our little effort. Three weeks later the results of their survey were presented, showing no substantial difference from what we had already learned. In the meantime, we kept on with our informal and very low-key formal listening and found that in the two weeks between sampling and presentation, the issues were changing substantially, as were the perceptions. However, because the experts from the big firm had convinced the client that our informal listening was of no value, the ongoing listening had little impact on strategic and communication decisions. This would not prove helpful to the client in the long term.

The effectiveness of a communication effort needs to be measured. Managers are soon taught that you can't manage what you don't measure. Public relations professionals, in my mind, too often hide behind the general perception that public relations results can't be measured. The reality is that public communication is highly measurable because the only thing that matters is the perception of the audience, and this is very measurable on both a large scale and a small scale. The communication process is not the picture of a hose squirting information in a single direction, it is a waterwheel collecting information and distributing it. Critical information is collected about how the company is doing. This information is vital to keep the communication process rolling.

Voice: Who Needs to Deliver the Message?

One of the most profound insights of John Naisbitt's 1982 bestseller, *Megatrends*,[2] was that there was a relationship between the use of advanced technology and personal communication. This simply said that as technology becomes an ever more pervasive force in our lives, we have a compensating need for more personal interaction. This has been clearly demonstrated in the use of email, one of the most startling and significant communication innovations of all time. One might have assumed, like express package shipping or faxing that preceded it, emailing might have been primarily a business tool. It is indeed a powerful business tool, but it is much more a personal communication tool. Email and its close relatives—chat rooms, instant messaging, and so on—are used primarily for interpersonal, nonbusiness communication. In a world in which work and careers are driving people out of small communities, new communities are being formed and personal ties are maintained by a high-tech tool initially envisioned more as a business tool.

A major focus of this book is the use of technology in communication. Technology has transformed the media and is threatening its monopoly status. The only response of those facing reputation risk in this instant news world is to fully engage the technology available to provide speedy, direct communication. However, technology requires a counterbalance, and that is the personal touch.

The CEO of Exxon defended his decision to stay at his headquarters on the basis that communication technology allowed him to effectively manage the response from his office. He was right, but it didn't wash. President Putin didn't claim that his dacha was properly wired for him to manage the *Kursk* business, but the effect of both their decisions was the same. The media reported their absence and the public interpreted it as personal disengagement.

The people at the top need to be highly visible and very involved in the situation. Anything less looks either like hiding or obliviousness. An outstanding example of executive involvement was the role played by Alaska Airlines CEO John Kelly following the crash of Flight 261 in January 2000. What will undoubtedly be studied by communication specialists in the years to come as the ultimate example of executive leadership in an overwhelming crisis is Mayor Rudolph Giuliani of New York City. His presence and very human but straightforward communication style during those horrifying days following September 11, 2001, resulted in his being named *Time* magazine's person of the year in a year dominated by other people at the center of historic events.

One thing that must be considered in this new world of direct communication is that the chief executive can only go so far. Giuliani and others who have done well in the public eye have done so in part because they made themselves highly accessible to the media. However, doing this diminishes the time and availability for other key stakeholders, such as customers, stockholders, employees, and so on. The burden of personal and direct communication must be shared. The entire executive leadership team must take a role in personal and direct communication at the time of the incident. This is, of course, not to say that their entire responsibility should be communication, as they have their job to do as well. However, part of that job needs to be communication.

MEDIA: HOW SHOULD WE COMMUNICATE?

Of all the questions dealt with in this chapter, this is the one that reflects the greatest change as a result of the instant news world. We identified the audiences to be communicated with earlier, but this isn't new. All those audiences were there before. It's just that the understanding for most of them was that the only option for fast communication of information was through the traditional news media. Because reporters were the ones beating down your door looking for information, it was natural to focus on meeting their needs and to presume by doing so you were meeting the information needs of everyone else.

The Internet has changed that because it creates the possibility of direct communication. Those deeply affected by what was going on always had a strong desire for relevant information, but they had no expectation of it because there was not really a practical way to communicate directly. It was natural in the media world for them to expect to receive the relevant information from the media only. Now there is a growing realization of the potential for direct, personal, fast messages to those people who have a reason for wanting that information. As that realization grows, companies or organizations that ignore that expectation will do so at their own peril. That is the real opportunity and risk of the coming postmedia world.

Those people living next to an industrial facility that experienced a large fire and who sent an email to the company asking if they should evacuate had some expectation that they would get a response. In fact, they probably had an expectation that they shouldn't have had to send an email but should have been informed directly. Instead of being proactively informed before inquiring, these people did not even get a response for more than two weeks. Did they really think it was because the company didn't have the computer or Internet resources or the people resources to answer their life and death question? Clearly not. Their only thought could be that the company didn't care enough about their well-being to even get back to them. The company communication manager's response was that their job was communicating with the media. It was this same company that was severely criticized by the media because the information they needed for their stories was only available from the fire departments and agencies responding.

The best and most effective way to communicate has always been direct and face to face. Romance by love letters has its attractions, no doubt, but the lovers usually write about the day when they can communicate face to face. Rarely when the lovers are together do they pine about how eager they are to get back to writing letters from a distance. We made the point earlier that the executive team must be actively involved in public communication. Ideally, the CEO would meet personally with every person affected by the events. That isn't possible, so a sort of information triage is always the order of the day. If we can't have what we really want, which is direct, personal, face-to-face communication between those who matter and those who can do something about it, what is our next best option? We mentioned earlier that getting other executives involved is very important in extending this personal outreach, but even that will only take you so far.

If the basic principle of effective communication is to make it as personal and direct as possible, we can establish a hierarchy of communication methods, as follows:

1. Face to face
2. Telephone
3. Personal letter, fax, or email
4. Special section on Web site
5. General Web site
6. Media

As you go down the list, each method becomes less personal and less direct. It is immediately obvious that the use of the media to communicate to those whose opinions matter deeply to the organization is not ideal. It has been commonplace in a breaking news event simply because there were no options and because speed was always primary. A front-page news story would outpace a letter any day of the week. The 6 p.m. news would certainly outpace most of the methods of getting information out quickly—even within organizations, such as to employees.

The Internet changed that. Now direct, personal, and immediate communication is possible. If it is possible, it will become expected, and it already is in many respects. A company can send an email out to its employees within minutes. Every company of any size also has the opportunity, should it decide to make use of it, to use the Internet to communicate proactively with all the key stakeholders whose perception holds the key to its future. Even though they have the capacity because the technology is very much available, very few companies have the will or the current capability. This can only be explained by a failure to understand the current media environment.

The audience wants what it has always wanted. If the information is relevant, or if it bears directly on their present or future hopes or plans, then there is a pressing urgency for the information. When they know it is possible, the urgency changes into a demand, and not meeting that demand can be catastrophic.

There can be little question that the use of the Internet is already and will be increasingly more critical for a company to protect its reputation and maintain a too-fragile public franchise. The Internet offers the opportunity to provide immediate, direct, personalized information: one-to-one communication on a mass scale. Done right, it blends high tech and high touch in a way that Naisbitt could not have imagined. Communication strategy in this instant news world that does not focus on the requirement for getting direct, personal, and immediate information to critical people is doomed to failure.

Endnotes

1. Baron, Gerald, *Friendship Marketing*, Grants Pass, OR: PSI Research, Oasis Press, 1997.
2. Naisbitt, John, *Megatrends*, New York: Warner Books, Reissue Edition, 1982.

CHAPTER

8 Preparing the Organization and Team

Executives are an insecure lot. As a result of watching the very public destruction of countless corporate reputations, executives are very well aware of the risks they face every day in a world dominated by instant news, infotainment, and the Internet. They have seen the steady decline of CEO tenure and have observed that in many cases, the public embarrassment of the company has been the primary reason for premature CEO departure. Several studies since September 11, 2001, have shown that more than 80 percent of executives feel their organizations are unprepared to deal with a significant crisis. They are smart enough to know that if their organization is unprepared to deal effectively with a news-making event, as the leader they are extremely vulnerable. What makes this strange is that although there is a powerful need, there is little being done to prepare for the new realities of public communication.

Having dealt with dozens of companies at various levels over the past few years on this issue, it is clear that the primary obstacle to effective preparation is the organization. There are within most organizations enough obstacles to adequate preparation that only those leaders and concerned employees with great commitment and stamina are able to overcome them. Ultimately, organizational problems are problems of leadership. In plain truth, that so few companies and organizations are prepared to manage a reputation crisis is a failure of both communication leadership and top executive leadership. Only strong commitment from one or both of those groups is sufficient to overcome the inherent opposition that exists to effective preparation.

One top manager of a large industrial facility clearly understood the need for adequate preparation. The person in his organization who would be responsible for the public communication in a major event was unconcerned. His computer keyboard was stored on the top of his computer and he has likely never touched it. He was within a year of retirement and learning something new was simply not a high priority in his life. He had long-standing working relationships in the community and believed that should disaster strike, his job would be to answer the questions from the media and then go on with his normal routine. He's a nice guy, well-liked, with a long history of loyal service to the organization. Aside from replacing him, working completely around him, or forcing him to change, the manager decided he had little choice other than to wait out the time remaining before his communication manager would retire.

One large multinational company convened a global teleconference to discuss its preparations, including the ability of its technology infrastructure to handle a major news event. Although there were some on the call very aware of the new media environment and the importance of adequate preparation, the prevailing viewpoint was that it was sufficient in a time of crisis to simply post some information to the company

Web site. If the demand for information exceeded the few thousand hits per day that the company servers could handle, it would be acceptable if the site went down while they worked to put together a more robust solution during the crisis. This is an extreme example of a head-in-the-sand response, but, as I was told, "We are not interested in paying for insurance." In other words, there was no leadership inclination to invest in the ability to publicly communicate effectively in the event of a crisis. This story would not be so illustrative if the company in question were not a leader in an industry that was seriously damaged in the public eye because of one company's failure to communicate adequately.

One of the most consistent obstacles to preparation is the disconnect between various areas and departments in a larger organization and the fact that they do not share common agendas. The Internet is a technical issue and therefore Internet infrastructure, access, use policies, applications, and so on typically fall under the purview of the information technology (IT) department. In a public communication crisis, the communication team and executive leadership need to have full and unimpeded access to the communication potential of the Internet. However, this kind of access normally conflicts with the natural desire of IT managers to maintain their position of masters of the technology. The very natural fear is that providing nontechnical people with the tools they need to make full use of the technology will diminish their role and value in the organization. There is inordinate fear of the curtain being pulled back to expose the wizardry they perform. They are exceptionally cautious about any effort that might result in this kind of exposure. They also seem to be afraid that if a new idea or new technology is brought to the attention of top management and it didn't originate from them, it will weaken their position. The "not invented here" syndrome is very much alive. In all fairness, some of this "turf war" is related to the responsibility that IT managers have to maintain the integrity of their systems. The Internet, being an open, uncontrolled, and largely uncontrollable sort of technology, represents huge risks to IT managers whose job it is to ensure the safety and security of the organization's technology resources and business data.

Leaders who understand the importance of preparation and planning are not stymied by the obstacles, no matter how many there are and how entrenched they might be. They subscribe to the old saying, "Don't tell me how rough the water is, just get the ship in." Getting the ship in, in this case, means addressing the three key elements of preparation: policies, people, and platform.

Policies

Communication policies exist on two levels: a broad statement of intention that indicates the commitment of the organization to communicate effectively with those people who need information from the company and a plan that details more specifically how the intention will be implemented in practice.

To communicate or not to communicate? How quickly and with whom? These are the core questions that must be answered at the very highest levels of the organization, and the difficult nature of these questions is one of the main reasons why far too many top executives would rather shove the public communication question into the corner. Establishing policies means making decisions and in the case of public communication in this new era, it means making some difficult decisions with the entire enterprise at stake. Very few executives come to the task with a professional background in communication. Most come via financial, legal, managerial, or technical training and experience. This is not to say they are not interested in or ineffective in communication because it is highly unusual to rise to top positions without considerable communication skills. It does mean that communication is frequently not seen as central to the business and therefore best delegated to those whose responsibilities are also, therefore, limited.

Although communication policy at the highest levels can be seen as a board-level decision, certainly no one can establish policy as critical as this for the future of the organization other than the CEO. However, frequently a communication manager or even communication team member concerned about these issues can instigate the discussion and facilitate the process of developing an appropriate policy. These are some of the key questions in developing such a policy:

1. How vital is the role of communication to the existence and mission of the organization?
2. What does a successful communication response look like and how will it be measured?
3. Does the organization consider it important to communicate information of high public interest?
4. Recognizing the dramatically changed nature of news and public information, what is the organization's goal as it relates to speed and accuracy of information?
5. What groups or audiences will receive priority in communication?
6. Will the organization be reactive or proactive in the distribution or publishing of information?
7. What role will the organization's leaders play in the communication process?
8. How will it be determined whether a crisis exists and what level of response is required?
9. To what lengths is the organization willing to go to protect its credibility?

Each organization must answer these questions independently and with integrity, but a primary purpose of this book has been to provide the background about changes in the public information environment that requires new thinking and a new approach to some of these questions. Some guidelines that might apply to your organization are offered as a means of starting the discussion.

How Vital Is the Role of Communication to the Existence and Mission of the Organization?

In the previous chapter we discussed the concept of the public franchise. This is simply the idea that a company or organization cannot effectively operate without at least the tacit support of the public. From a marketing standpoint we can look at this as brand value. If the brand has become tarnished and confidence is lost, the company is severely damaged and might even need to go to the extreme measure of abandoning the brand entirely. ValuJet took this measure, and it appears that Firestone is doing the same, as its parent company, Bridgestone, is rapidly expanding public exposure of the Bridgestone brand in the U.S. marketplace. The public, in effect, has veto power over the goals and aspirations of the company. What makes this so frightening is that the franchise can be lost not only by misdeeds on the part of the company, but by the actions of activists, misinformation, or an overly aggressive reporter intent on telling a good story for ratings purposes. The only real protection is the ability and willingness to respond very quickly to reputation threats.

We also discussed how the value of an organization was linked to a great extent to the value placed on it by key people: stockholders, customers, employees, community leaders, and so on. When it is understood that there is actual economic value attached to these perceptions, the shepherding and protection of these perceptions take on a very high priority. It is these issues that should help determine the organization's response to this important policy question.

WHAT DOES A SUCCESSFUL COMMUNICATION RESPONSE LOOK LIKE?

A communication policy, like a public relations plan, should include a clear statement of goals. The goal of most communication is relationship building. The goal of a communication effort for a company or organization should be to create, enhance, or protect the relationships with the people who are important to the enterprise's present and future. A crisis represents a considerable threat to established and future relationships, but as mentioned earlier, it can also represent an opportunity. Handled properly, an effective crisis response and its communication can build an organization's respect, credibility, and brand value. An appropriate communication policy statement should state in some way that it is the intention of the organization to manage the response and the communication of that response in such a way that the credibility of the organization and the respect with which it is held are enhanced. In other words, based on the way the crisis is handled, the goal is to have the people who matter to the company place an even higher value on the company's existence.

DOES THE ORGANIZATION CONSIDER IT IMPORTANT TO COMMUNICATE INFORMATION OF HIGH PUBLIC INTEREST?

The basic question here is whether the organization's leaders wish to speak to the public and interested audiences themselves or be content to allow others to speak for them. Others include the media, activists, opponents, competitors, employees, industry pundits, government officials, and so on. It should be obvious, but in viewing the actions of many companies caught in the headlights, it appears that their communication policy states they want everyone else to speak for them. This appearance, in the age of instant media, is likely caused by the speed issue. In other words, by the time the organization is prepared to speak, others have already spoken for it and the media and the public have gone on to the next breaking story. The effect on the public is the same: The company has not spoken.

That means in this new era, the decision to communicate is a decision to communicate very quickly: It is virtually instant communication or no communication at all, which leads to the next question.

Recognizing the Dramatically Changed Nature of News and Public Information, What Is the Organization's Goal as It Relates to Speed and Accuracy of Information?

The evidence of instant news is all about us. Each day and night on television we see it clearly and each day as we use our Internet devices to gain instant information the point is made. Yet, when I recently asked some industry communication people about their expectation about getting an initial press release out in a drill scenario, they indicated that if it got out the first day they would be doing well. The first day? The reporter referred to earlier made it clear that if they don't have a statement from the company when the news breaks, they will go with what they have. It is now or it is too late. A communication policy and plan should clearly identify when statements from the company about fast-breaking events should be issued. This compelling reality brings the instant news world problem home. If the organization cannot find a way to communicate effectively and properly in that golden hour, the first hour after the event, it is flat out not prepared for today's instant media world.

It is obvious that it is not sufficient to simply state, "We will respond with a public statement within one hour of the initiation of the incident," because the critical question is how? No doubt a very fast response is required. Other important plan, policy, and technology decisions need to be made to make certain that this speed policy is feasible. Our government might state its policy to land a person on Mars next year. However, without a realistic commitment of resources and the technological capability of doing it, creating such a policy is an exercise in futility. Much of the further discussion about policies, people, and technologies is focused on how to make a fast, accurate public information response feasible.

WHAT GROUPS OR AUDIENCES WILL RECEIVE PRIORITY IN COMMUNICATION?

This question has been a nonissue in public relations since the days of Edward Bernays, recognized by many as the first spinmeister or public relations professional. To many involved in public relations today, the question still does not make sense because public relations has long been equated with media relations. However, as pointed out, the media have simply served as a necessary intermediary to communicate with the audiences that really matter. In this postmedia world, their role and significance is undergoing fundamental change. This does not mean that reporters should now receive a lower priority; it simply means that today every one of the audiences is a priority audience. Their demand and expectation for immediate and direct communication is the fundamental change that defines the postmedia world.

If you have to choose between communicating to the governor or taking care of the county executive of the county where the facility exists, to whom do you respond? How about the governor, the county executive, the publisher of the local paper, *The Wall Street Journal* bureau chief, your stockholder, and the eldest son of a worker who was killed in the accident everyone is interested in? What is your priority?

These are the very difficult and very real situations that executives and communication managers need to deal with. It might be more comfortable to let things sort themselves out in a real situation, but undoubtedly a price will have to be paid. A crisis can almost be defined as a situation in which circumstances and demands overwhelm the capability to deal with them. That will most certainly be true of communication demands. In communication planning, the keys to this dilemma are technology and delegation. The technology available today allows for instant and direct communication with the key people—provided there is the proper preparation. Delegation makes it possible to prepare the team in advance to cover all the bases. Perhaps while the CEO is given the responsibility of dealing with the families of those involved, another senior-level executive or the director of communications might be the one to coordinate the governor's visit.

Will the Organization Be Reactive or Proactive in the Distribution or Publishing of Information?

No doubt it is my bias that makes me marvel at the companies and organizations at the beginning of the 21st century that consciously pursue a communication policy of having others tell their story for them. It is well established that public speaking is many people's number one phobia. Does this phobia extend to the highest levels in a corporation and to the degree that they wish reporters whose job it is to deliver as large an audience as possible, and activists whose future depends on creating a sense of public outrage, to speak on their behalf? This is exactly the policy defended by communication professionals in some of the world's largest and most successful companies. Although some explicitly state that the media will speak for them, a far greater number have a policy that states they will provide and disseminate information. However, the fact that they are completely unprepared to do it in a way that meets today's media and audience demands means they have a de facto "no communication" policy. It does no good to say you will be open, direct, and straightforward in your communication when no preparation has been done to make that possible.

What Role Will the Organization's Leaders Play in the Communication Process?

This simple question contains one of the most important communication policy decisions to be made. In a reputation crisis, the organization's leaders must be visible, engaged, and, if appropriate, on the scene. In a large-scale event, the communication task is overwhelming enough that perhaps several on the executive level will need to be very actively and visibly involved.

There are certainly circumstances in which the CEO, undoubtedly talented in many areas, simply does not come across well through public media. In that case, the situation must be confronted directly, and other company or organization leaders designated to be the face of the company. Many reporters have a strong preference for getting their information from executives or managers rather than spokespeople who are professional communicators. Perhaps they believe that despite extensive media training, executives are more likely to slip up and give information or juicy quotes than trained professionals. More likely they believe that better, purer, less laundered information will be provided by those responsible for making decisions within the company. As a general rule, reporters respond best when they are given access to the decision makers, and this often results in better reporting.

There is no doubt a lot of misunderstanding about the role of spokespersons, and not only on the part of reporters. One company I talked to that had little inclination toward open and direct communication said it had designated a low-level administrative assistant as its spokesperson for the primary reason that this person wouldn't be in a position to really know what was going on and therefore wouldn't be tempted to give out information the executives felt was inappropriate.

In addition to determining the role that executives will play in putting a public face on the company during a reputation crisis, another important policy decision relates to the information approval process. Who will decide what information goes out under which circumstances? Who has the right to approve public information? What role will attorneys play in these decisions? What about other outside consultants such as crisis experts or experts on specific response topics? How will the editing, vetting, and approval process work in actuality? In a media world where now is too late, the answers to the question of approvals might make all the difference between an effective and a botched response.

There is probably no more important role the organization's leader must play than refereeing the almost inevitable battle between the legal team and the public communication team. It has become increasingly common for company attorneys to take a very prominent role in decision making about what the company says (and does) in a crisis. It has even become common for attorneys to speak on the company's behalf. There are very good reasons for this, primarily because a crisis seems to inevitably involve legal action, either immediately or down the road. Many attorneys are very effective in the role of public spokesperson, which is not difficult to understand given their usual gifts with language, persuasive ability, and knowledge of the law. However, executives who decide to use attorneys in this role, or who base their public communication decisions on legal advice, need to be very aware of the considerable dilemma involved. In my experience the most serious reputation damage occurs unnecessarily as a direct result of attorney involvement, and that experience has been confirmed by conversations with numerous other communication professionals.

An attorney's single charge is to protect the enterprise in the court of law. The charge of the public relations manager or communication manager is to protect the enterprise in the court of public opinion. It is far more common than not in a newsmaking crisis that the best course to protect the organization in one court puts it at considerable risk in the other court. That's why the conflict between attorneys and communicators is almost inevitable.

Most attorneys' natural reaction to an event that will likely lead to legal action is for the company to say little or nothing. That is understandable given the highly fluid nature of the events and the fact that anything that is said publicly can and will be used against the company in court. Accepting responsibility, expressing sorrow, expressing a strong desire to prevent such actions or accidents again, and expressing a past record of preventive activities all represent very genuine risks in the court of law. However, not speaking, speaking in legalese, or couching everything that is said in terms and styles clearly intended to protect the company in court is counterproductive to the main goal of the communicator, which is to protect and enhance credibility in the minds of the people who really matter to the future of the enterprise.

What is the solution? It should first rest with the attorneys and communicators. It is easy to get into a power game at this delicate stage of a crisis. The issue quickly becomes not what is in the best interest of the company but who can establish dominance or control of the situation. I have observed both attorneys and very experienced communication professionals allow their arguments to go to ridiculous extremes, making it clear it wasn't about protecting the organization, it was about protecting their individual ability to influence the direction taken.

An increasing number of attorneys are very aware of the inherent conflict between these two courts and will give their advice with that understanding. They might say, "If I look at it purely from a legal perspective, here is what you should do or say. However, I understand what that would mean for the company's credibility and therefore you should consider if the long-term consequences to the company are more significant with loss of credibility than the legal risk." Communicators, on the other hand, need to take the time to listen to the attorneys and find out what the legal risks really are. In many situations, if there is some discussion and the power-tripping is ended, a solution can be found that minimizes the legal risk while allowing the company to speak in a way that protects its credibility, but not always, unfortunately.

That means that the CEO or organization leader has a critical role to play here. The CEO's job is to protect the present and future of the organization. The dilemma between the two courts is very real, so tough decisions need to be made. A legal cost must sometimes be paid to protect the public franchise and the viability of the company in the future. Sometimes a decision must be made that harms the organization's credibility to protect the company's legal position. In those cases, I prefer to make an honest statement about why the company cannot speak or why it is taking the position that it has because of the potential consequences in court, but taking such a position often leads to a new round of warfare with the attorneys.

I am making a strong point of this because it is a crucial issue and because too often I have seen CEOs take the position that protecting the organization means turning decision making over to the attorneys when a large legal action is involved. Clearly they believe that protecting the company's legal stance is the best way to protect their positions. My only reminder to CEOs who have this philosophy is to assure them that most CEOs today experience a short tenure not because of adverse legal action but because the customers and/or the public has lost confidence in them. Do not be too quick to assume the best way to protect the investment of the owners or shareholders is by allowing the attorneys to take control.

How Will We Determine Whether a Crisis Exists and What Level of Response Is Required?

There are many excellent resources on defining crises and appropriate responses. We won't cover well-trod ground here. The point to be made is that the communication and crisis response managers need to have clearly in their minds the circumstances that require various levels of response. In the aftermath of September 11, 2001, the National Guard and other agencies such as the Coast Guard have developed various alert levels with fairly clear definitions of which threat conditions require which level of response. Some agencies have four levels, others use three. A company or organization that plans properly for reputation threats will likewise have various levels of response with a corresponding response plan for each level. The greater the threat, the more of the leadership team and response team is pulled into the response, with clearly defined roles and expectations for each member.

It is not always easy to see in the early stages of an unfolding story how it will play out and how much of a crisis it might become. That is one good reason to have an experienced crisis communication professional available to provide threat assessments and guidance in evaluating the direction a story might take. I have been involved in many situations that had the appearance of becoming major reputation-threatening crises but never developed. To overreact in the early stages could have caused damage and could have actually precipitated media coverage and stakeholder concern that wasn't necessary. On the other hand, situations such as those of Arthur Andersen and Firestone/Ford make it clear that crisis momentum can get rolling quickly and if the company underestimates the impact, it is forever behind the curve with little possibility of catching up.

When a client was faced with what promised to be highly publicized legal action, we prepared a response and a press release to convey that response. The question became whether to release it or not. To release it without a large-scale effort on the part of the plaintiff's attorney would likely create a story that otherwise wouldn't exist. To delay or not release it would mean that our side of the story would likely not get told. When the plaintiff's story appeared on the AP wire, I could see that the story was released in a very early stage. We emailed the release to all reporters we thought might be interested. When very little media coverage appeared, we concluded that one possibility was that with our response, reporters could more easily see that the plaintiff's attorney's release was a publicity-seeking story and decided it didn't have strong news merit.

To What Length Is the Organization Willing to Go to Protect Its Credibility?

This is the fundamental preparation question. It starts with an assessment of brand value and the potential risk to the enterprise's future should its public franchise be damaged or destroyed. From there it goes on to the establishment of a clear link between credibility and reputation. When raising my three teenagers, I appropriated the great NAACP college ad slogan, "A mind is a terrible thing to waste" to repeat to them more frequently than they wanted to hear, "Trust is a terrible thing to waste." I appropriate it once more here: For a respected company or organization, credibility is a terrible thing to waste. The loss of credibility is the loss of public confidence and the potential loss of the public franchise.

Credibility is a character issue and character values are ascribed to organizations as well as people. Firestone's trust was lost once it was believed, fairly or not, that information about tire manufacturing problems was ignored or hidden by management. Large tobacco companies are spending millions and millions of dollars attempting to restore credibility by talking about their good work in war-torn areas such as Kosovo, but the reality is for years executives hid the truth about what they knew about the risks of smoking. Their bald-faced lying will perhaps never be forgiven and the willingness of the public to respond with draconian measures that put civil liberties at risk is an example of the cost of loss of credibility.

The real problem with this issue arises with an honest discussion about what credibility means in the instant news world. This is discussed at length in a later chapter dealing with the future and the need for truth filters, but as companies and organizations more often find themselves taking on the role of the media in public communication, credibility expands in importance beyond anything we have yet seen. People reading information from a Web site or from an email message coming from the company need to know that the information is reliable, that it does not represent the company spin, and that it is completely honest and truthful.

Credibility, as former President Clinton discovered, is more than the clever use of the word *is*. It is fundamental honesty. It is not just a matter of how carefully you choose your words. It is much more a matter of speaking the truth clearly in a way that is understood and that contains the whole truth. The most difficult challenge to credibility in communication emerges when it becomes known that people within the company did indeed make mistakes, were negligent, or even operated illegally or unethically. If this information is not public, should the company communicate it or wait for it to be revealed by other sources? This is the real meaning of the question of to what length a company will go to protect its credibility. If credibility is important or critical, the answer to that question is obvious. If protecting the company financially in a court of law is the ultimate value of the company's leaders, then credibility will almost invariably be lost. There is very little no man's land in this highly dangerous battlefield.

A quick perusal of news stories in this age of instant news and infotainment shows that cover-up is a most consistent theme. A company that knows something and does not explain it straightforwardly is almost always accused of a cover-up. The lead accountant on the Enron account for Arthur Andersen destroyed key documents relating to the Enron situation. He protested that he was following the advice of the company's attorney, who responded that she only said to follow document destruction procedures. The legalities are a moot point. What is crystal clear is that the credibility of Arthur Andersen was at stake and already damaged by the decision of one of its partners. He might have followed legal advice and company policy, but the result was the appearance of a cover-up, and that is toxic to a reputation. Although the company responded by firing the partner involved, and he subsequently pleaded guilty to federal obstruction of justice charges, these actions did not substantially help the company. By that time their waffling on matters of character and policy, their stated intention to fight the criminal charges, and the inconsistency between what the company officials were saying and their lawyers were saying resulted in a profound loss of public confidence and a flood of account losses. A March 30, 2002 *New York Times* headline summed up the problem: "Leaderless at Arthur Andersen When Direction Is Needed."

There are no simple answers to this difficult question but a communication policy needs to address it because it lies at the heart of the entire response. Hypocrisy will be exceptionally visible when a policy says one thing and company leaders do something else. It is essential that communication leaders, executives, and the attorneys they will rely on sit down together to specifically discuss and hammer out a policy and plan to answer the question of how far the organization will go to protect its credibility.

After the fundamental questions have been answered in a document that represents the organization's communication policy, that policy must be implemented through a well-prepared plan. Here are a few questions to consider in developing that detailed communication plan:

1. How will the communication team be organized?
2. How will the communication organization evolve based on the scope of the issue or incident?
3. What are the key roles in managing a communication effort and who will be assigned to those roles?
4. What equipment and resources will be required to communicate effectively?
5. What key organization messages need to be communicated during a public event?
6. What approval process will be used to ensure that messages and information released are accurate, appropriate, and reflect the values and priorities of the organization?
7. How will outside participants such as lawyers, consultants, communication contractors, and so forth, be integrated effectively into the effort?
8. How will the many questions from the various audience groups be managed and answered?
9. How will we coordinate and manage participation from the various units in the organization?

PEOPLE

When my children were young in the early 1980s, like almost all their friends, they got into video games. Like most parents, we questioned this use of time and what it might mean for their futures. Aside from the frustration of not being able to make Mario perform with anything near the degree of skill they demonstrated, it was my view that they were indeed preparing for the world of the future. "This is the way the next war will be fought," I opined to my wife. Not only that, but because an entire generation was being raised on fast-paced action on the computer or TV screen and the intense movements on a handheld controller, I was convinced that employers of the future were going to have to replicate this kind of action in their work or have a generation of workers who were terminally bored.

This has become reality in ways I could not have dreamed. Most automobiles are now manufactured using mouse and joystick controls handled by a few highly trained and very bright computer engineers operating billions of dollars of technology. We bomb the caves of Afghanistan from 50,000 feet guiding smart bombs and "daisy cutters" into the smallest spaces with computer-aided devices using controllers not unlike what my kids were running with Nintendo. Today, we communicate with millions around the world with gamelike digital production interfaces.

The postmedia world—the world of instant news, instant media, and infotainment—demands a new kind of communicator. The "slap you on the back, everybody's his best friend" style of public relations professional that dominated the capital and media world is as out of place in this new world as the Kalishnikov rifles proudly owned by the horse-riding mujahadeen are in the new world of pilotless aircraft.

There is no doubt in my mind that the primary obstacle to change and to adequate communication preparation is the fact that the very people who have risen to the top of their profession are too often living in the comfortable media world of the past. To tell them that their new world will live on an Internet platform, and that they must be conversant with advanced database management, broadband communications, and digital image production is to tell them that much of what they have built their careers on is now irrelevant. No wonder there is resistance.

The solution is not to throw that valuable experience away, nor am I suggesting that no one born prior to 1975 can succeed in the instant news world. However, change is necessary, inevitable, and must be demanded. Age is not the issue. My father, who has been interested in technology since he hid a radio from German occupiers in his native Holland during

World War II, is an avid computer enthusiast who spends countless hours learning the latest digital video and image-manipulation technologies. My mother, also in her early 70s, has recently discovered what a marvelous tool the Internet is for keeping her children and their spouses, grandchildren, and great-grandchildren connected.

Those involved in public communication today must clearly understand that technology is a primary driver in their lives. The ones who will succeed and grow in the new news era will embrace this fact and anticipate the changes rather than resist and dread them.

Communication leaders today must also step up to a new level of responsibility within their organizations. We have seen the elevation of the corporate communication manager in the decision-making hierarchy in recent years, but in many organizations this function is still relegated to lower level junior managers or a subfunction of human resource managers. Communication managers need to take a strong role in the company strategy and decision making because so much of the present and future of the organization rides on the effectiveness of public and stakeholder communication. Lines between marketing and public relations simply do not make as much sense in the era of instant, direct communication. If the purpose of the organization is to develop and maintain high-value relationships with the right people, it should be obvious that effective communication with those right people is a fundamental element of what the business or organization is all about.

At a recent gathering of public relations professionals, one of the most popular sessions had to do with "gaining a seat at the table." The speaker offered suggestions on how public relations contractors or corporate communications staff people could become more strategic. Although the topic was timely and the presentation well received, many suggestions were less than meaningful. Being strategic means making contributions that are important to helping fulfill the mission of the organization. Yet there was essentially no discussion about the critical role of communication in the function and operation of the business, or about learning to think like a CEO. A communication professional of real benefit to the executive team is one who deeply understands and is committed to the mission of the organization. He or she understands the role of internal and external communication in fulfilling that mission and has the ability to develop, build support for, and implement communication solutions that are effective in advancing the organization's mission.

One task today's communication leader must assume is preparing a team to manage the communication process in the event of a reputation crisis. If the organization does not have a communication leader with the qualities already described, the CEO or other senior executives need to assume this role or bring in the outside expertise needed to prepare an effective communication team.

Training and drilling is the most effective method for preparing a team and it is more important than ever in this world of instant news. A team can be effective only when everyone clearly understands the goals and the roles they and others on the team must play to achieve those goals. Another way of putting it is to use the game analogy: A team can't win if it doesn't understand what winning means, and a team can't win if each member doesn't know what he or she must do as part of that team.

Much of my experience in crisis communications has involved the Joint Information Center (JIC) model. This model provides an excellent template for developing a fully staffed and efficiently operating crisis communication operation. The JIC was developed to flesh out the public information function of the Incident Command System (ICS). ICS was developed in the 1970s by the fire service as a means of quickly developing an effective management structure to respond to out-of-control fires. It has subsequently been adopted and refined by most major federal agencies responsible for responding to major public crises, including the Federal Emergency Management Agency, the EPA, the Coast Guard, the FBI, and others. It is a primary training and management tool used by these federal agencies to extend their capability to the local level through departments of emergency management, police agencies, and local industry coordinating groups.

The ICS provides a ready-made organization structure to quickly and efficiently manage a large-scale event such as a fire, a school shooting, an earthquake, an oil spill, and so on. It is especially useful when there are multiple government agencies involved, including federal, state, and local agencies. It clearly defines the command structure and the entire organization plan and eliminates the very real potential for mission-diverting discussions like, "Who's really in charge here?" and "What are the boundaries of my role?" Although it is especially helpful for a company (called the "responsible party" in ICS terminology) that finds itself at the center of an event in which government agencies are responding, it is also a very useful model to study, adapt, and drill for companies who face reputation crises without the likelihood of agency involvement.

The JIC was developed out of the ICS structure as a way of coordinating public information when multiple agencies are involved. Again, even if your organization's most likely crises are legal actions or product recalls, which might not involve police, fire, or federal regulatory agencies, the JIC model is still very useful as a means of efficiently organizing and managing a crisis communication team.

The Information Officer is the communication manager responsible for overall public information. He or she has a direct link to the Incident Commander, or in the case of a multiagency response, the Unified Command. Closely related to the Information Officer is the Liaison Officer, whose role is to provide the link between the various agencies and in some models, also manage communication with government agencies and officials. The major roles within the JIC include the JIC manager, Assistant Information Officer, Internal and Assistant Information Officer, External. The internal manager is responsible for development and production of needed materials, communication within the response organization, and communication to the employees of the organization. The external manager is responsible for communication with outside audiences such as the media, neighbors, local officials, and other key stakeholders. Further roles are defined to divide the responsibilities under each of these key managers. The model is easily expandable and with even minimal training and drilling, the communication response team can be organized and efficiently managed.

Some of these specific activities are explored in more detail in the chapter on crisis response. The JIC manual is published by the National Response Team chaired by the EPA and can be downloaded from the Web at *www.nrt.org* by selecting NRT Publications.

Whether the JIC model is adopted and adapted for use by the organization or whether a custom-designed model of crisis communication team organization is adopted, the key point is to develop the organization structure, and then train and drill.

Training involves getting the team members together, explaining potential crises, and identifying desired outcomes and major tasks that need to be done and by whom to achieve the desired results. This can be done in a didactic method of telling people what it is they need to do, but it is more effectively accomplished through hands-on experience. Short of a real incident, which is not a good time to train, the best method of preparing the team is through a drill.

Drilling involves setting up a scenario and either walking through it in a tabletop exercise or running a real-time drill. There is no better method for preparing a communication team than a full-scale drill. This is particularly true if the communication response involves the use of technology unfamiliar to at least some of the team. In a full-scale, real-time drill, a group needs to be involved to provide the inputs to the drill, as well as people to be reporters, neighbors, executives, employees, investors, government officials, and so on. Sometimes called the *simulation cell* or *simcell,* these people should be experienced in crisis communications and need to take their roles seriously even as they become the worst nightmare for the communication team.

A major advantage of a drill is the chance to identify the strengths and weaknesses of various team members. Some might be more effective at information gathering, drafting, and editing of materials. Some might do well in media interviews, whereas others might be best in personal, face-to-face discussions with stakeholders. The CEO or executives who will be involved in making decisions during a real event and those who will provide the "face" of the organization need to be involved in these drills as well, and their strengths and weaknesses must be honestly assessed. Given the seriousness of a real crisis to the future of the organization, this assessment of strengths and weaknesses and required skill levels should be seriously undertaken. Hard decisions made at the drill or post-drill stage can have an impact on the organization measured in the millions or billions of dollars.

That is the most important point to be made about the people issue in crisis or corporate communication in this era. Quite frankly, some are suited for this kind of work and others are not. There are some able to adapt and grow with the changes in the media environment and others who will serve as obstacles. Communication managers and top executives need to constantly ask themselves, "What is at stake?" When the importance of a fast, effective information response is deeply understood, the tough people decisions will be made. As an observer from the outside looking in at some of the organizations and the unqualified people they have in key communication positions, I can only conclude that the leadership either does not grasp what is at stake for the entire organization or simply does not have the leadership qualities to make the difficult decisions involving people they might like or who have a long tenure in the organization.

Platform

The technology for communicating has always been an important issue, but never more so than today. It has become a cliché to claim that "the medium is the message," and yet it is quite obvious in a reputation crisis how important this is. Take, for example, a family member of a person injured in an industrial accident. How they respond to and feel about the company's apology for what has happened will vary greatly depending on the medium used to convey that apology. If they receive a personal visit from the CEO who communicates warmly, sincerely, and with genuine sorrow, their response will likely be considerably different than if they received a letter or fax, much more so if their only message of condolence or regret was expressed by a news anchor on the evening news reading a statement from the company that says, "XYZ Company expresses its regret over this incident."

The hierarchy of communication should always go from the most personal to the most impersonal. If the CEO could communicate directly and personally with each and every person involved, and each and every reporter, that would obviously be the ideal. The reality is that such a response is impossible, so the challenge for the communication manager is to come as close to that ideal as possible given the media, the technology, the people, and the resources available.

Although personal is best, it does not follow that the more recent technological means are therefore most impersonal. This is where Naisbitt's insight has done us a bit of disservice. High tech is not always the polar opposite of high touch. The extensive use of email for tying families and friendships together, the use of the Internet for locating old classmates, and the replacement of the telephone (another tech/touch medium) with email and Web sites for locating missing relatives on September 11 all illustrate the personal nature of the most high-tech of all communication devices. One of the things that makes this discussion difficult is, with current technology, we can mass personalize. When I sign on to *Amazon.com* or some other advanced e-commerce sites, I get personalized information about my past buying history, recommendations on new products that I might like based on past purchases, and other help personally designed for me. Is this personal? Hardly, because there was no person involved other than the one who designed the program, but it's not as impersonal as a catalog and it certainly cannot be described as a mass solution. I am treated as an individual and I know that the information is there uniquely for me and uniquely tailored to meet my needs.

I have already described the role of technology in creating the instant news world we currently live in and particularly the postmedia world we are moving into. A technology-driven information world requires that technology be part of the information strategy of any company or organization operating in this environment. The issue is not whether you will use technology in your communication plan, but which technology platform you will use and how effectively you will use it.

We explore some of the basic technology issues here, but the next chapter discusses specific applications required to meet the instant response demanded in today's public information milieu.

A basic assumption of communication technology involves the use of computers. In the most basic uses, computers are used to draft and edit documents, write reports, and store data such as facts about the organization and mailing lists. The main issue today isn't whether or not to use computers, it is how they are linked. George Gilder, in a *Forbes* magazine article in 1994, highlighted the Sun Microsystems slogan, "The network *is* the computer."[1] Much more than an advertising slogan, this is a profound insight because how computers are linked together makes all the difference in their power as communication devices and whether or not their true capabilities will be unleashed. From this standpoint, we can say today that the Internet is the computer.

All but a very few executives and communication professionals currently are linked to hundreds of millions of other computers through the Internet. This is the most significant change in the emerging postmedia world. It is essentially this light-speed linkage that creates this new public information environment. However, when it comes to using this capability, most communicators are severely hampered. The obstacles to effective use of the Internet in public communication include fear, lack of awareness of the technology, budgetary constraints, and IT policies. It is like a medieval king having available a machine gun or a tank to help him fight his battles, but he cannot use it because he either doesn't know how or the person in charge of weaponry simply won't make the tool accessible to him.

The Internet is the only realistic platform for communicating in this instant news world. More specifically, an Internet-based communication management application operating on a crisis-capable Web server is rapidly becoming an essential tool of today's communicator. As a platform, the Internet offers the opportunity for a team to work effectively together on a common desktop to create, edit, approve, and instantly disseminate the information needed. Information can be mass customized. All types of information can be presented quickly and at virtually no cost for distribution—information such as audio interviews, video, all manner of printed materials, and every conceivable kind of photographic or illustrative image. A virtual command center can be established instantly and new team members can be quickly incorporated by issuing passwords and security levels.

Today, there are a few professional communicators who have at their fingertips the opportunity to instantly summon a global team of communicators. They can work together in real time or as their own clocks allow to draft, edit, review, approve, and upload any kind of media and instantly distribute any information they desire to an audience of one or many thousands, and they can do this without a single Web programmer in sight. In other words, a few communicators currently can command the full capabilities of the Internet for both team and external communication, but most cannot.

Most communicators today, although certainly adept at computer skills, are limited because company policy operates around a local area network (LAN) mentality. This is understandable because IT managers see the work that people need to do as restricted to those inside the company and the LAN has traditionally offered a higher level of security. Add the opportunities now afforded by virtual private networks (VPNs) and the reach of the LAN can be extended through a secured connection with the Internet.

In simple terms, the problem with the LAN, and even with VPN, is that it does not easily provide universal access. The perceived problem with the Internet is that it does provide universal access and therefore is a security risk. The reality is that opening up the Internet as a platform for public communication challenges IT people to their very core: control of the resource. Security issues are relatively easily resolved, but turf issues are not.

Top executives of today's "at-risk" companies need to be completely aware of this situation. Tools are currently available that enable you and your communication team to respond quickly and efficiently and meet the "now is too late" standard. However, making these tools available runs counter to the inherent control issues of most IT leaders. Their power is gained by controlling access to technology when their role should be seen as power through providing access. There is no reason today's communicators should not be able to fully and completely command the capabilities of the most powerful communication implementation ever devised even though the thought of programming or increasing technological knowledge is abhorrent to them. What keeps most people from making use of this is either their fear or internal obstacles relating to IT policy.

There are two major issues involved in this difficult situation: first, not understanding the value of an open but controlled access platform for team communication and second, not understanding the criticality of crisis-capable Web service.

On the issue of universal access, in a crisis situation today, open but controlled access is essential. *Open* and *controlled* means using the Internet but controlling access through various methods, including multitiered passwords. In an example based on a real event, let's assume you are the head of communication for a large hospital. You find out that a legal action is being filed and the attorney for the plaintiff is a publicity seeker. You get a call from *Good Morning America* or the *Today Show* courteously informing you that the attorney, the plaintiff, and a physician friendly to them will be on their show discussing their lawsuit. You ask if you can be there also. They say no, but if you can get them a statement of response in a half an hour, they might use it on the air. The problem is that the CEO of the hospital is on the other coast, one attorney involved is in Denver, and the other is in San Francisco. The attorney's reaction, of course, is to say nothing, but you press and get agreement to work out a statement that the attorneys can live with and the CEO will approve. But how? Email? Much better than letter. Fax? With four or five different people involved, all making changes to your document? LAN-based application? Are these outside attorneys going to have access to your LAN, even with a VPN? The best application is one that is Internet-based, allows the communication manager to provide needed passwords that control access only to the portions of the application needed, and allows real-time drafting, editing, and distribution.

In this case, the company involved did have access to that kind of technology. Three different attorneys, the CEO, and the communication manager all had their licks in on the document. The news producer on the other side of the continent got the response by email in 20 minutes and the statement was read on the program the next morning.

The other issue involves crisis-capable servers. There are very good reasons companies and organizations should have their public communication technology including press room and incident dark sites on Web servers completely separated from their regular operational servers. Most Web servers today, except for those at companies relying on heavy traffic for e-commerce, are not capable of handling the bandwidth required for millions of hits. Yet, we have shown that a great many companies and organizations are vulnerable to these kinds of hits in a major news event. The cost of upgrading can be substantial and few IT departments are willing to spend the kind of money needed for the remote possibility that they will need that kind of capacity.

At the same time, new services are being offered to share crisis-capable servers across many users. Similar to insurance, these services offer multimillion hit capacity and share the cost across many at-risk users. Is there a chance that a number of different companies in different industries would experience multiple crises or catastrophes on the same day? Yes, but it is far more likely that each crisis will occur independently and the cost of preparing can be shared.

When using such a service, if the company's press room is hosted on such a server it will automatically take the hits in the event of a major news crisis. If not, traffic can be quickly diverted from the company's main site by using a crisis-specific domain name in the initial release and all subsequent public information about the event. More and more companies are taking this approach and are setting up response-oriented domain names that drive traffic to the crisis servers and away from the main business servers.

The primary obstacle to this is the IT department's requirement that any and all company sites be hosted on their own servers. Again, it's an easy pitch for the IT department to make to the executives: Why wouldn't we want that? It saves money, adds security, and gives us control. Yes, but it leaves the organization highly vulnerable to reputation management crises and highly vulnerable to a Web service crash that will take the entire company's Internet operation down.

This situation can result in a kind of catch-22 of rather ridiculous proportions. One high-level communication manager wanted to make use of Internet-based communication management technology for crisis management. However, the large company he worked for had a policy of no outside hosting of company sites. Why not put the software application on the company's servers then? Because the company's servers can only take a few thousand hits and if a crisis hit, the traffic would bring them down. Then why not make use of the service that hosts crisis information sites and relieve the company's servers of any hit burden? Because company policy won't allow outside hosting of company Web sites or services. This is a global company with a very high risk for international-level news interest.

As usual, when the demands of various departments collide, it is the executive leadership that must decide. In this case, it needs to start with executive awareness of the issues and how important they are to the future prospects of the company. It is the responsibility of the communication professionals, either those inside the company or outside experts, to inform and educate the executives on what is at stake and what solutions are available. It is also their responsibility to make clear the internal obstacles that stand in the way of implementing the solutions needed to make certain the organization is fully prepared to respond.

We have identified and discussed three important elements of preparation and their related obstacles: policies, people, and platform or technology. Three legs of a very important stool, these must be thoroughly addressed for today's organization to be adequately prepared. The good news is that preparation is very possible. The bad news is that tomorrow will be different.

Endnotes

1. Gilder, George, "The Bandwidth Tidal Wave," *Forbes* magazine, Dec. 5, 1994, p. 162. Used by permission.

CHAPTER

9 The Role of Technology

The first notice came from the border patrol manager at the international boundary between the United States and Canada. The local Department of Emergency Management (DEM) was notified and the volunteer Information Officer was alerted and activated. The situation: Someone had stopped a large motor home at the border crossing and a cloud of steam or gas was escaping from the air conditioning unit on the top. When approached by agents, the driver ran off and escaped on the Canadian side. The agents on the scene suspected it was a bioterrorist attack and the gas escaping contained a toxic substance, possibly anthrax. This occurred 4 p.m. on a Saturday afternoon.

The Information Officer was home mowing his lawn when he got the call. He quickly went to his home office with his computer and broadband Internet connection. The local DEM public information site had been prepared for just such an eventuality. He opened up the "dark site" and filled out the templates for public notices and press information. The incident dark site had been prepared in advance and was available on the Internet for immediate public launch, but was not visible to anyone except the communication team.

Using the internal message center and chat room functions built into his communication management system, he confirmed some of the latest information and completed a draft of the initial statement. The ICS was just beginning to be implemented and the local police chief was serving as Incident Commander while other agencies such as the FBI and the Royal Canadian Mounted Police were notified and activated. The Incident Commander approved the draft public notice and press release and the Information Officer pushed another button, posting the approved documents to the incident site, and then clicked another button to launch it as a public site available to anyone.

He also then reviewed the contact names contained within the system. He selected all the reporters in the immediate area and some of the major media reporters in the region, then he clicked a button to send the release. He decided that this release would go out via email and telephone. The system automatically converted the text of the release to voice, and across the region reporters began to receive telephone calls with the information. At the same time, the press release popped up in their emails, and if they didn't have email, their fax machines were humming with the startling news.

The Incident Commander said he wanted all agencies involved to be kept informed of the event and the unfolding response and activities. Simultaneous with the release of the press information, the Information Officer selected prepared mailing lists of community leaders, as well as local and state government officials. They also received emails or faxes with the news, as did the local hospital, the Red Cross, the local and state health departments, and every police and fire agency in a 30-mile radius.

It was now 4:30. Reporter calls were coming in, but many of the reporters were following the advice offered on the release, indicating that the best way to submit questions would be through the media inquiry function on the public Web site. The Information Officer monitored the inquiries coming in even while he activated the JIC team of volunteer and agency information professionals. He activated them using the system to send a simultaneous email and telephone message. He monitored their involvement by seeing who had "signed in" to the password-protected intranet site that served as their common desktop. He decided given the urgency and time, it was best they operate a "virtual JIC" for a couple of hours. They would operate from their homes or offices until a command center with sufficient computer resources was established nearer to the scene. He assigned one of the JIC staffers as Assistant Information Officer External and redirected calls coming in to his busy cell phone to the new Assistant Information Officer's home phone. The assistant grabbed a couple of other JIC volunteers and assigned one to handle local media, public, and government inquiries, whereas the other was to take state, national, and international inquiries.

The inquiries coming in by phone were captured by the team entering the relevant information into the communication system. Other inquiries coming in via the public Web site would show up on the "uncompleted inquiries" list. To complete the inquiries, information responders would answer the question and click a button to automatically email them, at which point they automatically moved into the "completed" category. Inquiries were shifted among team members by another click of the button. Meanwhile, the Information Officer could observe all this activity from his home office and send messages to responders when they were getting off track or weren't using the latest approved information. Using the internal email and secured chat room to communicate among team members meant they never needed to leave their common work platform, the intranet site, and the New Message button would light up when a message was directed to them.

The Assistant Information Officer Internal was given the duty of keeping up with the rapidly unfolding events and preparing the needed updates. One person was sent to the scene to be the liaison on scene with the Unified Command. A computer was now available at the scene so he used this to keep a running update of the rapidly unfolding situation. Multitiered access levels allowed key members of the information team as well as leaders of the responding agencies to review this minute-by-minute document online, whereas others on the team, such as those responding to inquiries, were not granted access to this "raw" information to prevent inadvertent release of unconfirmed or unapproved information.

An hour into the event, the hit counter on the crisis-capable server was moving into the hundreds of thousands of hits, but it was built to withstand millions of hits so it was in no danger of crashing. Members of the public, the media, and the government who were not on the initial release list were now taking up the offer to get automatic email updates and were adding their names by the hundreds to the mailing list available on the public site. The next email update was sent to all those who had just signed up. A press conference was scheduled and all reporters, including those who had added themselves, received an email notice as well as a phone call alerting them to time and place. An additional and connected Web site was established, this one without public access. The Information Officers for the response agencies were given passwords for this private site so that their agency leaders and top U.S. and Canadian government officials could get immediate access to the most complete information before it was released to the public. This site was launched and managed by the Information Officer, still operating from the vast high-tech control room that used to be his daughter's bedroom.

Did this event happen? No, but an international bioterrorism drill playing out this scenario did happen in August 2000. Called Northern Exposure, this drill brought together more than 40 federal, state, provincial, and local agencies from the United States and Canada in a table-top exercise to prepare for just such an event. I served as the Information Officer and the technology just described was available. If the drill had not been a table-top exercise, the communication technology could have been implemented in much the same way as described.

The new media environment requires that today's executives and communicators have a different picture in their heads about communicating with the public and the many stakeholder audiences. The old picture revolves around sending out press releases by broadcast fax and holding a press conference or conducting media interviews. The new picture is more like managing a control room in a highly complex industrial facility where multiple processes are occurring at the same time and everything needs to be carefully managed and controlled. Such a complex operation cannot be managed by sending runners out to check on this unit or that operation and having them report back to the office. Complex process management, in which speed is the driving element, requires all aspects to be networked together, with monitors displaying real-time information about what is happening.

New communication management technology provides the means to manage the most challenging issue or crisis situations. Even a relatively small team can manage the quickly escalating demands of multiple audiences wanting immediate, direct, and individualized information. This technology is entirely Internet-based, providing universal access. However, it is highly secure and controlled with multiple levels of user access. The most important advantage of using the new breed of communication management technology is that it puts the full potential of the Internet as a communication tool in the hands of executives and communicators and removes control from technicians, Web programmers, and IT managers who understand technology but don't understand the communication demands of the instant news world. You might note that in the scenario just described, not a single programmer or technician was part of the information team and there were no delays or additional steps required to make use of any aspect of the Internet.

The term *communication management* must be distinguished from the now commonly used term *content management*. There is a critical difference. Content management is focused on allowing a group of users with password access to jointly manage and control content on a Web site or Web sites. Communication management incorporates the content management function but goes considerably beyond it. Content management is aimed at "pull" communications, where viewers come to your Web site when they want and view or download information that they are seeking. Communication management incorporates interactive communication and "push" communications. Interaction involves the give and take, input and response, of most human communication. *Push* means directing the information to specific individual users via email or other more traditional means such as fax, telephone, or mail.

The many tasks to be managed by the communication team can all be supported by currently available technology. We'll break these tasks into various elements, understanding that in an instant news event, they flow seamlessly and simultaneously together.

Information Development

If we look at the task of the communicator as getting the right information to the right people, right now, the first facet is the right information. Information development involves collecting the facts, data, comments, images, and all other elements needed, and then drafting those elements into an appropriate form such as a press release, backgrounder, fact sheet, or other type of document. Normally, the draft needs to go through a review process. The more important it is in terms of the company's or organization's reputation and credibility, the more thoroughly it will be reviewed. The editing process might put it through many hands and eyes, with a variety of people marking changes. It is not uncommon for people outside the organization such as attorneys, consultants, or communication professionals to be consulted or to actively participate in this process. Finally, it must be approved. A communication manager might have approval authority over most such documents but when the company's present and future rests on what is said, the CEO or another top executive might be the final approval authority. In a crisis situation, this is most frequently the case, and if the ICS is implemented, nothing can go out without the approval of the Unified Command.

All this can work relatively smoothly using today's common computer and Internet tools, such as word processing software and email programs. Documents are stored on network servers, outsiders participate via email, and their changes are incorporated back into the drafts on the server. The problem with the normal way is the need for speed. In a crisis situation, the normal way of doing things is almost always too slow. The instant news environment and the expectations of Internet users require a process that takes just minutes rather than days or hours. The urgency of getting it out is matched by the urgency of getting it right because no other releases or documents might be more important to the viability of the organization than the first few releases going out after a major event has occurred. Equally important is the development and distribution of information inside the organization to employees, managers, and families.

The only viable solution today is to place the process on an Internet platform. Document and information development needs to be accomplished completely on a common desktop made possible by the Internet. Team members can participate regardless of location, provided they have password access. Current technology provides for intranet sites specifically designed for this purpose. Drafters can create new documents in advanced Web editing tools that present a word-processor-like functionality. These same advanced editors provide those used to common word processing software the tools to place images, design pages, and fully control how they want the information to look.

Images and files can be uploaded for placement in documents or on a public Web site simply by browsing for the file on a desktop or network server. Each person with appropriate password access who signs into the intranet site can then see which drafts are available for editing and what changes to earlier drafts have been made by other editors. Designated "approvers" are established by the intranet site manager, and only they have the approval buttons on their screens allowing them to move the document forward, posting it to the public site or sending it for automatic distribution via email, fax, or telephone.

The very significant speed versus accuracy issue can only be effectively resolved by having a team prepared to work together instantly and providing a platform that makes that possible. Having document creation, editing, and approving set up on a universally available but highly secured intranet site is the only practical solution for this problem. It has proven its worth in numerous crisis situations, demonstrating that it is possible to resolve this difficult dilemma.

In addition to providing an Internet platform for document creation, more companies and organizations are also preparing for the demands of the instant news world by preparing incident *dark sites*. These are fully prepared Web sites that are not available to the public but can be made available in very short order when launched to provide the information that the public and the media are looking for about an event. These sites are exceptionally helpful in getting a headstart in providing information, and they provide an important opportunity to get ahead of the information curve.

However, most of these sites are built with common static Hypertext Markup Language (HTML) technology, which means they are dependent on technicians or programmers to keep them updated as an event unfolds. This might not be a problem for an event that has no changing information, but such events are quite unlikely. By building dark sites on a fully dynamic communication management platform, a company has a better chance of staying ahead of the curve. Drafting, editing, and approving information online is one critical element, as is the ability to instantly post existing digital documents without technical assistance. The option, of course, is to have an exceptionally efficient and responsive Web team able to keep up on a 24/7 basis for an indefinite period of time. The cost and inefficiency of this suggests that the technology platform is a more suitable solution.

Information Distribution

Information distribution remains one of the most challenging aspects of high-speed communications. Many professional communicators rely on their email program to manage media contacts and in the event of a crisis will email releases from their desktop, faxing them to people who might not have email addresses. Others rely on outside news distribution services for distribution of all releases. These solutions represent significant problems in the event of a crisis.

Crises rarely occur during business hours when you are sitting behind your desk looking for something to do. If you are away from your office, accessing your contact list might delay the release of information from minutes to hours or even longer. As we have discussed, these delays can be very consequential. Additionally, in a crisis, many of the reporters and others seeking information (e.g., a U.S. Senator or local state representative) might not be in your database of contacts. A large number of names, phone numbers, email addresses, fax numbers, and so on, will need to be added. The new additions need to be kept in a place where multiple members of the team can access them. Using an outside service invariably means that although the service will distribute to their previously developed lists, the important names you collect during the event will need to be managed independently.

If you take the reasonable approach that these predeveloped contact names and the ones captured during the crisis should reside on a server within your LAN, you still have the very real issue of the access of team members to the LAN. Will they always be in a position to access that critical data? Unless you have developed a means of capturing names from the public site and automatically having your LAN-based database updated, there is an important manual step that must be included in your planning and execution.

The rather obvious solution to this, just as in the document creation issue, is to put the contact database on an Internet platform. Having the contact database available to all team members via password access enables any team member, anywhere, anytime, to get at the contact names. When integrated with other Internet-based communication management functions such as inquiry management and automated distribution, the data management element becomes much more manageable and contributes to the speed of response.

Standard data management capabilities need to be available if the data resides on the Internet. Communicators without technical skill beyond that required by basic word processing software need to be able to sort, find, organize, and set up sublists of all kinds within databases. The data management system should also be able to easily accommodate not just media, but all potential stakeholders and audiences who might seek information, including shareholders, employees, executives, neighbors, elected officials, and so on. In other words, the data fields need to be flexible to handle the different types of data you might want to collect on each of these types. This is one critical difference between a system such as this and the many wire services that many communicators use. To use only a media list and not an integrated list including all key stakeholders is strong evidence of operating in the media world of the past and not the instant news postmedia world. Managing these contacts must be simple enough so that communicators can "slice and dice" the data on the fly without requiring a database programmer or technical help that might not be available at 3:30 a.m. when you are trying to prepare and distribute information while on vacation in Bora Bora.

With both document preparation and data management available on the same intranet site, the real power of the Internet as a communication tool becomes accessible. The Internet is the best platform for getting the right information out quickly to the right people. Current technology allows you to take the press release you created and approved online and distribute it instantly to databases of reporters and stakeholders managed within the same intranet site. With a click of a button, the document is simultaneously posted to the public Web site and instantly emailed to the mailing lists you select. It is a simple one-step process.

Faxing is accomplished in the same way. Currently available technology enables you to automatically fax the same document to any name you select that does not have an email address attached to it. If you prefer, for safety's sake, you can both email and fax to each name on the list.

A third automated distribution option is also available: text-to-voice conversion and automatic telephone messaging. Voice engines take written documents prepared on the private intranet site and when approved, convert the words to a synthesized voice. The phone numbers on the list are dialed and when answered either by a person or an answering machine, the system delivers the text message in a remarkably human-like voice. Voice options include male or female, with even regional accents as options.

The implications of this kind of currently available technology are quite significant. Fenceline neighbors, for example, want and have a right to know about activities within a plant that might affect their safety, security, and peace of mind. The telephone notification system makes it possible for a communicator to quickly type up a message and distribute it via mass telephone calls to the neighbors surrounding a plant. That message or a modified version can simultaneously be emailed, faxed, or telephoned to reporters or anyone else needing the information immediately. In an earlier chapter we discussed how expectations and demands for information change when it is understood that technology makes needed information available. What becomes possible becomes demanded. The commonsense reality of this situation means that every company and organization now needs to become aware of the technologies others are using to see what standards are being set and how that is adjusting the expectations of their audiences.

INTERACTIVITY AND RESPONSE

The two-way nature of communication is often given lip service but not seriously addressed. Admittedly, most of the focus in this book has been on quickly getting messages out to specific people and audiences. However, the ability to listen is also greatly improving with technology and there is much evidence that, similar to the demand for information, the individual's demand to be heard also corresponds to his or her realization that the technology exists to facilitate listening. The surprising popularity of radio talk shows is one example of how in this media-saturated environment, people are longing to be heard.

At the most basic level, a communication system today must allow interested people to register their interest, and the easier and more inviting the method, the better. A Web site that has no contact button or no email address to send questions or comments to or does not encourage response is a Web site that subtly communicates "We don't care much about you." If a system is used that places the contact databases on a Web platform, it is very easy to have dynamic and automatic database development from the public Web site. This is done more and more, and it helps eliminate double entry of names. More important, it helps communicate that you are eager to communicate with your audience. When this technology is used, visitors to a public site are encouraged to register themselves and those names are automatically added to the database managed within the Internet-based communication management system.

A second level of interactivity is facilitating questions, comments, and inquiries. A government agency found itself in the middle of a sizable public controversy. It offered an toll-free number for citizens to register complaints or comments. I asked how incoming calls were managed. I was told, somewhat sheepishly, that they were gathered on an answering machine that could handle 60 calls. I asked how many calls they had received. The answer was 1,400. When the machine was filled, they erased the calls and reset it to receive the next 60. If the public calling in had an inkling that this was how their efforts to communicate to their government were being handled, their anger would have increased.

Because we live in a mixed-media world, inquiries and comments can and do come from a variety of different media:

telephone, fax, email, and even mail once in a while. Email is now one of the most important means of interaction, but it also represents significant management issues. In 2001, it was reported that Congress received more than 80 million email messages and that the burden of those emails was simply beyond managing. Personal experience in attempting to contact federal elected officials confirms that although they might have the automated response down, they do not yet have the ability to manage the email messages they receive. This same problem will plague any company or organization finding itself in the news.

Although some email management technologies currently exist and no doubt will emerge to help address this significant problem, one of the best ways to manage inquiries today is to incorporate them into the communication management system. This is done by providing an inquiry function on the public Web site so those inquiries are managed on the team intranet site. Aside from the technology, which is becoming increasingly common, reporters and members of the public or other key audiences must be directed and encouraged to use the inquiry management system available on the public site. A public site inquiry form should ask the person inquiring to indicate if he or she is a member of the media or a member of another identified audience group (e.g., elected officials). It should also provide a convenient form for indicating the topic; the specific question; the time the response is needed; what company, media, or organization the individual is with; and other pertinent information that will help build a valuable inquiry history.

An inquiry that lands on an intranet or private communication team site without some notification is trouble. What if no one checks the inquiry list? Current technology alerts the communication team or designated members that an inquiry has been registered. As a user of such technology, I receive an alert on my text pager whenever inquiries land on client communication sites that I am managing.

A third level of interactivity is more directive listening. Questions can be directed to public site viewers or can be sent directly to specific individuals via email. Current technology facilitates this by providing simple survey-building tools and a viewer survey or poll on the public site, with the results monitored and analyzed on the private intranet site. Communication managers can select whether to share results with the public on a real-time basis or keep all results private. This technology also enables surveys to be published to lists managed within the system. Examples of this include use by government agencies or elected officials to get snapshot views of public reaction to new proposals or controversies and by companies to gauge public reaction to new initiatives, proposed actions, or even just to get a sense of how they are doing in communicating to key audiences.

Interactivity also includes tracking what reporters write or present. There are many technologies currently available for media tracking from a variety of vendors, both as packaged software and as hosted Internet applications (sometimes called Application Service Providers, or ASPs). Integrating these functions into a comprehensive communication management system means that a single system can complete the communication management circle.

INQUIRY MANAGEMENT

Inquiry management can make or break a communication effort. Earlier I quoted a frustrated communicator who spent two days responding to reporters. However, the company was criticized in news accounts for being unresponsive simply because the stretched communication team couldn't get back to everyone in a timely manner. You also read the disturbing story of neighbors near a plant that had experienced an explosion and fire emailing the company to find out if they should evacuate, only to have their emails answered two weeks later. The best of communication efforts will fail in the minds of those people who have asked a question and not received a response.

Technology has a very important role to play here, as do training and communication policies and plans. Technology can provide the means to collect, organize, track, and report on inquiries. Technology can facilitate getting the appropriate responses to the right people and also help a communication manager or company executive monitor the effectiveness of the response in real time or in detailed reporting after the crisis has passed.

With the communication management technology now available, inquiries are captured from the public site and by members of the communication team recording telephone calls or email inquiries and adding them to the inquiry list maintained inside the private team intranet site. By having all inquiries recorded and available on this site, all team members can work in concert to manage inquiries, even if it is 2 a.m. and they are scattered around the globe on vacations or business trips. An effective inquiry management system will show which inquiries have been completed and which ones have not. It will also allow a communication manager to act as a sort of air traffic controller, directing specific inquiries to the most appropriate member of the team. It will enable each member of the team to see who is working on each inquiry, whether they have responded, and how they have responded. It will also allow a communication manager to view all inquiry activity to determine the nature of the questions, to see if rumors are arising, and to evaluate both the speed and effectiveness of the responses. The system will also enable communicators to write the responses, forward the drafts to others for review, and send materials directly from the system via email to reporters or inquirers without having to exit the system.

In a large organization, such as a global manufacturing company, the communication team might be responsible for handling inquiries on a wide variety of issues from around the globe. Reporters are known to develop direct contacts with several members of the team and go from team member to team member asking the same question. The problems for the communication team are the risk of inconsistent answers and having multiple team members spend time on the same question. The only way to improve efficiency, quality, and consistency of response is to have communication management technology that allows every team member to share the information in real time. Today, that reality essentially forces the technology onto the Internet because of its accessibility; it also requires that the communication system be highly secure.

Another advantage of this available technology is record keeping. Where drills are required by law (e.g., in the oil industry), the documentation of drills can be very significant. In drills where this technology was used, the complete record of all communication activities, including all inquiries and their responses, was prepared simply by requesting a report from the system. The resulting printout recorded the full communication activity during the drill, including details on each inquiry and their responses. Even more so than in a drill, such automated record keeping can be invaluable as part of a debriefing after a crisis and can supply highly useful training material for the communication team to better prepare for the next event.

Web Site Control

The Internet is arguably one of the most powerful and flexible communication tools created. Yet for most communicators, that power remains largely leashed. With the current content and communication management systems available, it is quite surprising that more communicators and communication managers are not protesting the restrictions that artificially limit their ability to make use of this vitally important tool. To gain control of the Internet means more than being able to fully and completely manage the content of public Web sites. However, that is a basic starting point that the vast majority of communication managers have yet to get to. The company's public site is one of the most important faces the company puts forward in a time of crisis. To be forced to go through even one layer of personnel or policy to control that site, let alone multiple layers—as is now quite common—makes the Web a tool with limited usefulness to the communicator when it is needed most.

With the many options for commanding Web content available today, there is no policy or security reason that should prohibit communicators from taking command of the content. It should be clear when I say "taking command" that I mean being able to fully control, including changing or adding content without requiring the involvement of any technical resource, even if the communicator is only able to perform the most basic of word processing functions. Today's Web content management technology allows this; the question is whether or not the company will allow it. That is a matter of understanding the critical role the Web will play in a crisis.

This role is better understood when executives understand how a reporter reacts to initial information about a story. The first and natural reaction now is to hit the organization's Web site. It is the fastest, most convenient source of basic information about the company, including location, what it produces, number of employees, size, and so on. Knowing that this is the behavior pattern of reporters will lead forward-thinking executives and communicators to realize that the telling of the story that is unfolding can be best facilitated through the company's public Web site.

That is not to say that the public site used by the company for general information or for conducting routine business should be used in crisis communications situations. There are two good reasons why a separate site should be used: to avoid the dual problem of obliviousness and overreaction, and to take the burden of public information traffic off the normal business infrastructure.

Let's say you are a food manufacturer that has a serious problem with a batch of product, requiring a public recall. When the news breaks, the reporters will hit your Web site, as will many customers or consumers looking for details about which products have been recalled. What will they find? Business as usual? Nice statements about how long you've been in business and your long-standing reputation for safety and quality? That's obliviousness. It communicates a powerful message that the company just doesn't get it. This is scary for people and serious for the media and people directly affected by the product's problems. On the other hand, if the Web site is totally subsumed by huge warning messages and all other information is lost in the information about this one particular product, the damage to ongoing business could be much greater than necessary. I went to one well-known national food manufacturer's Web site without knowing anything about a product recall. The site was completely dominated by safety warnings and the product recall information. If I had been a customer looking for some basic information, it would have given me serious pause.

A related problem is the issue of traffic. In a major public news crisis, there is very great potential for heavy traffic. Most companies' public sites are not designed for crisis communication traffic. A site that works well managing hundreds of thousands of hits will likely crash under the burden of millions. Even if it remains operational, significant slowing can result in viewer frustration and the use of other means to communicate, such as picking up the phone. Then, one of the most important and efficient tools will have gone silent both for ongoing business and for communicating about the rapidly evolving crisis.

The solution to both of these problems is to have crisis communications managed on a separate site hosted on crisis-capable servers. This is the direction more companies are taking, despite the very serious obstacles raised by many IT departments. IT departments face the uncomfortable dilemma of committing precious, limited budget dollars to building crisis server capabilities or altering their policies to allow outside services to host these special-purpose Web sites.

Having a separate site on separate servers manage the public communication provides the opportunity to divert traffic from the public site for both appearance and infrastructure benefits. An objection might be raised that people will go to the public site anyway and therefore you don't avoid the hits by having a separate site. The answer to that is when the initial information is submitted, it needs to include a Web address specifically for the public information site. An increasing number of organizations are securing domain names to be used in the event of a major crisis. For example, XYZP Consulting Services might have a regular domain name of *www.xyzpconsulting.com* and set up a domain name such as *www.news.xyzpconsulting.com* or even a simple *www.xyzp-responds.com*. Those receiving the initial information will know which site to go to; those who haven't—the majority—will go to the main company site looking for information. A link on that site directing them to the specific incident site should be clear and unmistakable, but it need not dominate the site or significantly detract from the company's ongoing operations. Two problems are thus solved—the organization is seen as neither oblivious nor overreactive, and the Internet infrastructure of the business is protected.

The topic of incident dark sites was mentioned earlier. These sites are prepared in advance specifically for this purpose. If they are built on the kind of Internet-based communication management platform described in this chapter, they not only fulfill the public Web site function, but offer fully integrated communication management. However, to meet "now is too late" instant news demands, these sites need to be able to be launched by an executive or communication manager anytime, anywhere. To activate a Web team or to get the IT staff moving in the middle of the night to activate a Web site is not kind, practical, or necessary. Today's technology provides for launching such sites at the touch of a button by authorized staff with the appropriate passwords.

This ability to launch new and specific-purpose Web sites is one important element of taking control of the Internet. Today's well-appointed press rooms have all the functional capabilities described in this chapter. They are fully loaded with background information about the company; releases can be drafted, edited, approved, and posted online by clicking the right buttons. Information prepared in the press room can be instantly distributed to infinitely flexible contact lists via email, fax, or even telephone. Databases of contacts are built at least in part automatically by users registering on the public Web site, and inquiries are recorded and fully managed within the system. Now a crisis hits.

As an example, we'll say it is a legal issue involving a top-level executive. The story is not going to go away. No incident or dark site has been prepared for this particular eventuality. The communication manager launches a new site based on the existing press room site. She selects all the existing information to be transferred and all the existing databases. The new site is then built and launched. The horde of new reporters and other audience members who register on this incident-specific site are captured in that database and do not taint the original press room database. Information specific to that incident is created, approved, and posted to that public site. Team members like attorneys who need access to that site are not given access to the inside of the press room site. The incident's communication activities can be managed and controlled much easier through a specific site dedicated to the incident. The ability to launch, transfer data, and independently manage this "spawn" or subsite is a key part of today's communication management technology that is being effectively used by a number of companies, agencies, and organizations.

Group Communication

Web sites are not just effective for public communication. Group communication or semipublic sites are growing in popularity. Communicators might wish to use Web browsers and Web sites to communicate with specific individuals or groups while keeping the public out. Some public relations managers prefer to keep media communication from the public (although in my mind the policy is questionable because knowing the information is also available to the public helps reporters treat the information carefully). Group Web sites are appropriate for associations, private communities, or internal communication. Communicators need to not only be able to launch and completely control the content of all of these sites without technical assistance; they also need to be able to determine whether or not they want these sites to be public, private, or semipublic. The communication management technology available does allow communication managers with the highest levels of security to determine if each site they control is to be public, available to a limited group, or kept private for authorized users only.

Internal Communication

One of the most discussed items coming out of the events of September 11, 2001, was the need for effective internal communication. Many companies became very concerned about what systems and policies were in place to inform employees within the organization about what was going on, provide instructions on what actions to take, and locate employees to make certain they were safe. Even minor events such as the Nisqually earthquake in Puget Sound in February 2001 demonstrated that the cellular phone system is easily maxed out. In the first hour after that event, only fortunate users were able to check on family or friends by either land line or wireless phone. The Internet remained very much intact. Company officials from the rest of the country resorted to email and internal Internet communication, such as through the communication management system, to ascertain the condition of employees and operation of the facilities in the area impacted by the quake.

Internet technology needs to be part of the comprehensive plan for employee and leadership communication in case of large-scale internal or external crises. The Internet-based communication management system described earlier can play a key role because of the ability to launch new sites on the fly and the ability to control access to any site. An internal-only site can be launched to keep employees informed and a different site can be launched exclusively for the management team. One user of such a system uses a site specifically for employee information related to weather conditions. During bad weather, employees can check the site to determine if there are changes in work locations or work hours or if they are just to stay home. Of course, they need not check the site for the information because the same information can be instantly pushed to them via email and telephone.

It is becoming common practice among users of such systems during drills and actual events to establish secured documents on the private site for executives only. Different security levels can control who can see which documents, so that incident status reports containing raw information not yet confirmed can record events as they unfold. Images such as helicopter overflights or photos or videos of the activities can be loaded and retained for internal use only. As executive leadership is increasingly dispersed in this global economy, making use of these communication tools simply to provide management with the information needed to make fast and effective decisions is extremely important.

One user of the technology described here is the communication manager for a global oil company. A large tanker carrying gasoline ran aground in a sensitive environmental area on the East Coast of the United States. The incident occurred after work hours at night and the communication manager launched a site using a prepared incident dark site from his computer in a spare bedroom. Built within that system was a database of more than 1,800 reporters. He used a template to complete an initial statement release that described the grounding and what was being done. The information site used a special incident response domain name that was registered in advance for just such eventualities. Company executives in London were able to view this site from their homes or offices and keep up with the very latest information. A widespread release was never sent because the tanker, a new double-hulled ship, was floated off the bar at high tide and no gasoline or anything else was spilled. It was a potential nightmare that ended happily, particularly for the communication manager who demonstrated to executives in the company that he was exceedingly well prepared to manage communication not only with them, but with the entire world if needed.

User Access

References have been made to multiple levels of user access in such communication management systems. There are a couple of different business models used by suppliers of Internet-based communication tools. Many providers of Internet-based software price their service on a per-month, per-user basis. They sell what is sometimes referred to as *seats*. This limits the number of users who have access to the tools appropriate for routine day-to-day communication activities. A problem arises when a sizable incident happens because at that point a number of people from the CEO or chairman to outside contractors might be quickly pulled into the communication team. In that case, the model used by other providers is more suitable: A license fee is paid monthly or one time for the system and unlimited users are allowed access.

Because a large number of users can be provided access does not mean that you want all functions of the communication system to be accessible to all users. Certain functions, such as signing in new users, assigning passwords, creating secured documents, posting information to a public site, and launching whole new Web sites need to be accessible only to the highest level communication managers. These communication management systems accommodate this by providing multiple levels of access, in some cases providing grids of functions that can be assigned to specific users, in other cases assigning functions to multiple levels of access codes. A user assigned access Level 1, for example, might only be able to view and edit certain documents or view and respond to inquiries. A person with access Level 10 can launch new sites, assign system administrators, change basic site information, and manage other such high-level uses.

Hosting

All Web sites, including private intranet sites, must reside on a server somewhere. Hosting of communication management systems is an important element of the infrastructure. This issue is one of the most common reasons communication managers who want to implement the functionality of these advanced systems within their companies or organizations are prevented from doing so. IT policies might prohibit outside hosting, and even though the software might be available for licensing on company servers, the company servers typically are not suitable for crisis communication applications.

The ability to absorb a heavy traffic load is the essential element. Traffic really consists of the number of people attempting to get information from the site and the type of information they are viewing or downloading. One user viewing streaming video will absorb much more server and bandwidth capacity than a number of visitors viewing static pages. Companies and organizations today need to be serious about their ability to take the hits and deliver the information. IT departments and executives alike must be informed, probably by their communication managers, that in today's instant news environment in which the Internet is moving us into a postmedia world, communication ability depends on servers. Whether ultimately they take the approach that they will absorb the cost themselves by building crisis-capable server capacity or decide to share costs by using outside hosting services, the decision needs to be made to provide for the potential demand.

How many hits? The heaviest hit load on Web sites in early 2002 measured in excess of 10 million hits per day. In 2002, Internet access among the American population hit 50 percent, with an additional two million users being added every month. Hit loads are increasing significantly. A company or organization with any potential for creating national or international news probably needs to be prepared to absorb at least five million hits. That number will likely increase at a rate of 10 percent to 20 percent per year until Internet access has reached the saturation point around the world.

Earlier we said that there were three important elements to effective communication in the instant news world: policies, people, and platform. The technology platform exists to enable communicators to take much greater control over the Internet than ever before. The issues come down to people and policies: Are the people prepared to make use of these technologies? This question is more about willingness to change than about technical ability. Resistance to change and ignorance about the changes in the world are the biggest obstacles to implementing the necessary changes.

Most significantly, does the company policy encourage or prohibit the use of such technology to enhance the ability of the organization to communicate quickly and accurately? As we have seen, there are many obstacles within organizations that prevent the changes that are needed. Leadership is the key. Leadership must recognize the new demands and be willing and able to push through the obstacles to put into place the policies and technologies needed to protect the organization's future.

CHAPTER

10 Crisis Preparation: What To Do Before It Happens

For companies or organizations that have the potential for reputation-damaging public issues or crises, communication strategy can be viewed in three parts: before the crisis, during the crisis, and after the crisis. This might seem a bit negative or pessimistic, but in reality it is not. If you do those things needed to best prepare your company or organization to withstand a crisis of organization-threatening scope you are doing the best possible job of routine public relations or image building. Having significant crises in mind when constructing a corporate communication effort is one of the best ways to focus the strategy on those things that really matter. It is similar to walking through a cemetery as you are contemplating life's decisions; a deep understanding of your mortality and the shortness of life help concentrate the mind on those things and relationships that matter the most. Some might view this exercise as morbid, but others see it as a wonderful way to concentrate the mind, see what is truly important, and help make important decisions.

We know what it looks like when a crisis occurs and the company is not prepared or does not respond well. The brand value is destroyed, key employees leave in droves, recruitment is difficult, stock value hits bottom, customers defect, and others in the industry shake their heads in a sort of "there but for the grace of God go I" sense of relief, pity and bemusement.

We also know what it looks like when a company emerges from a crisis stronger than ever. Johnson & Johnson emerged as a highly respected company in the aftermath of the Tylenol scare of the 1980s by using a textbook case of crisis management. Haggen, a Pacific Northwest food retailer, emerged with its reputation very much intact after its aggressive, proactive stance following a hepatitis outbreak linked to an employee. In early 2002, Alaska Airlines was reported to be the only major air carrier experiencing significant growth in a very troubled travel economy. The remarkable story here is that Alaska had been seriously criticized in the national and regional press following the January 31, 2000 crash of Flight 261 off the California coast. There were serious allegations and some genuine problems that were identified in the intense scrutiny following the crash. Yet Alaska's reputation, although threatened and damaged to some extent, was neither destroyed nor sufficiently sullied to require rebranding or large-scale retrenchment; in fact, within two years the company has emerged as a bright spot on the travel landscape.

A case can be made that these good and bad stories coming out of crises depend entirely on the response during the crisis. However, a stronger case can be made that the brand or reputation equity held by companies and organizations will have much to do with how well it emerges from a major reputation crisis. Haggen enjoys an outstanding brand reputation as a quality food retailer, with strong sales for a retailer with a high price position. Alaska Airlines' safety record was one of the best in the industry and matched by a reputation for quality service that led them to advertise that their outstanding service did not equate to high prices.

A stellar reputation depends on much more than effective communication. Product and service quality must be excellent and consistent and the entire organization must operate, plan and market to maintain and build that reputation. However, the communication manager or executive responsible for communications has a key role to play in making certain the operational excellence translates into desired perceptions held by customers, industry influencers, stockholders, and employees.

We are going to make the reasonable assumption that the crisis you need to plan for will involve accusations of wrongdoing in some form. Certainly not all crises involve this, but a vast majority do—even those involving accidents. Our society has evolved the notion that there are really no such things as accidents and that inevitably someone will be found to have intended the consequences at worst, and at best was seriously negligent. In preparing for such a crisis, the most critical element will be credibility and, as we will see, not necessarily your credibility, but the credibility of those who stand in support of you. That being the case, the most effective preparation is to focus pre-crisis communication efforts on those people whose relationship to the company is most critical now, as well as those whose relationship to the company during a crisis will determine its viability.

To illustrate some of these key points, let's use a hypothetical example. One Saturday morning you wake up, pick up the morning paper, and read that an acquaintance has been accused of masterminding a scheme to bilk his company out of serious money. Your immediate natural reaction is to weigh the evidence that is presented and pronounce him guilty or not guilty. What process do you use? There are three basic questions: How well do you know him, and do the accusations fit with your knowledge of him? How well do you know his accuser or accusers, and do the accusations fit with your knowledge of them? What are others you know well and greatly respect saying about this person or the accusers?

If you know the person well and have had enough experience with him to believe that you are in a good position to judge his character, you will base most of your opinion on that personal knowledge. If your personal experience strongly contradicts the charges, a higher level of evidence is required to overcome your skepticism. Match that against your knowledge or perception of the accuser. If you also have some knowledge of the accuser and know him to be a drug-abusing, wife-beating, habitual liar, it will have a serious impact on your judgment on the charges. If, on the other hand, your experience with the accused leads to you to believe that it is entirely conceivable that he would do such a thing, relatively flimsy evidence and the lack of credibility of the accuser will not likely dampen your judgment that the accusations are likely to be true.

However, if you do not have direct personal experience or strong perceptions about either the accused or the accuser, you will likely suspend firm judgment until you have heard from others. If someone close to you has direct and personal experience with the person accused, and you know he or she is an honest and trustworthy person, if that person tells you that he or she believes it is true, then your judgment will most likely quickly go against the accused. Similarly, if the person you know and trust says the person making the accusation has a personal agenda or other reasons for making the accusations and is not to be believed, then you will likely assume innocence for the accused.

This simple parable provides a basis for exploring many of the key issues relating to communications programs aimed at positioning an organization to withstand a major reputation crisis.

It's All About Relationships

The underlying philosophy of this approach to effective external and internal communications is that business and life are all about relationships. It is not unreasonable to say that the economic value of most companies is related to the relationships they have and their ability to leverage those relationships into new ones in the future. For example, an accountant will value a company by looking at its assets and liabilities. A manufacturing company might include equipment, inventory, raw materials, cash, receivables, and so forth. What are all those items, particularly the manufacturing equipment, raw materials, finished goods, and such good for? They are only valuable in the potential they offer for someone to employ them as a means of developing valuable relationships. The products and the potential to create those goods have no economic value without the willingness of people to buy them. The stronger that buyer–seller relationship is, the higher the economic value of those relationships. Loyalty, also defined as more resistance to price-based competition, translates to economic value. An office full of the latest computers and networks is of no value without the ability of someone to take those tools and build working relationships with others that are valued by those served.

Certainly the same is true of nonprofit organizations and even government agencies. Although government agencies might appear to have a life untouched by performance, accountability, or meeting expectations, their existence depends on those who vote on budgets and who approve funding requests. Nonprofits live or die on the perception of those whose contributions make their existence possible. Relationships are at the heart of virtually every enterprise.

This makes the communicator's job easier to understand. Communication, after all, is primarily about building relationships. That might come as a surprise to some who view communication as providing information, but what is the end purpose of providing that information? In most cases it is to create, enhance, or protect the relationship. Certainly this can be seen on the personal side, but it is equally true on the business or organizational side. This is frequently forgotten when there is bad news to communicate. Bad news to stockholders will result in loss of share value. The real bad news for the company is when the stockholders lose confidence and trust in management. This might happen for performance reasons, but it happens more quickly when there is a perception that management is hiding information, covering up problems, or being less than forthright—even about bad news.

Many women instinctively understand the real nature of communication better than many men. John Gray pointed this out in his book, *Men Are from Mars, Women Are from Venus.*[1] Women tend to view a conversation about a problem as relationship building. The information conveyed and the potential solutions discussed can often be secondary to the value of having discussed them and shared the problem together. Men tend to view the information content as primary and want to get quickly to the solution, viewing the value of the conversation only in terms of its problem-solving effectiveness. That women are more "right" about this than men is evident in the response to listening. Listening is the most powerful key to relationship building, in part because it does provide the information content needed to serve effectively. Perhaps more important, genuine listening demonstrates value and communicates respect in ways that cannot be replicated by anything else. Listening is unique in its power to establish and build relationships. As a result, listening should be at the heart of most corporate communications programs. Unfortunately, there is little evidence that this is normally the case.

If the executives of an organization view at a fundamental level that their success in leadership will be measured by the quality of the relationships of the people whose perceptions are vital to the organization, it changes in profound ways their understanding of the job. Put another way, a CEO's primary task is to enhance loyalty among the people who matter most to the organization. This concept should also change to some degree how the success of the enterprise is measured. Financial measurement is one very important indicator, but it is not the only one. One big disadvantage is that it is all backward looking. Relationship valuation measurements are forward looking. Current relationships are the best predictor of future performance. The ability of the organization to develop and strengthen relationships and leverage strong existing ones into powerful new ones is perhaps the most critical factor in evaluating the future prospects for an organization. In this view, the role of communications manager becomes highly strategic. The chief communication officer should be, and in some cases is, the executive with overall responsibility for translating the organization's operations, administration, and all other elements into strong, long-lasting relationships and leverage those into the appropriate new ones.

That job might seem overwhelming until it is understood that for the vast majority of companies and organizations, business depends not on relationships with millions but with a relatively small number of people who are critically important to the organization. In our consulting business we have come to call these "the right few." Much to my surprise, when I began focusing on this element of business success, I discovered by accident that there was an exceptional concentration of strategic relationships in most business. Business volume can normally be traced to a very low percentage of key customer or key customer referral relationships. We used to talk about the 80/20 rule, but in reality it is more concentrated than that so we could reasonably talk about the 90/10 rule or even the 95/5 rule. This doesn't just apply to customer or external relationships. When I have asked the question, "How many people does your business truly depend on so that if you were to lose those it would cause serious risk to your business?" I discovered a very common answer: from five to seven. This was true of businesses doing volume in the hundreds of millions as well as one-person businesses.

Whether this formula applies to your business or organization is not really the point here. What is important is that if you do a careful evaluation of the people whose positive perception of your enterprise is vital to your future, you will almost certainly find that those people are both fewer and more significant to you than you thought. Clearly, if those people are the right few, it becomes critical for the communication manager and the top leadership to focus on what can be done to strengthen, improve, and leverage off those important relationships.

Building Reputation Equity

In the example presented earlier about the accused swindler, it is clear that the judgment of those reading about the accusations will be based primarily on their experience. This is the key to building reputation equity. An organization with strong reputation equity has "banked" positive perceptions that can be drawn on at those times when credibility and reputation is being questioned. The more equity in the bank, the better able the organization is to withstand serious accusations and even serious wrongdoing. However, it is not just a general, positive perception that matters most. The most important element of this effort is the direct, personal experience of the relatively few people on whom the company's credibility will rest at the time of crisis.

The most important people are those whose opinions about the company matter to those who matter to the company; in other words, people who have strong influence on those individuals whose opinion about you is important. It is simply not possible to have direct and personal relationships with everyone whom you wish to think positively about the company. However, for those people who might be neutral on your character and therefore don't have a basis for making a judgment on the accusations they read in the paper or hear on the news or read on an Internet page, the most important basis for making a judgment is the opinion of those they respect.

This phenomenon is what makes celebrity endorsements so powerful in advertising. The public tends to believe that they know celebrities personally. Witness the general grief when a well-known person such as Princess Diana or John F. Kennedy, Jr. dies tragically. These celebrities are also accepted and respected and therefore their opinions carry weight. Certainly, there are exceptions to this respect idea; for example, heavyweight boxer Mike Tyson might have been respected for his boxing skills, but his incredibly poor behavior has diminished his respect to the point where his opinions on matters of ethics or behavior bring amused laughter rather than respect. The "borrowed credibility" of celebrities is sufficiently powerful to overcome even the public's natural skepticism about paid opinions. The public seems willing to suspend their disbelief about people such as Michael Jordan and Paul Harvey, preferring to believe they would not represent a product they couldn't endorse no matter how many millions were offered to them.

This is not to suggest for a moment that public relations managers for pulp and paper mills or microprocessor plants using toxic materials need to go out and find a celebrity to say good things about them. What they need to do is to figure out who the people who do not know the company well will turn to for an opinion on the crisis and accusations. As an example, let's say the mayor of a smallish community is well-liked and respected, serving her third term. A natural gas supplier encounters a serious problem with gas delivery during the height of a winter storm and longtime critics are complaining that the executives are incompetent, or worse, they are cutting costs to preserve their profits at the risk of freezing poor people in their homes. If the gas company has a strong reputation and is well respected among its customers and throughout the community, it can quite easily withstand those kinds of attacks. If not, judgment will rest with those whose opinion counts in the minds of the public. If the well-respected mayor stands up and says, "I have worked with Nelson Blothmore, the CEO of Blothmore Gas, for many years and I know that he is doing everything he can to meet the needs of these people," that opinion will carry weight. At that point in time, the mayor is perhaps the most strategic relationship for the future of the company.

Building reputation equity, the essential task of the communication team in the pre-crisis phase, depends on identifying the strategic relationships, the right few, and focusing communication and relationship-building efforts at them. Every situation is clearly different. However, every communication situation involves the process of identifying the right few and focusing efforts where they will create the most significant results. Strategic relationships are ripples in a still pond. The right few have enormous influence.

FLYING UNDER THE RADAR

In the past 15 to 20 years, the public information and news environment has changed significantly, as we have already discussed. Environmentalism, consumerism, public health activism, and activism of all sorts have become the most potent forces for change in our society. This is true not because of some vast conspiracy but because both activists and the media have noted that people care about these issues. We are currently in a time, the first in some time, when some of these issues are taking a back seat to national security concerns, understandable in the months following the death of more than 5,000 citizens going about their daily business.

Nevertheless, this environment of activism, media activism, and heightened public concern has led many companies with activities that have potential environmental or public health or safety to concerns to adopt a stealth strategy wherever possible. In talking to a number of executives about their community relations efforts, the most common explanation I have heard for why there is reluctance to put relationship development programs in place is that "we prefer to fly under the radar."

This is an entirely reasonable concern. To actively promote the fact that you want to place a fuel pipeline through a community, or run new 230,000-volt power lines through local farmland, or that you want to build a high-tech plant that uses no fewer than 20 materials considered toxic by the federal government that could cause serious problems in a worst case scenario, is risking attention and opposition not desired or needed. However, there is a big difference between asking for attention to these issues and putting in place an appropriate corporate or community relations communication program.

In a situation repeated many times, one company sought a state permit on a quiet basis. After doing everything to meet the permit requirements, they had every reason to believe they would receive the permit. They didn't count on the politics of it. Rabid opposition mounted, quietly at first, but then it suddenly exploded in a burst of zeal and misinformation that built huge momentum over a year. The activists' intentional emotional characterizations of the issue and their supposed evidence of extreme public risk played well to the media's need for a good story with white hats and black hats. The strongly negative media coverage blossomed quickly, resulting in rapidly escalating public opposition. The permit was denied by a body specifically put in place to reduce nimbyism, not on the basis of failure to meet conditions. The squishy words used clearly revealed the political nature of the decision. The company reapplied but now faced huge political opposition and an understanding of the potency of activism and media support for it. Although opposition could not have been prevented, if the company had been prepared with solid, quiet community leader support, if it had been prepared to counter the rapidly rising accusations, and if it had laid the groundwork to gain solid public support, the story would be different. All those things happened, but under the extremely trying conditions of vociferous and effective opposition, which makes the support-building task infinitely more difficult.

The company did not need to fly above the radar to prepare, but it did need to prepare, primarily by quiet and judicious relationship building with the right few. It also needed to prepare by being more equipped to counter the opposition in the public with effective presentation of the facts and effective countering of the misinformation.

Goal Setting

Communication efforts are very measurable, and they need to be measured. That might come as a surprise to many executives and perhaps a few communication professionals. There is some comfort in operating in an environment without accountability. However, that environment also has serious risks. As a communications professional, I want the leaders I am serving to have a clear idea of what their investment will produce in terms of results. I want to know what "winning" is from their perspective. If an effort or campaign or project is completed and I consider it highly successful but the executive doesn't, it must be because we did not start with an agreed-on, clear, and well-defined definition of winning. Communication managers (or for that matter, all professionals) who work toward ill-defined or undefined results are taking serious risks with their reputations.

We discussed communication goal setting in a previous chapter. Building high-value relationships is the goal of most organizations and is also the goal of most communication efforts. A general goal states what winning is, such as, "We want to be able to emerge from a serious crisis with our reputation for credibility enhanced and to be able to continue and grow our business." Beyond that, measurable objectives need to be put in place. What does it mean to emerge with reputation intact? The ability to move forward can be measured objectively in business sales or profitability, but what about the relationships?

Perception measurement is an essential element of practically any communication effort. Because we are talking about focusing on the right few, we are not necessarily referring to large-scale, scientifically accurate perception surveys. These have their place, but typically not in the kind of relationship-oriented reputation equity effort we are discussing here. People answering questions posed by zombie-sounding college students with minimal training, where it is obvious they are simply filling in a form to be entered into a computer, do not consider this or treat the experience as real listening. Typically, such surveys have neither the benefit of providing valuable relationship information nor the benefit of communicating to those participating that they are valued. Objective perception measurement is much more effectively done by focusing the questions on the right few and doing the interviewing in person or, if personally isn't convenient or cost-effective, by a conversation-style telephone interview.

Goal setting is not just about perception evaluations. In specific campaigns, setting specific objective goals can be very helpful. In the situation described earlier in this chapter, where the industrial firm found itself with strong opposition in gaining a facility permit, specific goals were set to gain community support. Those goals included the number of letters written by community leaders to the governor of the state, the number of cards indicating support sent to the state committee, and the number of prominent community groups providing public endorsement. The goals even included the numbers of people speaking at upcoming public hearings, including a diminishing number of people speaking in opposition to the project. This was important because a considerable effort was expended at dispelling misinformation with the primary purpose of countering the efforts of activists to secure passionate opposition through emotional accusations and misinformation. Those goals were also important because a public permitting process is unpredictable. It was important to establish objective goals in addition to the overall definition of winning, or securing the permit. Failing to secure the permit would constitute failure of the effort, but meeting all the objective support-building and opposition-diminishing goals would result in at least a moral victory. With this company, there was great clarity of strategy and purpose between the communication team and the organization's leaders.

Strategic Relationship Development

The natural inclination of many in public relations when the go-ahead has been given to build public support is to mount an advertising campaign. This natural tendency is one reason executives tend to be leery of giving the green light to the communication team to attempt to build support. A highly public campaign can have potentially negative effects, such as heightening opposition, opening the organization to accusations of using slick, Madison Avenue techniques to gain government approval, and highlighting issues that might otherwise remain dormant. There are definitely circumstances when a public effort involving paid advertising is advisable and even necessary, but it should always be seen as a support method to the fundamental task of building reputation equity, which is strategic relationship development.

The first step is to identify the who. Who are the people whose perceptions are vital to the current business and future health of the organization? Who are those people with whom you ought to have strong relationships, but do not? On a global corporate level these people are going to include high-level elected officials from many countries. They will include major customers, customer referral sources, key industry reporters, key stockholders, executives, industry influencers, labor leaders, policy makers, regulators, and so on. On a local level, strategic relationships might include neighbors, local elected officials, local reporters, major customers, owners, key employees, consultants, and so on. Whether global or local, the basic principle remains the same: A relatively small number of people carry the present and future value of the organization around in the perceptions they hold about the company, the benefits it offers, and the perceived value of their relationship with the key people in the enterprise.

The next step is listening. As mentioned earlier, listening does two critically important things: It tells you what you need to know to meet the needs and expectations of those important people. Even more important, if done right, it communicates that you respect and value them. Listening is the most important element of effective relationship building. However, there is a risk. Listening without response can be deadly. To create an expectation of value and of meeting needs and then to not effectively respond with communication and delivering the goods can mean the positive results gained by listening can turn to negative results in the relationship. Another way of saying it is this: Listening and responding are both essential.

Effective listening will result in a much greater understanding of the benefits the right few either receive or want to receive from the existence of the organization. Sometimes the benefits are entirely predictable. For example, employees are likely to want good pay and benefits, opportunities for growth, stability, and pride in their place of employment. Shareholders can be expected to want a competitive return on investment, but they might also seek involvement, participation, recognition, influence, and so on. Sometimes the benefits are not as obvious. In evaluating what it takes to establish a high-value relationship with community leaders for a sizable industrial facility, I discovered that they wanted assurance and stability. The jobs and taxes this facility provided for the community were critical for their futures, but with frequent ownership changes they did not feel certain that the facility would be there for the long term. This valuable piece of information was extremely helpful in crafting messages that, although not promising what could not be guaranteed, provided information that helped reassure them based on what was happening in the industry, facility performance, and insights about ownership changes.

One of the other important information items gained by the community leader research was their desire to have personal contact with plant managers. Community leaders have influence in part because they are perceived by others in the community to be "in the know." This perception is considerably enhanced when they can mention casually in conversation that they had lunch or coffee with Mr. Smith or happened to run into him at a cocktail party and they discussed such and such. This desire doesn't always correspond very well with a busy executive's schedule, which is focused on problem solving and operational issues. However, when executives understand how important these relationships are to the present and future of the organization and how vital they can be during a reputation crisis, they can usually set aside a small amount of time, as long as it is judiciously administered by the communication manager. In this particular case, a monthly "coffee with the manager" was instituted and community leaders were invited to participate. Those conversations with a group of 10 to 12 diverse community leaders provided the opportunity for continued listening as well as the opportunity to address specific concerns or issues. Nearly everyone invited eagerly attended and the comments filtering back through the community and the annual perception survey validated that this approach was highly successful in creating the high-value relationships that were the goal. Without conducting the listening in the first place, it is highly doubtful if this strategy would have emerged or have been supported by a very busy management team.

This coffee meeting anecdote further illustrates a key point in strategic relationship building: Start with the most personal and work downward from there. In this high-technology world, a premium is placed on personal, face-to-face interaction. There is great power in this in developing a strategic relationship program.

The listening processes ultimately will result in having solid information on which to build messages aimed at specific groups and individuals. Those key messages should form a consistent whole and should directly address the "what's in it for me?" question of every strategic relationship. This is the next step in the process: formulating and disseminating key messages. These messages must—above all—be true, they must be as personal as possible, and they must be relevant (i.e., address directly the sought-after benefits). How to communicate them? I have already suggested one method that is both efficient and personal: meetings with groups of people who share some common interests. If personal time with managers is not feasible, as it will not be for the vast majority of those whose positive perceptions are sought, other methods need to be chosen, with a priority placed on those that are the most personal. For example, a personally signed letter from the CEO is considerably more personal than a beautiful four-color newsletter that addresses the same issues. A presentation at a service club is more personal than a videotape or an interview on local television. An email directed to an individual, addressing specific concerns and inviting interaction, is more personal than a Web page. Even Web sites, however, can be used in more intimate forms of communication through the use of private sites or private areas on Web sites where certain people are allowed access to nonpublic information.

REPORTER RELATIONSHIP DEVELOPMENT

Reporters are important people, too. For most public relations practitioners, it seems silly to treat reporters almost as an afterthought. They are their reason for existence. A primary theme of this book has been that in the postmedia world in which direct communication is becoming more and more common, reporters become not the end-all and be-all of communication, but one more very important group requiring effective relationship building.

The methods for building relationships with reporters are not fundamentally different from those for any other group or person. First, prioritize: Who is most important? To whom should most effort be directed? Second, listen: What are their needs? What do they want, need and expect from you? What benefits can you offer that support important personal and career goals they might have? Finally, respond: What messages are you sending, not just by what you say, but by what you do?

Reporters get to keep their jobs if they get the information needed to present to their editors and audiences and if they do so with the credibility and balance expected by their editors. They have the opportunity to excel and advance if they prove extraordinarily effective at capturing and presenting information—particularly unique information—of high public interest. The communication professional's job is to help them do just that. I'll put it even more strongly: As much as possible, given the absolute necessity to advance the cause of the organization for which he or she works, the communication professional's job is to help reporters succeed.

A communication manager's job description should include making life easier for all reporters who seek information from them. Credibility is the major tool and major goal. The best way to damage or destroy relationships with reporters is to be disingenuous, to lie, to mislead, to break promises, or to be untrustworthy. There are times in the course of normal interaction that you cannot provide information that you possess. Reporters understand that, but they also understand that it is their job to do their level best to get that information, if not from you then from others. This situation does not threaten credibility. Telling them one thing when you mean another, not showing up when you said you would meet them, or suggesting that you can give them something greater than what you can cause loss of credibility.

One public affairs leader for a large government agency said it was the agency's goal to be the first and best source of information about events in which it was involved. That is a highly appropriate goal for each and every communication manager for companies and organizations. You want reporters to understand that there is no faster, better, more accurate, or more complete information about what is going on than what they can get from you. They want to know that you will be proactive, and that you can be counted on to deliver information to them without waiting to be asked.

This position has caused some raised eyebrows when practiced in tradition-bound organizations that normally exercise the don't ask, don't tell policy of public information. A small-scale event occurred at a facility. Emergency notification procedures had been activated, which was standard for even minor events such as this. Because the local media were tuned to emergency radio frequencies, they would know that something was up. I opted to proactively send out a short press release explaining the circumstances, what was happening, the nature of the event, the response, and so on. Top management approved this decision, but lower level management, who saw absolutely no point in alerting the local press to something they might not even notice, strongly attacked the decision. They certainly had a point. No one goes out of their way to seek out press coverage of accidents or other events that could harm a reputation. The point I made to management, however, was that I wanted these reporters to trust me. I wanted them to know that for any event or situation that might be considered newsworthy, I would be a reliable source of fast information and I would do everything in my power to get the information they needed when they needed it. Most important, I wanted them to understand that when a major event happened, they could trust me to help them do their jobs while I was doing my job. Because this was a considerable change from the previous management of public information, the reporters were initially surprised and skeptical. However, it wasn't long before the nature of the relationship between the local media and the facility began to change. In the case of the minor event when we issued a release, not a single local media outlet considered it worthy of coverage, which I considered a victory.

In building relationships with reporters, it is helpful to understand that they have unique needs as well. Print reporters have different requirements than local TV reporters, who in turn have needs different than national cable and network reporters. Trade publication reporters have different needs than general news publication reporters. Of course, reporters themselves are individuals with individual quirks, personalities, expectations, and pressures. It is also true that communication managers might not always be dealing with qualified, experienced reporters. Local papers, even dailies, are training grounds for rookie reporters. As the news business continues to change, many substantial publications have reduced their staffs of experienced reporters, replacing them with lower paid reporters with much less experience. These circumstances can make the communication manager's job more difficult, but they also provide an opportunity because the basic rule is to help the reporter do the best job he or she can.

Responding to Minor Events

The minor incident just described illustrates another point. The best opportunity to build relationships in the communities or networks in which your important audiences live is when a relatively minor crisis occurs.

In a previous book, *Friendship Marketing*,[2] I explored the concepts of loyalty and trust in more detail. Trust is built when someone perceives that the other person in the relationship is willing to sacrifice their own interests, needs, desires, and selfishness for them. The opportunity to observe this most clearly is when there is a problem. Billing problems, quality problems, and expectation problems all provide the opportunity for one to observe the behavior of the other. Because we all understand our intensely self-centered nature, when I demonstrate to you that I am willing to place my interests second to yours or you demonstrate that to me, trust is established. This does not mean that one should go out and cause problems with customers, supervisors, or strategic relationships to build trust. It does suggest that one should view those problems as unique opportunities to emerge with a stronger relationship. That might indeed be the meaning behind the Chinese character for crisis that simultaneously means risk and opportunity. Each crisis, particularly minor ones, should be viewed as an opportunity to build relationships and reputation equity.

A minor crisis provides the opportunity to demonstrate to the strategic relationships you have identified the character and nature of the organization. Quick, effective, comprehensive, proactive, personalized, and direct communication with those people about something that has gone wrong with the company or organization can communicate a tremendous amount about the trustworthiness of the organization.

Assume for a moment that you are a strategic relationship of another organization and they encounter an internal problem that might not see the light of day. However, you have been made privy to the information and the company has explained what happened, why it happened, the culpability of the company in it, and what is being done to prevent future recurrences. Now assume that this same company is involved in a far more significant crisis and they are accused by reports in the press of stonewalling, covering up, or outrageous malfeasance. These accusations counter your experience with the company that you perceive to be honest, forthright, and willing to confront problems directly. This is the equivalent of the example that opened this chapter, where you read about an acquaintance accused of swindling. Your previous experience with this person will largely determine your judgment. Those minor crises provide the opportunity to establish a record of proactive communication that reveals the character, values, and principles of the company or organization.

Use of Technology

So far, there has been nothing in this chapter that hasn't been applicable to the old world of slow news and media exclusivity. However, we are now in a world of instant news, entering a postmedia world. In this world the fundamentals don't change. Relationships are all-important. Character, truth, honesty, values, virtue, and principle all matter. Knowing the people who are most important to you is critical, but it always has been. Listening and responding remain the bedrock of relationship development. Something has dramatically changed, though. The tools by which these tasks are accomplished have changed tremendously and with them the expectation of how people communicate and interact.

The same technology discussed in the previous chapter that is used to communicate rapidly and effectively in a crisis event is also being used daily as part of community and strategic relationship development programs. The demands are the same. The only thing that really changes is the extreme urgency and overwhelming multiplicity of tasks that characterize a communications crisis. Understanding that distinction is where the power of Internet-based communication tools resides.

There is probably not a single communications department or operation in a company or organization today that does not believe the demands placed on it are greater than the resources available to meet those demands. The suggestions about thorough evaluation of all potential strategic relationships and establishment of proactive programs to communicate with them were likely met with some audible groans by communication managers struggling to keep up with the demands of the media alone.

Communication management technology designed to effectively manage crises is aimed at one simple goal: doing the most with the limited resources available. There is no guarantee in a crisis that a fully qualified Web team ready and able to meet your every whim will be available on a 24/7 basis. As a result, the technology requires no technical expertise, enabling even confirmed Luddites to easily manage Web content, distribute to email lists, upload and post images, and even launch entire new Web sites. Similarly, in a crisis, there is no certainty that a room full of seasoned veterans with adequate telephones, computers, and fax machines will be able to handle the potentially hundreds of calls from reporters and others seeking information. The technology is aimed at limiting calls by instant and proactive distribution, feeding inquiries into an inquiry management system, simplifying responses, and sharing information to improve the quality of responses. In a real event, this kind of technology has demonstrated that much more work can be done by fewer people—exactly the point of technology in the first place.

The same productivity tools aimed at improving crisis communications can be and are effectively used in routine day-to-day communication. The primary result is that fewer people are doing more effective communication. Although some in the communication profession might take this as a negative, executive leadership will welcome this increase in performance and productivity. For those who fear this change, I would remind them that a few years ago when graphic design was done with wax, X-acto knives, and drawing boards, the computer threatened the occupation of graphic designers. "Everyone will be able to do this stuff," some complained. To some degree it has proven true. Everyone's design quality and production has been dramatically improved by desktop publishing technology. Yet, there are far, far more people employed in the graphic design profession and doing graphic design at all levels than ever before. The real skills of graphic design are in more demand than ever. However, if your communication skills are the equivalent of operating an X-acto knife safely, you do indeed have reason to be concerned about the new highly productive communication management technologies.

The same technology designed to help speed press releases via instant and integrated email, fax, and telephone distribution is also being used to connect ever-larger groups of individuals into closer intimacy with the company or organization. The same tools designed to increase interactivity are being used to build the bonds needed for reputation equity. The same listening tools can and should be used to support the listening process of strategic relationship development. In this case, when speed is not so much the issue, productivity is. So much more can be done. As Federal Express and Intel have proven, if more can be done, more will be demanded.

Reputation Equity Summary

There could come a time when as a CEO you need to turn to people outside your company for help to survive. The help might be in the form of letters addressed on your behalf to U.S. Senators, or it might be in submitting op-ed pieces to the newspapers. You might need good and respected people in your community to say to their fellow citizens that what they are reading in the paper about you isn't true. You might need key stockholders to come to your defense and you could need the strong loyalty of managers and employees. At that time of great need, the reputation equity you have in the bank will be worth the gold in Fort Knox, or more than that, because the very life of the organization could depend on those important friends whose trust has been cultivated in advance.

However, that equity does not appear on its own. Too many executives busy with their operational issues assume that the world knows all the good things they are doing and the communities in which they operate understand the benefits of their existence. People who enjoy the benefits of your organization's existence every day do not necessarily think about it or even become consciously aware of those benefits. The taxes you pay that support the school district are largely invisible to most parents. The contributions you provide to charities and local causes impact only a few if only the organization knows about it. The benefits of good jobs and the multiplier effect in a community are forgotten by most whose lives are enriched by those benefits.

In 2001, Boeing shocked the Seattle community by announcing it was leaving Seattle. The local television news reporters hit the streets to get public reaction. Some expressed dismay, but one young man, with sheer delight on his face said, "Great! I hope they all leave so we can have this city to ourselves." The "ourselves" he was referring to no doubt had trust funds or independent means to be unconcerned about the potential loss of thousands of jobs and the economic devastation of a city. He imagined a city filled with beautiful buildings, well-tended streets, and overflowing coffee shops without the burden of major employers. To him, there was no benefit to a company like Boeing providing tens of thousands of well-paid jobs. Suffice it to say, he is not likely to become one of Boeing's, or any other major employer's, strategic relationships.

Now, we turn to the reason for all this preparation—the organization-threatening reputation crisis. With a solid base of strategic influencers loyal to the organization, with a track record of fast, direct communication with reporters and stakeholders, and with the policies, team, and technology in place, you are ready for the challenge.

ENDNOTES

1. Gray, John, *Men Are from Mars, Women Are from Venus,* New York: HarperCollins, 1992.
2. Baron, Gerald, *Friendship Marketing*, Grants Pass, OR: PSI Research—Oasis Press, 1997.

CHAPTER

11 Crisis Management: What To Do While It Is Happening

"While it is happening" means while the white-hot glare of news cameras are on you, and you wake up each morning knowing you face more headlines in the paper. A crisis is not a singular point, it is a continuum that flows out of everything you do, and who or what you are. After the moment in the spotlight has passed, the crisis flows on, usually remaking you and redefining your future. Here we focus on that flash of time when it seems the whole world has focused its brief attention span on you and your organization.

We follow two different crisis events, both very loosely based on a combination of real situations and drills.

Notification

It was late on Thursday afternoon when the owner of a small public relations firm got a call from a sometime client. The client was the CEO of a fast-growing chain of dermatology clinics that had established a strong reputation for leadership in a popular new form of aging treatment. Women and men were flocking to the small clinics for the laser treatment and the results in almost all cases were outstanding, so that the vast majority of new patients came by referrals. Nevertheless, the company advertised heavily and the brand name was becoming well-known as the leader, and also viewed as more commercial than some felt comfortable with for a medical clinic.

"We've been hit by a class action lawsuit and I need your help," Aaron, the CEO, said. Steve took some small satisfaction in this, in that he had been unable to establish a solid, ongoing public relations or crisis communications plan with this client.

"I just got a call from the producers of the *Today Show* and Matt and Katie are interviewing two ladies and their attorney who are claiming we botched their procedure," Aaron explained.

"Was it true?" I asked.

"Yes and no," he replied. There were some relatively minor problems, but the ladies refused treatment to fix them, which could have been addressed by more treatment. They instead went to an attorney. The attorney was well-known for taking high-profile cases and noticed an opportunity in this new procedure. He needed to build a class of victims and to do that he needed publicity. He'd been on this route before and he knew the right people to call.

"Will they allow us on the show with them?" Steve asked.

"No, but they are putting a doctor on with them who is a supposed expert in this field and who has a large but undisclosed investment in one of our competitors. Not only that, but the attorney has sent out a press release and my assistant is fielding calls right now from reporters from all over the place."

"What is she telling them?" Steve asked.

"What our lawyers told us to say, that it's a legal matter and we can't comment on pending litigation."

"Oh, boy," Steve said under his breath, or something to that effect.

"What did you say?" asked Aaron.

"Uh, never mind."

The fireball could be seen for 50 miles, making it plainly visible to many residents of the nearby large city. The well-placed bomb had taken out the refinery's distribution center, including the pipeline that fed jet fuel to the nearby international airport that served the entire region. The fuel pipeline was the only source of fuel for the airport, and laws passed in the previous years had restricted fuel truck tankers, so that without the pipeline, flights would have to be seriously curtailed.

The explosion was loud enough to rock the house of Mark, the refinery's assistant human resources manager and designated Information Officer. It was 3:30 a.m., but he jumped out of bed and stared in disbelief at the huge orange glow coming from the refinery. He was booting up his computer at home when he got the page. Full-scale response was underway with all required agency notifications taking place.

"What happened?" Mark asked when he got the safety manager on his cell phone.

"Don't know, but security did grab three guys who were trying to get out who didn't have any business being there."

"How'd they get in the fence?"

"Don't know."

"Anyone hurt?"

"Yes, we know there were several workers near that area at the time and we haven't accounted for them yet. I'll let you know as soon as I hear more."

"Wait, one more question. What about fenceline neighbors? Any homes damaged or need for evacuation?"

"We have no reports of neighbor damage or injuries but we have notified the local Department of Emergency Management that we want everyone along Franklin Road evacuated."

"I'll send the telephone alert to that area," said Mark, and the manager agreed.

A command center would be established in a predesignated area in the visitor complex, with the JIC in the trailer behind the medical office. Based on the sketchy information from the safety manager, Mark guessed this would be treated as terrorist activity, resulting in much higher press attention than if it were an accident. Before heading to the command center, Mark turned to his computer, entered the prepared incident Web site, and typed a quick announcement to the neighbors living along Franklin Road. He selected their names from the database in the system, clicked the Urgent button, and ran a quick test telephone call. When he received the test call on his cell phone confirming the message, he clicked the button to call those neighbors and phones along Franklin Road immediately began to ring with the request that they immediately evacuate to the designated Red Cross shelter.

That completed, he filled out the initial release template with the minimal information available. He would launch the site, post the initial statement, and distribute it by email and fax with a few mouse clicks, but first he needed the approval of the Incident Commander. After he launched this new, incident-specific site, everyone would be directed to use this site rather than the refinery's regular Web site. For those people going to the regular Web site looking for information, a button on that directed them to the new incident site. He alerted the communication team with email, text pages, and telephone messages using the text-to-voice feature of the communication management system, quickly dressed, and drove the 10 minutes to the plant.

For Mark, it was now that the policies, plans, people, and platforms that had been prepared came into play. The communication team could work effectively if there was a clear policy direction established in advance; if there was a simple but effective plan that would tell various people where they needed to go, what tools they needed, and what they were to do; if the people who were to help manage the response had been trained and had a good idea of what was expected of them and what would unfold in the coming hours; and if the communication management platform had been put in place to facilitate group communication leading directly to public communication.

Golden Hour

The golden hour is golden because much is determined about how the story will be told in that first hour. As the old saying goes, you have one chance to make a first impression. Slow is, unfortunately too quickly interpreted as not caring. This is a new concept for many in public information and crisis communications because they do not understand that with the trend toward instant news and the new technologies used by broadcasters, news coverage of an event begins the instant broadcasters become aware of the event. Not just broadcasters, either, because with the Internet everyone becomes a broadcaster, which means that all newspaper outlets also report news much faster on their Internet sites.

The goal of the most enlightened communication managers is to be the first and best source of the news. That goal can only be realized by putting in place the processes that will allow them to gather needed information quickly and then distribute it at the speed of light.

Preparing the Clinic's Response

Steve's challenge was to get a reasonable response to the producers of the *Today Show* in very short order. He got the names and email addresses from the clinic CEO of the four attorneys working on this case. Two were in one office, but one was in a different city and the other was out of town. She also needed to be included in the decision of what to say. Steve opened up his Internet-based communication management system, assigned all of them passwords, and got all of them signed into the system by alerting them by phone or email. Once inside, they used the secure chat room to discuss options. Several attorneys did not want to respond. Steve argued that no response in this situation would likely be reported on the show as saying the clinic declined comment, which would be tantamount to accepting guilt. Steve drafted a statement that said this was a legal matter and the clinic was not able to discuss the details; however, the allegations were without merit and the clinic looked forward to the opportunity to demonstrate that in a court of law. The statement also declared that the procedure was one of the safest medical procedures used today and that this clinic had one of highest success rates of any clinic performing this procedure—a statement the CEO said could be verified by readily available data. Each attorney reviewed the draft and marked it up with comments. Everyone was online working on the same virtual desktop, and so could review the changes made in each draft as they were completed. A lively discussion took place between attorneys and Steve, with the clinic CEO making a final determination based on what he was willing to live with. Once agreement was reached, Steve clicked the button that said Post This Draft, so it appeared on the public Web site. He then clicked another button that emailed it from within the system to the *Today Show* producer. Steve called the producer immediately, and she said she had just received the email with the statement.

The Refinery Incident Evolves

On the short drive from his house to the refinery, Mark got another call on his cell phone from the safety manager. He got a quick briefing on scope and status of the fire, along with the information that two bodies had been recovered but there were still three missing. He also found out that the three young men caught by security were now in the hands of the police and that they were of Middle Eastern descent. He was told that Jack Wyles was Incident Commander. In his car, Mark dialed the number of the Houston Crisis Center, which had already been alerted by the response team. He confirmed a full-scale response from the information team was needed and confirmed they would arrive by company jet in six to eight hours.

When Mark arrived at the command center he quickly grabbed one of the laptops, pulled up the still-private incident Web site, edited the initial statement draft with updated information, and printed it out. He quickly found the Incident Commander and told him he was serving as his Information Officer and had an initial statement ready to release. The Incident Commander held off the others clamoring for his attention long enough to carefully read the statement, initial it, and hand it back to Mark. Mark walked back to his computer, clicked the Approved button, noting who approved it and when, launched the site, posted the release, selected the full database of 1,249 reporters he had prepared for a full-scale media alert, and clicked the button that emailed and faxed it to all reporters on his list. The elapsed time from the explosion was 33 minutes. A fully loaded public Web site was available for the public and the press and a release was prepared and distributed to all reporters in the region. During this time, Mark's cell phone rang four times with reporter calls. In each case he quickly told the caller that the information would be available at the refinery's press room on its Web site within a few minutes, that he would email the release to them, and that he could speed future inquiries if they logged them into the system.

Organization and Personalities

With the task for getting an immediate response completed, both communication managers needed to move quickly to put in place a communication team that would enable them to respond quickly and communicate proactively in the coming hours, days, and weeks. Steve's task was much simpler than Mark's because the scope of media and public attention would be considerably less. However, Mark's task was made easier by much more careful and thorough preparation and by the fact that government-mandated oil spill drills had prepared a response and communication team to deal with events of this magnitude. Steve had been suggesting quite vigorously to his friend and client, the clinic CEO, that some preparation should be put in place including an incident dark Web site that would contain the information reporters would want to know about safety and effectiveness of the procedure. Also, he suggested that they identify media spokespersons and do some media training to prepare for this kind of public attention. However, those suggestions had been placed on a lower priority list as the clinic moved forward with major technology investments and rapid growth.

Steve would manage the communication function but he needed a spokesperson. The clinic CEO was simply not the right person. Steve's recommendation to the CEO was that the chief of the medical staff should represent the business. Steve had immediately asked that all media calls be referred to him and by now he had fielded several. His answer was that the clinic had just received the complaint, was reviewing it, and would provide a response to the media as soon as the review was complete. It bought precious little time because he understood the regional press would be running with the story soon. He drafted a quick media statement and question-and-answer document to be used by the head of the medical staff, and sent a notice to the attorneys and CEO that it was available on the communication management site for them to review. Then he called his spokesperson to discuss what could and could not be said. He found an argument. The medical staff person was in no mood to take instructions from some outsider who didn't know anything about dermatology.

"This isn't just about dermatology, this is about legal issues and protecting your clinic's reputation," Steve argued.

"The hell it is," said the doctor.

Steve ended the conversation and called the CEO. Either the doctor would get with the program and participate with the communication team or Steve would have to serve as spokesperson. About 10 minutes later the CEO called back saying his medical chief understood the situation better now and would support Steve.

By now the attorneys had worked over the statement. A brief chat room conversation within the communication system resolved a couple of wording difficulties and the statement was ready to go. Steve approved it for release in the system, posted it to the public site in a moment, emailed it to the medical chief and phoned him to prepare him for the first interview.

Mark's challenge involved many more people. The first three members of his communication team were assigned roles immediately. One would be JIC manager, setting up all the logistics needed for a full-scale JIC operation. The communication team would soon consist of PIOs from various agencies such as the Coast Guard, the police department, probably the FBI, the state department of environment, local emergency management staff, and so on. These people needed computers, desks, phones, and some of them likely needed brief training to participate fully in the Internet-based communication system. Mark assigned one person to be Assistant Information Officer, External and another Assistant Information Officer, Internal. External would manage inquiries coming from the outside including media, government, neighbors, community, and so forth. Internal would handle employee and in-company communication and also coordinate with the Incident Command staff, prepare needed information, secure approvals, and so on. They knew these jobs from previous drills and got to work. When a more senior or experienced communication team member arrived, Mark would quickly make an assignment change. Each of these managers in turn took in newly arriving communication team members and made assignments to help collect status reports, draft the next release, or hunt down answers to new questions as they emerged.

The state department of environment public information manager arrived about 90 minutes after Mark began the process of establishing the communication center. By then two releases had been put out, a press conference was scheduled, and inquiries were being managed with dispatch. Sandy was intent and officious.

"My boss, the on-scene commander for the state, has demanded that I serve as Information Officer," she announced.

"I will take it up with Unified Command in a few minutes," Mark said. "In the meantime, would you be willing to help out with media inquiries?"

"Afraid not," she said. "I'm to take over."

Mark finished reviewing an early draft of the next release, marked a few changes, and then went to discuss the situation with the Unified Command. In the ICS system, the incident commander is in charge. When an appropriate authority for the lead federal agency shows up, he or she automatically becomes part of the command team, now called Unified Command. The lead responding agency for the state also has a position on the Unified Command team, as does the lead local responding agency. However, the incident commander for the company involved, known as the responsible party, always has a place in Unified Command. Tribal leaders, when their land or property is affected, also become part of Unified Command. Should an impasse occur, final authority rests with the Federal On-Scene Commander (FOSC). Mark conferred with Jack Wyles, the Incident Commander for the company, who said he would confirm it with the other members of Unified Command. At this point the FOSC was the lead EPA representative. At the point it was determined to be a terrorist activity, the federal command position would switch to the FBI. Mark observed a brief discussion among the Unified Command, the state commander shrugging his shoulders, shaking his head, and turning away. "Carry on," Jack told him.

"I've been confirmed as Information Officer for now," Mark told the woman. "Now, if you would be so kind, please help out with media inquiries. Sally here is the JIC manager and Al is Assistant Information Officer, External so he will get you caught up on inquiry responses." The woman glared and then walked away.

Turf wars, power struggles, personality clashes, and all the weaknesses of humans working together in tight quarters and stress-filled circumstances play a role in crisis communications. The most important element in managing these difficulties is strong, competent, experienced leadership. The second is preparation and an organization structure that is prepared in advance and is understood prior to the incident by everyone on the team.

Mark was strongly aided in his difficult task by having incident commanders who understood the vital role of public information in a crisis situation and who also understood the absolute need for speed. The commanders recognized that they could be major stumbling blocks. I personally observed one incredibly officious and uncooperative state official block vital public information in real situations and drills, in some cases for up to two hours, for the apparent purpose of demonstrating that he had the power to do so. The fact that he was successful in doing so demonstrated that his primary concern was establishing his own power position rather than contributing to the team effort, and also that command did not demonstrate the requisite leadership needed to put an end to the frustrating nonsense.

PRIORITIZATION

Within an hour of the explosion, Mark's communication team was settling into their tasks and the JIC was beginning to function relatively smoothly. Mark decided he needed to take a few moments, so he stepped outside where he could clearly see the bright glow of burning fuel. Priorities, he thought: employees' families, company leadership, government officials, neighbors, community leaders. Oh, yes: reporters that are local, regional, national, and international. He jotted a few notes and returned to the JIC.

He called a brief meeting of his management team, which now included the assistant information officers for internal and external, the JIC manager, and their deputies. "We've probably got eight hours before the team from Houston arrives," Mark told them. "I want to get maximum information out to our various groups to help minimize the inquiries coming in, or else we will get buried in a hurry."

Mark directed that a private Web site be launched for company leadership with a direct transfer of the reports inside the main crisis site that would allow them to follow incident status as it changed. All appropriate company officials would be alerted by email and some by phone of the general password used to enter this site. Employees' families would be provided the approved public statements as soon as they were distributed to the media by email and those without email addresses would get a text-to-voice telephone message. Neighbors in the five-mile radius identified in eight different sectors in the database would be similarly notified. All government officials and community leaders would get a modified version of the public statements emailed or faxed to them concurrent with the release of media statements.

"Critically important," said Mark, "is to include the incident URL, *www.fairawayrefineryresponse.com,* in all messages going out including the phone messages. Also, please request that if they have questions they should enter them through the inquiry function on this site. If we can maximize use of this, we'll limit phone calls and cover the most ground."

Mark understood there are two important realities to prioritization in crisis communications: Everyone is a priority, and there are still priorities. So he gave one final instruction to the assembled communication team: "We want those whose opinions matter the most to understand that this refinery, this company, these agencies working together are unified in their efforts to minimize danger to people and damage to resources, and that they can count on us for the fastest, best, most accurate information about this event."

With the approval of the Unified Command, Mark's team had been posting digital images, and even a short video, of the response team at work. Mark took a call from the CEO of the company. "Wow," he thought, "I've never talked to the CEO before." The CEO congratulated him on doing a good job and then told him he had received a call from a lead attorney for the company vigorously complaining about the images on the public Web site. "I think we need to take those off," the CEO said.

"We certainly can and I will be happy to comply," responded Mark, "But you need to know that the result of that will be that reporters and members of the community will go to this local online news site that has pictures and stories of what is going on. Check it out at this Web address," Mark said, giving him the information. The CEO checked it out. The question was whether the company wanted this small independent news operator with great photos that everyone was screaming for to become the primary and best source for information about this event. That job was what the JIC was established for, but if company attorneys were fearful of how the images might be used down the road and wanted to pass control of the information to people outside the JIC, then the CEO needed to understand that the company attorney was changing company communication policy, Mark explained. The policy clearly stated that the company or the JIC in which the company operated was to be the first and best source of information about the incident.

The CEO decided to leave the images up and said he would get back to Mark if and when he needed to remove them. "Keep up the good work," Mark was told. He never heard back.

BROADENING THE CLINIC'S MESSAGE

After the *Today Show* statement had been received, Steve also turned his attention to priorities. He was fielding media inquiries and working with the medical officer, who was now much more cooperative in providing the approved and appropriate responses. Steve handled those inquiries coming in via the public site about the legal action himself, quoting the medical officer as the source. There was more that needed to be done. Steve was very aware that the clinic's tens of thousands of patients would shortly be getting news of this action and they would get it in time to tune into the *Today Show* and see what Steve fully expected would be a hack job. The black hat would be placed on the clinic's head. Steve saw that the CEO was still online in the private communication system intranet site, but also that one of the attorneys—one of the least public-relations-sensitive attorneys—was also still online. Steve decided not to use the chat room, but phoned the CEO instead.

"Aaron," Steve said, "I want you to consider something." He went on to explain that he felt it would be a good idea to email a letter to all 43,219 patients who had been served by the clinics owned by the company in the past four years.

"Let me get this straight, Steve. You want me to tell my patients who represent 85 percent of my business through their referrals that they should watch the *Today Show* tomorrow while we get hammered?"

"Uh, yes," said Steve. "They would get the story eventually, through the press reports, watching the show, or hearing about the show from their friends and neighbors. We have the chance right now to tell the story to them first. Tomorrow we won't have that chance. Yes, there is a downside risk in that you are drawing more attention to what might very well be a negative story. However, the upside is their understanding that you are communicating directly, honestly, and truthfully with them."

"What about the attorneys? I can see where they would be concerned that this could hurt us in court."

"Losing the confidence of your patient base could be the end of your business, Aaron. It's your call, of course, but even a significantly increased risk in court doesn't compare to the risk of negative opinions of those people who are most important to your future."

"I get your point. Let's get on the phone with the group."

The email was sent. Unfortunately, only half of the patients in the database had an email address so a few went by fax and the rest went by mail. They would not hear from the clinic prior to the show, but they would know the clinic had communicated with them as quickly as it could.

In the instant media world, decisions about priorities go far beyond the question of which reporter's call to return first. Those people who control the future of the institution by the positive or negative perceptions in their head are all important. It is absolutely true that while we are moving toward a postmedia world, we are still very much in a media world so that reporters, editors, and producers are still vital in opinion making. However, that is shifting, and with the Internet, the opportunity to communicate immediately and directly is shifting that balance. The ability and willingness to use that capability determines whether or not a company or organization will trust its future to the media or will take at least some control in its own hands.

Inquiry Management

If Mark did not have the option of communicating quickly and directly to the various nonmedia groups, or if he decided to wait until later to communicate, the burden of inquiry management would have taxed the ability of even the most well-prepared and well-managed information center to respond. In the second and third hour of the refinery explosion, Mark's workload would be reaching a climax. Inquiries would be pouring in at accelerating rates via email, telephone, and from the growing number of reporters, videographers and producers in the satellite trucks arriving at the refinery main gate. The governor's office, U.S. Senate and Congressional offices, and the White House would be calling in for briefing updates. The airport manager would be expecting a call. The CEO of the company that owned the refinery and the company's entire executive level would be pressing for ongoing information. Neighbors, the mayor, the county executive, and assorted other elected officials and community leaders would be emailing and calling.

Even if the latest Internet technology is used and the most proactive communication actions are taken, the inquiry burden will be very great. Reporters will be flying overhead, driving up in satellite trucks, and certainly calling every land line and cell phone number they have in their PDAs to get the answers they are looking for. At a minimum, a written record of every inquiry should be logged. This provides communication managers with the opportunity to review what questions are coming in and provides some measure of quality control over the answers provided. However, a two-part form simply cannot match the functionality of available Internet-based inquiry management.

Inquiry management is not just a crisis communication problem, but it is a part of everyday life for communicators in most larger companies and organizations. This function is certain to grow in complexity and demands as we continue to move toward a postmedia world where growing categories of stakeholders will have the same high expectations for direct, instant, and accurate communication as reporters now have. The demands are higher today than they need to be because of inadequate technology platforms used. For example, one large corporate communication team recently explained that it is very common for a reporter to contact different members of the team with the same question. These people might be scattered in different parts of the country. Two problems occur: A loss of productivity occurs because now perhaps two, three, or even more communicators are working on the same issue or response. Second, if the answers provided are not entirely consistent, quality control becomes a concern. Internet-based inquiry management technology solves that problem by allowing all members of the team to work on a common desktop, enabling them to view the inquiries each member is working on. This avoids duplication of effort and inconsistent responses.

With this technology, inquiries are instantly logged as they come in. Inquirers are encouraged whenever possible to log the inquiries themselves using the public Web site, which is directly linked to the secure inside communication management site. Either way, contact databases are automatically kept up to date by direct link to the inquiry system. Inquiries coming in from the external site trigger an email notification, which means that designated team members will see an email appear in their regular email or on their text pager or email-capable cell phone. Inquiries can be directed to the members of the team best positioned to answer them, and when a response is completed, it is emailed directly to the responder from within the system, avoiding an additional step of re-entering the response into regular email. The system records all details, including date and time of inquiry and date and time of response, as well as what the response was and who responded. The inquiry management screen alerts the team to all the uncompleted inquiries as well as giving them shared and easy access to all past completed inquiries. This adds greatly to efficiency, as a responder can quickly check to see the same or related questions and see how those questions were answered.

This technology provides communication managers and executives far greater oversight of the inquiry management process than ever before. They can view in real time the questions and answers, spotting emerging trends in questions, misinformation, or rumors. They can also quickly identify when any member of the team is supplying inconsistent, inaccurate, or inappropriate information.

Although productivity and quality of communication response are the primary advantages, this new technology can also decrease administrative burdens in other ways. In industries in which response drills are required by law, detailed documentation of the drill is also required. Because every detail of the inquiry function is maintained in databases, these systems usually provide detailed reports that meet or exceed all regulatory requirements.

Steve was also using the inquiry management function of his Internet communication management system. Although the call volume was insignificant compared to Mark's challenge and he and the medical officer plus an assistant in his office were the only ones actively managing the function, he found it very helpful to review the inquiries and responses with Aaron and the legal team in the days following the *Today Show*. One thing the reporter inquiries demonstrated is that they had some level of understanding that the aggressive press effort orchestrated by the attorney was an attempt to create the publicity needed to generate a victim pool to warrant class-action status. As a result, Steve noted to the CEO and the attorneys that the press coverage of the story was far more muted than what they might have expected.

Mark was relieved of his position as Information Officer 13 hours after first hearing the explosion from his bed. The crisis team from Houston arrived nine and a half hours after receiving notification and the experienced Information Officer from headquarters assumed Mark's role after a two-hour transition that enabled her to get fully up to speed on what was happening. By that time, his team had released five public statements including various versions for the stakeholder groups, and had conducted two press conferences. One he had conducted because the Unified Command got tied up on critical operational issues just prior to the announced briefing time, and three members of the Unified Command participated in the other. Mark hung around for a half an hour or so to make certain things were running smoothly and went back home. He had managed to get a couple of calls in to his wife, who was understandably concerned. As he pulled into his driveway, he could feel the burden being released, but he sensed his work wasn't done.

RUMOR MANAGEMENT

Nearly every student has played the communication game in school where a story is whispered to one student who must whisper it to the next until it passes throughout the class. At the end of the line, the story is almost always unrecognizable. Person-to-person communication passed through many ears and mouths is notoriously inaccurate. Add to that the reality that not everyone wants the information to be accurate. Negative twists and turns are not always entirely innocent.

Rumors and rumor management are a necessary part of communication management, particularly during a crisis when a reputation is on the line. Rumors have sometimes been likened to cancer: Detected early they can often be treated, but left to spread undetected or without response, the damage can be very severe. That means that the first and best line of defense is early detection. Part of preparing the team must include instructions on how to recognize rumors. When spotted, the rumor should not be laughed off, but instead reported quickly to the Information Officer or communication manager.

Steve encountered the rumors very early, involving the clinic's past legal history. Steve soon detected that the reporters asking questions about the legal history were on more than a fishing expedition—they had some information that the company had a history of legal actions. An email and response to the CEO clarified the situation. The clinic had never gone to court. However, there were two instances in which a patient experienced some difficulties, hired an attorney, and reached a settlement with the clinic that included retreatment. As usual, the rumors had a portion of truth, but the truth was stretched or distorted almost beyond recognition. Steve drafted a statement in the communication system that explained clearly that in two previous situations in which patients had been less than satisfied with results, the patients had agreed to retreatment and their complaints were satisfied. In this case, the patient had refused retreatment. The holding statement also made clear that the clinic's patient results were among the highest in this area of medical practice and that although legal action in this area was growing due to the rapidly growing number of patients and clinics providing the procedure, the action facing the clinic was the first legal action of this nature it faced. After brief legal review and the obligatory wording changes, Steve approved the holding statement and released it only to those three reporters who had asked the question. He did not want to raise the question of legal history if it wasn't necessary, but now he and the medical officer serving as spokesperson were fully prepared to respond if and when a question should arise.

Mark's problems with rumors involved the question of injuries or fatalities. The initial report he received was that two bodies had been recovered. Later information revealed that only one was dead; the other was rushed to the burn center in the nearest large city and was in critical condition. There were still at least three people missing. Injuries or fatalities trigger the portion of a crisis communication plan that everyone dreads the most. The shock, horror, and disbelief of losing coworkers is combined with the great difficulty of relaying the information to family members. This burden is exacerbated in the era of instant news because the families need to be notified by company officials, usually the highest ranking company official available, and not by the media. That's one important reason why extreme caution in dealing with public information about deaths and injuries is an absolute must. Perhaps the only thing worse than having a family member find out about the death of a loved one on television is to have that death reported, only to find out later it wasn't true. Accuracy is critical and speed here refers more to the speed of getting absolutely accurate information to the families.

Whenever he had a spare moment, Mark was monitoring the inquiry screens. The fact that his team was putting out updated releases whenever new information became available was keeping the inquiry load and the number of routine, predictable questions down. Mark first noticed a couple of inquiries coming in that hinted at some knowledge about who the dead and injured might be. Then he was handed a phone by one of the media responders who whispered he needed to hear this question. The reporter told him he had it on good authority from an employee he interviewed as he was leaving the plant that a senior manager, possibly the operations or maintenance manager, was among those caught in the explosion. Mark knew it wasn't true because he had seen both of them in the command center, but he also wasn't absolutely sure that a senior plant manager wasn't involved.

He conferred with the Unified Command and they concurred with his recommendation. He amended the next release to explain that the information they had available indicated that as many as five workers involved in distribution center activities might have been in the area at the time of the explosion. One worker was seriously injured and had been sent to Mercy Hospital by helicopter. The status of others who might have been in the area had not yet been confirmed. He also decided that at the next press conference, which was coming up in an another hour, he would ask the plant manager, the operations manager, and the maintenance manager to attend and have the Incident Commander for the facility introduce the senior managers for the facility. They would not take questions but they would be visible.

While writing this chapter, I watched a local all-news cable channel seriously blow it. For almost two hours they offered up blaring breaking news headlines. A prominent politician in the state was in a coma following a skiing accident. They showed file pictures of the handsome state senator at work in the senate and repeated the story at least every 10 minutes. Then, suddenly the report changed. It was a family member of the senator who was injured. The misinformation was blamed on a hospital employee who told the news crew that the injured person was the senator. A troubling aspect of such a story is that many people viewing the news during those two hours saw the story, but didn't hang around to hear the rather quiet correction. An injured family member doesn't warrant continued breaking news coverage, so after the very short correction, the story was over. That meant that the majority of people who watched that channel believed that the senator was in the hospital clinging to life.

Responsible journalism and responsible communication require a great concern over accuracy. Communicators today need to understand the tremendous pressure news reporters are under, particularly to find and report on breaking news. Everyone needs to take a deep breath and remember that real lives, real heartbreak, real careers, real futures, and real pain are at stake.

NEGATIVE REPORTING

Rumors are one thing, but negative reporting is another. The two might be connected when a report is released that is critical of the company or organization involved and the report is based on false or highly distorted information. However, much negative reporting is true. It might be spun heavily to fit the black hat mold, but when based on undisputed facts and not misinformation or the 10 percent truth, it's simply a negative story that is damaging.

Lindi Diaz, the experienced communication manager from Houston, took over for Mark and immediately faced a growing concern. She was forwarded a call from a media responder in the JIC who felt the Information Officer should hear the question directly and respond. A report was circulating, said the reporter, that the refinery had failed miserably in a recent security check undertaken by the National Guard and the Coast Guard and that the presumed terrorists had walked through an unsecured gate near the plant's electrical generation facility. The reporter said he had the information from a reliable source and would put the story on the wire in a half-hour but wanted confirmation or a response from the refinery. Shortly after she told the reporter she would get back to him shortly, she noticed three new inquiries logged on the system with similar questions. There was no question that a story would break soon with these accusations.

As she walked to the Unified Command area, Lindi's thoughts cleared. She had no idea whether there was substance to the information, but this was not a JIC issue; this was a refinery and company issue. She spoke for a moment with Hank Peterson, who had replaced Jack Wyles as the responsible party incident commander. He agreed with her approach and she left while he informed the Unified Command of the pending story and how the JIC was going to handle it. Lindi got the refinery manager on the phone and suggested he be prepared to handle media inquiries related to the plant's security. She briefed him and a communication assistant who would help the plant manager, then she drafted a statement and secured approval for a general release to the media. The statement said the JIC was there to provide information about the event and the response and would not be in a position to provide information related to cause, including questions about security. Such questions could be directed to local police, the FBI, or the refinery. She briefed her assistant information officers on this statement, and they in turn briefed the responders. The statement was distributed to all reporters.

Ron, the communication manager now working with the refinery manager, went to work on the refinery's press room

Web system that used the same communication management technology now being used by the JIC. They hammered out a quick statement that said the refinery had passed all security inspections and that information was not available regarding the cause of the incident, nor could terrorist activity be confirmed. However, the refinery already had a team in place doing an investigation of possible causes including the possibility of terrorist activity and a security breach. This statement needed legal approval from the corporate attorneys in Houston. Time was running short. The attorneys were online and reviewed the statement, discussed some wording changes, expressed concern about even recognizing the possibility of a security breach, and agreed on a statement when the plant manager said time was up. Because the JIC communication management system and the refinery's communication management system were operating on the same platform, databases of reporters—including all those who had recently inquired—were transferred with the click of a button. An email went out with the refinery's statement.

Both Lindi and Ron soon noticed a shift in the general pattern of inquiries. Focus started turning from the response to the fire and potential impacts on area fuel supplies to questions about terrorism, security procedures, points of entry, identity of the suspects, and so on. As Lindi and succeeding information officers in the JIC focused on the unfolding events in the response, providing status on fatalities and injuries, and coordinating information about impacts on fuel supplies, security questions were referred to police agencies and the refinery. The FBI had been participating in the JIC nearly from the beginning but had not replaced the EPA as FOSC, and did not until two days later. The shift signaled a confirmation of terrorist involvement and further moved the focus from the incident response to investigation. Five days after the explosion, the JIC was shut down, in large part because the media coverage was related to the terrorism aspect.

The first question about security problems at the refinery had set off a firestorm of debate in the offices of corporate headquarters in Houston. Ron was communicating within the intranet communication system and on the phone to his counterparts in Houston. The head of public affairs for the company assumed the role of communication manager for the company and the CEO became directly involved in the response. Despite the warning, the team was still shocked to find the banner headlines: "Security Failure at Refinery Blamed for Explosion." The main source behind the serious accusation was the deputy director of the local Department of Emergency Management. He had been interviewed by a newspaper reporter, and, although he was not directly involved in the security procedures or reviews, he had heard his boss say after the last inspection that the refinery was dragging its feet on some important new security measures. This offhanded comment was now the basis for damaging accusations.

The fact was that the refinery management, the EPA, and the National Guard had been discussing new and very burdensome changes in security procedures. There was a dispute about what the refinery was able and willing to do. Some new requirements involved significant costs without any real apparent benefit, and none of those items were involved in this situation. It was also a fact that the terrorists' planning had been outstanding. They created a diversion that drew the refinery's beefed-up security team into a high response, enabling the perpetrators to cut through and enter the refinery fence at a strategic point far away from the diversion.

Ron suggested on a conference call that it was probably pointless for the refinery or the company to defend itself against the rumors and accusations about security problems. They had a good relationship with the local people from the EPA office and the National Guard despite the fact they hadn't agreed on every procedure. It was agreed they would hold a press conference at the refinery with the local EPA and National Guard leadership to discuss security procedures. The ground rules of the press conference were established, limiting the questions to security precautions, measures taken, and compliance issues. Those responding to questions would not and could not address the cause of the explosion, which was now a refinery, police, and EPA matter. Ron introduced the spokespeople present including the refinery manager, a colonel for the National Guard detachment and a regional manager for the EPA. The refinery manager spoke first, explaining that details about security precautions and new measures could not be discussed for security reasons. However, the company and the refinery understood very well the strategic importance of the nation's fuel supply and the role of the company and refinery in providing that and therefore took its responsibilities to add security very, very seriously. The refinery had cooperated fully with all agencies involved in security measures and was never out of compliance. Not all measures that had been identified were completely in place because there was an ongoing review of procedures and a constant process of adding new ones. The two people from the agencies echoed what was said and took a number of pointed questions, but at no time were the reporters able to get the agency representatives to point a finger at the refinery and blame the incident on a security lapse.

Although the issue did not go away, reporting on it diminished greatly. The deputy manager of the Department of Emergency Management was suddenly unavailable or unwilling to talk to reporters. Without getting agency representatives willing to point to specific lapses or specific problems, it slowly became a nonstory.

Steve had a similar problem and solved it in a similar way. One aggressive reporter was able to identify one additional past patient who seemed less than thrilled with the treatment and made comments about running a "cosmetic factory." The clinic was an active participant in the dermatology association linked with this procedure and Steve was able to enlist the active involvement of the head of the association, who had very positive comments to make about the clinic, the quality of the medical staff, the strong record of safety and effectiveness, and the unfortunate trend of unjust legal action against this new and very helpful procedure. Now it would be seen as the complainers against a respected industry leader—not the poor victims against a prosperous clinic bent on protecting its reputation.

Ahead of the Curve

A journalist laughed when I suggested the goal of effective communication response was to stay ahead of the curve. There is a sense of playing fast-break basketball. Just when you think you've done your job and won the point, the other team is three-quarters of the way down the court and impossible to catch. The only way to play this kind of game is to anticipate the break and think through the next step before you're even done with the last.

During one of the most significant news stories I was involved in, new information came to light that would set the reporting off in a new direction. It was significant news and although not positive to the company, it was not particularly damaging either. Being a junior member of the team, I urged them to release it.

"Why?" the veteran communication manager asked me with a smile. "That's their job to do. Why do their job for them?"

Why? Because that's what I thought this was all about: providing good information, building trust, letting the reporters know that we have nothing to hide and will not hide anything. If we provide it first, not just to the reporters, but to all those people who care about us and this situation, we get ahead of the curve. It was clear the communication manager and I were playing a different game.

Steve anticipated a shift in focus toward more medical field statistics about safety of the procedure. He had discussed the need for this type of information before with Aaron, the CEO, but nothing was readily available. Steve took a few minutes from media responses to contact the three medical associations with some relationship to the doctors who practiced this procedure. Information was sketchy, but he combined it with some quick Internet research into a fact sheet on dermatology procedures. Whereas some outlets continued to focus on the complaints of the two patients involved and the sound bites offered up by the media-savvy attorney, others began more in-depth reporting of the safety record of the procedure. They even compared this record against other comparable medical procedures such as eye surgeries, liposuction, and other elective procedures with some risk. The results showed favorably and the stories began to change.

Mark returned to duty after some much needed rest. However, he returned not to the JIC, but to the refinery where, unlike the JIC, things were beginning to heat up. The FBI had begun to take a stronger role and had released the identities of those who had been arrested by the refinery security people. An FBI spokesperson had also said innocently, "We don't know how they got into the refinery but we know they did because the bomb was placed well within the refinery's security perimeter." This was absolutely true, but it set off another firestorm of questions aimed at finding out exactly what happened and who was to be blamed. What was even worse was that the public was being warned that flights leaving the regional airport might be curtailed because of the possibility of fuel shortages. The legislature was trying to decide if they should pass emergency legislation to put an exemption on fuel-tanker truck traffic, but the well-practiced truck opponents were grabbing lots of space and time in the media talking about the frequency of accidents and the numbers of fatalities expected from increased truck traffic. Now there were three confirmed dead and three injured, two very seriously. A prominent local attorney who also served on the board of several important civic groups announced that two of the victims' families had retained him and he had information from refinery employees that security procedures at the refinery were "a joke."

The fire was out. The mess was being cleaned up. Workers were going home exhausted. For a day or two the main headlines in the papers around the region carried stories other than the blast. It was time to start thinking about recovery after a major incident—the next chapter.

CHAPTER

12 Reputation Recovery: What To Do After It Happens

In a serious crisis, a company's credibility is often seriously compromised. Reporters write their stories assuming the public franchise has been lost and the news stories become self-fulfilling prophecies. When the company leaders or spokespeople try to speak, their words sound weak and defensive, and the organization's leadership begins to adopt a bunker mentality. However, an explosive crisis is not the only situation that causes this loss of credibility and resulting weakness in communication. Companies actively engaged in controversial public issues such as permitting new facilities, fighting legislative or regulatory battles, or combatting ongoing activists' attacks share similar circumstances with those who have just come through a major crisis.

This chapter addresses how to communicate and rebuild a reputation when your standing in the public has been damaged or called into question, or when you are under continual, long-term attack that is eroding public confidence. It's been said repeatedly that credibility is everything. Credibility means the audience inherently believes you or at minimum gives you the benefit of the doubt. So, what happens when that belief is gone and your words are considered suspect? How do you speak and what do you say when no one will believe you?

There are three phases to this process: getting out of the bunker, restoring credibility, and then returning to normalcy.

How soon you can go from one to three, or whether or not you can get to three at all, depends on the seriousness of the crisis, the culpability of the organization in causing the crisis, and the effectiveness of the communication response and recovery strategy.

Getting out of the Bunker

Sometimes company leaders under attack do adopt a bunker mentality and other times it only looks like that. That is one of the key issues in reputation recovery in the instant news world because it can look like the company is unwilling to respond simply because its communication process is operating too slowly. In the weeks and months following the revelation that an Arthur Andersen partner in Houston destroyed key documents needed in the Enron investigation, there was a strong suggestion that the leaders were hiding out somewhere. The appointment of former Federal Reserve Chairman Paul Volcker to an oversight board, the resignation of Andersen CEO Joseph Berardino, the decision to separate the audit business from other Andersen activities, and the launching of a campaign to help protect the jobs of thousands of innocent employees were done in incremental steps over a four-month period. Because they always seemed late and slow in response to the ever-deepening crisis, they never had the intended impact. Neither did they help the company to emerge from the appearance of hiding out. None of these steps were certain to put an end to the reputation crisis Andersen faced. However, because each step was seen as "too little, too late," and leadership was not as visible or as loud as required, these actions were almost certain to have little impact, if any, on the continuing slide.

The bunker mentality was quite clear in the weeks following a tragic industrial accident. The company's leaders were tired of the media. For weeks they had been tracked down and hounded, and they had become somewhat accustomed to seeing satellite trucks outside their office door. When the immediate furor began to die down, it was understandable that they were not eager to spend any more time talking to the press. After all, they did have a job to do and they had been distracted from getting back to business by the incessant and insistent press of reporters. However, to those on the outside, to the key influential leaders in the community, this understandable desire to get back to the job at hand can and did look very much like a retreat to the bunker.

This tendency to keep one's head down when under attack is true for long-term controversies and public issues as well as in the aftermath of a major news event. When confronted with activist opposition during a permitting process, it seems the natural tendency of many companies today is to delay a public response until the heat becomes nearly unbearable. Instead, they tend to focus on preparing their pitches to the regulatory bodies holding the public hearings, believing that the only thing that matters is meeting regulations and convincing the regulators of that. Experience has shown in the past few years that the perception of public opposition—even when created by just a handful of dedicated opponents—is enough to delay or even terminate otherwise fully acceptable projects. The bunker mentality in these situations proves to be very expensive.

Following a crisis, or when opponents have turned up the heat, the temptation to quietly get back to business after the media storm has passed has to be fought. When credibility is at stake and when the attacks have stung, it is critical to move aggressively, publicly, and with considerable visibility. In the instant news world, with the tools of the broadcaster or publisher at hand, this job is made easier, regardless of whether or not the mainstream press has moved on to another story or another "breaking news" crisis.

There are two very important reasons it is important for the communication team and the organization's leadership to venture out into the light of day as the immediate pressure of the crisis is beginning to ease. One is to get an objective measurement of the damage done to the public franchise. The other is to make certain that those who are still observing the company and its action understand that there is nothing to hide and no reason to hide out.

Measuring the Damage

When a company or its leaders have been attacked and damage has been registered, a response is required. However, what level of response? How do you make certain you are not adding to the damage by overresponding? Time, effort, and money spent on repairing a reputation is wasted if the attacks or negative stories have not significantly impacted the standing of the organization in the perception of the public or stakeholders. A crisis, attack, or extended public controversy almost always requires a measured response. The question is what measurement the measured response will be based on. Leaders and communication managers who have been through this will most likely admit that the guide used to measure the sense of where the public response is at is their own gut instinct. This is gauged by reading the news reports, letters to the editor, and op-ed pieces, and by what is overheard on the street on the way into work. These same leaders, when confronted with this, would likely agree that they are in no position to accurately assess public or stakeholder opinion at this critical time. They are too close to the events, too emotionally involved in all the happenings, and too boxed in by others who are also too close to it. There is too much of a chance that those around them will tell them what they want to hear or at least color what they are saying to minimize the reality. At the same time, it is quite possible that by reading newspaper reports or watching the television news, those inside the events could come to the conclusion that the public is horrified and has turned completely against the company. Reading public opinion through news reports can often lead to overreacting and potentially increasing the damage. A measured response means measuring perceptions and not relying on gut instinct or the insider-only perspective.

The best way is to get out and find out what people are thinking. As I mentioned earlier, this does not usually involve a large-scale, sophisticated survey. There are times when such an effort is essential, but in starting the discussion about how the public and stakeholders are feeling about a controversy or events, some simple structured listening can go a long way.

Whose opinions really count? Are you concerned about how the county executive feels or a key city council member? Call them and ask them. Are you concerned about how the average investor might be responding to the news? Call a dozen and ask them. If you get 10 different answers, you might want to keep calling. If the answers are pretty consistent, you have at least a small measure of how investors are feeling about all the news reports.

If you're a member of the communication team or company leadership and your face hasn't been plastered all over the local newscasts or newspapers, get out into the community and listen to what people are saying. Catch people in casual conversation, or engage them yourself. Assign a few members of the team to call randomly selected people from some of the target groups. A picture will begin to emerge that can help in evaluating what public and stakeholder response is and can serve as a helpful guide to the communication response and ongoing reputation-building strategy.

Keeping Visible and Vocal

In the instant news world, a major story usually hits with remarkable speed and then, almost as soon as it appears, it can fade away with the burst of another major story. The company leaders at the center of the story assemble their crisis response team, confer with all the experts, discuss a strategy, and launch a response. They might set a press conference only to find that no one is interested any more. The storm has passed and while they were cooking up their response, the public already concluded that whatever has been said negatively about them must be true because they were "not available for comment."

The lack of visibility demonstrated by many organization leaders in the immediate coverage of a major event is usually not because they are hiding in the bunker, but merely because they haven't realized that they are living in a "now is too late" world of instant news. Maintaining high visibility is critically important in the early going of a crisis and it is also critical after the initial media wave has faded.

The question about visibility is relatively easy to answer when the reporters are calling and seeking interviews. What about when the media wave has passed, or when the opponents are creating momentum of public opposition but the press hasn't really taken much notice? This can be a much harder question because now you are not responding to the demands for visibility, but proactively seeking it.

Two questions need to be addressed: When do you proactively work to enhance visibility? How do you do it when the media is not of a mind to pay attention?

The answer to the first question is in the measurement. If the assessment is that the damage to the organization's reputation is significant and the company has gained a perception of being less than open, honest, and transparent, visibility becomes an essential element of restoring confidence. If there is no real damage, if damage is slight, or if continued exposure could cause unnecessary damage, the decision will be to do the needed reputation recovery work without proactive public visibility.

The answer to the second question is in remembering we are entering the postmedia world. You, too, are the broadcaster. You have the tools and technologies at your disposal to communicate with key stakeholders and influencers regardless of media interest. You also have the option of communicating your message through email, direct mail, and even advertising to speak directly to the news audience.

It's an important and frequently difficult call to make. However, if transparency and openness are at the core of public concern, the answer is usually simple: Be visible and be vocal.

Restoring Credibility

Credibility is gold and it is a terrible thing to waste. In reputation recovery and issue management we have to assume that it has been damaged or destroyed. Put in terms of the instant news world, the black hat has been securely placed on your head. The question now is what to do about it.

The Need for Speed

Two well-known American companies faced significant reputation crises in the early part of 2002. For one, the story erupted quickly in the news, had all the makings of an extended and very damaging problem, but quickly dissipated and now is forgotten in the public consciousness. For the other, the story resulted in the end of the history of a well-respected brand and worldwide enterprise. Although these organizations' crises were quite different and the difference in outcome was dependent on more than how they responded to the crisis, nevertheless the approach they took in defending themselves and recovering their reputations is very instructive. The company that emerged unscathed demonstrated that it understood the need for speed, and aggressiveness, and it knew that the black hat had to land somewhere. The other responded slowly and always from a defensive position without any apparent or effective effort to remove, replace, or recolor the black hat.

On Christmas Day, 2001, a Secret Service agent of Arabic descent was heading to join President Bush at his ranch in Texas. He was refused entry onto an American Airlines flight apparently because he was carrying a gun and he appeared to be of Middle Eastern descent. President Bush was absolutely livid, as all the national news broadcasts demonstrated. He struggled to find the words in his anger. There was good reason for his concern. All the efforts to gain support among moderate Arabs and Muslims in the fight against terrorism were dependent on demonstrating that America is friendly to these people and nondiscriminatory, and that America abhorred the isolated acts of violence against Muslims and people with an Arabic appearance in the aftermath of the September 11, 2001, attacks. The message that a major American company was apparently engaging in racial profiling—even against a person working for the President of the United States—could be seen as an embarrassment to the President and his efforts at coalition building.

The agent immediately hired an attorney, who repeated the claim of racial profiling vigorously and often in the news stories that followed. A lawsuit meant the story would have a long shelf life, and, if past history was any indication, the issue would be tried in the media with only the prosecution being heard from. American Airlines was not expected to respond publicly, but reserve its defense for the courtroom. After all, it was a legal matter and defense lawyers don't like to publicly comment on legal matters. American Airlines had the black hat securely on its head; the whole world had seen the President's fury aimed at the company and an angry victim with a well-spoken accuser was getting maximum media attention. However, in less than a week, the story went away so that now few even remember it. The reason is simple: American Airlines moved the hat. The day after the agent's racial profiling complaints were aired nationwide and an Arab American group expressed its outrage, the airline responded. The pilot was quoted by American Airlines spokespeople as reporting that the agent was angry, his Secret Service documentation was faulty, and he was abusive. There were very few in America, including the President, who would doubt the pilot's judgment that it was not prudent to allow an angry, abusive man carrying a gun on an airplane, particularly when his credentials didn't check out. Especially when only a couple of days before, another terrorist attack—a shoe bomb in this case—had been narrowly averted in the air.

When there were no vociferous denials on the part of the agent relating to his demeanor or paperwork problems, the issue was dead. The Arab American groups that loudly howled after the initial reports had lost some credibility. The attorney working for the agent would have to go in search of another high-profile opportunity, and it is pure speculation, but the agent was probably advised by his superiors that it might be in his best interest to show a little temperance in these tense times.

If the airline had decided to wait to respond to the charges, if its leaders had been convinced that the time and place to present the evidence of the agent's behavior was in the courtroom, the airline would likely have experienced serious reputation damage. As it was, they responded quickly and aggressively, and effectively defended themselves against what could have become a major business problem.

Arthur Andersen did not escape the black hat. Given the seriousness of the consequences to many in the Enron bankruptcy, Andersen's role as auditor, and most critically the actions of the Houston partner in shredding vital evidence, there is a real question about whether anything could have been done to protect the firm's reputation and future. Although its problems were more severe than the airline's, it is clear that Andersen leaders could have communicated much more quickly, aggressively, and proactively than they did. They did not do what American Airlines did: They did not maintain visibility, accept the responsibility the public expected of them, question the placement of the black hat, and commit to open and honest communication regarding the now visible problems. As mentioned earlier, they did take a series of strong and much needed actions, such as appointing a well-respected national leader to chair an independent oversight board. However, these actions all fell under the "too little, too late" category. Their only hope was to take strong and decisive action early.

Replacing or Recoloring the Hats

Both examples just discussed demonstrate the value of the old and highly useful adage about getting on the offense. Being on the defensive means the black hat is securely attached. A company cannot succeed in protecting its reputation with a black hat on its head visible to everyone on the outside and totally invisible to everyone on the inside.

Going on the offensive can be a very difficult proposition, particularly when the accusations are justified. When actions or inaction by company employees or leaders resulted in genuine harm to innocent people, the environment, or some other aspect of the public good, the black hat is there for a very good reason. However, an organization wearing a black hat needs it removed if it is to operate effectively in its marketplace and in the eye of the public. Time heals most wounds, but the time it takes for reputation damage to fade can be very costly. The best course of action is to take strong, positive, aggressive steps to restore a damaged reputation, the earlier the better.

There are several approaches to going on the offensive, listed here from most extreme to most conservative:

1. Attack the attacker
2. Shift the ground of debate
3. Focus on public benefit

Attack the Attacker

As noted earlier, we are in an era of public debate that is often raw and unseemly. Negative or attack ads are the predominant form of political communication. It seems Americans have become a people who are more quick to anger, eager to blame, and open to seeing the worst in people and situations. Negative ads have become predominant not because politicians have become more mean-spirited, but because attack ads work. Research has demonstrated repeatedly that people don't vote for someone as much as they vote against a candidate. Today's elected officials seem to have an understanding that they are in office not so much because they are loved and supported by their constituents, but because they were the "least bad" of the choices offered at that time.

Former President Bill Clinton demonstrated, much to the amazement of even his closest aides, his ability to recover his reputation from near collapse, not just once but multiple times. This remarkable ability, detailed in George Stephanopoulos's book *All Too Human*,[1] demonstrates that this was based primarily on Clinton's willingness to attack the attacker. Mere denial was not enough to defend against the accusations of a Gennifer Flowers, Paula Jones, or Kenneth Starr. The response would come down to an issue of credibility and Clinton was very successful in undermining the credibility of those who attacked him, thereby helping to limit the damage to his credibility. If he hadn't needed to resort to this very aggressive tactic so often, it is likely that his reputation would have emerged largely intact, due in part to his many contributions and strong support from many quarters. In other words, without positive public benefit, attacking the attackers is not enough. The negative aspects must include the positive aspects for there to be any hope of success.

Although this strategy of launching very personal and very aggressive attacks as a means of defense has been proven to be effective in some cases, executives and communication leaders are wisely reluctant to employ it, except in perhaps the most extreme circumstances. It is almost always better to attempt to elevate the debate than be the one to bring it to new lows. This is true despite the all-too-common situation of facing highly personal attacks by opponents who feel passionately about the issue. Those attacked by the "true believers" must remember in a mud fight with a pig, as the saying goes, everyone gets dirty, but the pig enjoys it. It should also be pointed out that although negative campaigning has proven distressingly effective, all elected officials have become victims of the general disgust that most Americans feel over the political process and the declining respect for politicians in particular.

Attacking the attacker refers to waging battle over credibility. Who is to be believed? Far too often companies and organizations under strong attack seem unwilling to engage the battle and point out when accusers are wrong. There certainly are times when the best policy is to ignore the other voices and carry on with a positive message. However, a lie repeated often enough becomes the truth, and too many companies seem willing to allow the accusations to be made without answer. One does not need to resort to *ad hominem* (against the man) attacks to undermine the credibility of the accusers. Usually there are sufficient overstatements, hyperemotional language, and flat-out factual errors to provide evidence that the truth is not being told.

This strategy proved its effectiveness in a hotly contested public battle over permitting an industrial facility. The company attempted the stealth approach first, working only with the regulators and doing little to gain public support. In the meantime, the strong activist opponents, including an elected official, built an exceptionally solid base of opposition, flooding public hearings with passionate voices. The opponents used hyperbole, misinformation, emotionalism, and personal attacks. They were remarkably effective, resulting in a decision by the permitting agency clearly based on political pressure and not on any determination of meeting requirements. In a second effort to gain approval, the company took on the opponents directly. A publication was prepared that used direct quotes from the opponents including the accusation that the company intentionally was setting out to kill people. Each statement of the opponents was carefully examined and facts countering their position were offered. The publication created a storm of controversy when published in the very newspapers that took a strong editorial position against the project. The publishers found themselves in the position of defending the right of advertisers to have their voices heard. Although the opponents howled, they could find no factual errors or misstatements to destroy the credibility of the publication. The results were seen in the next public meetings where far fewer opponents spoke and, except for the extremist leaders, most were far more cautious and judicious in their remarks.

The opponents were not attacked personally. The publication boldly stated that this was to address a campaign of misinformation. The attackers were accused of being dishonest, not by the company, but by the exposure of their statements contrasted to the clear and indisputable facts.

A similar approach was used in another highly charged public issue in which an activist was very effective in whipping up a highly emotional public frenzy. It resulted in repeated public votes against the company despite the clear problems with the policies. Few elected officials today have the courage to sit in front of a hostile council room and make unpopular decisions. However, when the supporters of this activist received a multi-page document detailing the many public statements of this activist and clearly showing the distortion, misinformation, and hyperemotionalism displayed, only a few die-hards were willing to speak at the next public hearings.

Many grassroots organizations have achieved a level of credibility with mainstream media that far exceeds the credibility granted to major corporations and even smaller for-profit organizations. There is a strong sense that because these frequently involve volunteer effort and are not motivated directly by stockholder demands or the profit motive that they are inherently more believable than for-profit organizations. At times it is appropriate, however difficult, for companies attacked by these groups to show they do not have the purity that they might pretend or that might be offered to them by the public and media.

An "environmental" group spearheaded a campaign to prevent a pipeline company from gaining needed permits. However, the primary funding for this citizens' group came from a fuel barge company that stood to lose millions if the pipeline permit was granted. The interesting thing was that when the newspaper editors were made aware of this, they could not bring themselves to fully expose it and lose the very convenient accuser, who was providing the basis for the stories they printed about the negative aspects of the pipeline. The company left it at that. In retrospect, the issue was important enough that it would have been worthwhile for the pipeline company to become the broadcaster and let those who cared about credibility know about the clear agenda behind the environmental attacks.

A more moderate form of taking the offensive is to create alliances around a common foe. Restoring credibility, like politics, can make for strange bedfellows. So does war. The unlikely alliance of the Western democracies and the Soviet Union in World War II could only have come about because of a common and very powerful foe. Reaching out and finding even unlikely alliances is important when under sustained attack.

The activist community is very adept at forming virtually instant alliances, particularly in the Internet age. It should not be presumed that the leaders or members of the various groups would agree with each other very much. Some are far more extreme in their values and methodology than others. Nevertheless, when they identify a project or a company that represents something they both agree is bad, there is no time for quibbling over disagreements. An alliance is formed based on their shared opposition to the project or company, and they have found a common foe.

Could Andersen have recolored the very dark hat it was wearing by attacking the attackers and finding common cause with the public? Possibly. Members of Congress were quick to jump on the attack and express their outrage at Andersen, as they have done in many other such high-visibility situations. Although accepting full responsibility for the shredding and remorse for the lapse in ethics and judgment it represented, Andersen could also have strongly suggested that this situation showed that it is time that Congress thoroughly examine accounting practices currently permitted by law. If it is true, as I have been told by accountants, that at least some of the accounting practices adopted by Enron were legal but highly suspect, then this becomes a matter of regulatory and legislative concern. Andersen or any other accountant cannot be expected to coerce a client into doing what is right when what they are doing is legal. Making deceptive but legal accounting practices the culprit starts to make much more questionable who is the accuser and who is the accused.

It should be noted that Andersen's ability to carry out this kind of strategy was essentially nullified by the shredding. If the controversy was only about accounting practices, the reputation risk would be serious but manageable. As with too many critical reputation crises, the cover-up becomes the crisis.

Shift the Ground of Debate

Before President Clinton launched his attack on Kenneth Starr, the entire controversy revolved around the President's personal morality and honesty. By making Kenneth Starr the poster child for the "vast, right-wing conspiracy" he shifted the ground of debate. He made common cause with all those who feared and distrusted the far right and said, in effect, that the issue wasn't about him; it was about politics. It was about future direction of policy. He said, in effect, "You and I and all those concerned about the right wing taking over this country and the damage it would cause are in this together. That's what this Ken Starr thing is all about. If he wins, we all lose." It was perhaps only the egregious nature of the moral problems at the heart of the story that kept this strategy from being fully effective. As it was, it succeeded in significantly undermining the moral authority of the special prosecutor.

The "destroy Starr" strategy could be seen as an ultimate example of attacking the attacker, but it also demonstrates the value of shifting the ground of debate. This can be effectively done without resorting to the inherent risk and nastiness of personal attacks against those attacking you.

In the example of the public permitting controversy involving a very strong opposition group discussed earlier, the ground of debate was established by the opponents. It was environmental. Strong accusations were made about predicted environmental damage. The company was continually on the defensive: "No it won't, no it's not true, our impacts will be minimal, blah, blah, blah." However, when the publication referred to earlier was launched with a bold headline stating that the company was addressing a campaign of misinformation, the ground of the debate was changed. Were opponents intentionally misleading their supporters? Were government officials failing to take notice of the facts? Is it possible in our democratic society that important public decisions can be made based on completely false information? Using their own words rather than attacking them directly, the company put the attackers on the defensive. They had to answer the questions about the truthfulness of their statements. When the accusers are on the defensive, white hats and black hats get very confused.

Once that new ground of debate was established, when opponents launched new attacks on the environmental consequences, the response was, in effect, "There they go again." Because their only rhetorical tools were misinformation and hyperbole, their attacks were turned against them.

In a different battle, the opponent was extremely effective in controlling the debate. Operating from a base as an elected official provides great advantage for populist-style activists, as many are discovering. The willingness of the local paper to print the colorful accusations, the passionate, if outrageous, statements, combined with the unwillingness of the company to do much to counter these made it a one-sided debate with the black hat firmly fixed. However, a quiet but nagging issue was raised: What about the cost of all this? The government involved had spent hundreds of thousands of dollars in foolish legal actions, all destined to fail, but the elected officials did so willingly rather than vote against the angry crowds. The fiscally conservative council members became increasingly uneasy when the issue of the cost of continuing the legal battles was consistently raised. It was a ground of debate on which the activist opponent could not possibly win. Although it did not end the debate, nor did the company ultimately succeed in the issue, the strategy created a two-front war. It provided the grounds for creating public support and counteranger—that is, anger that countered those who were angry about the accusations against the company. It also made the situation more complex for the elected officials who needed to make decisions in the public eye on the issue.

Focus on the Public Benefit

The strategy of taking the offensive is always a matter of a two-front effort. One effort might be aimed at countering the accusations, claims, or credibility of the accusers or opponents. The other must always be to present the positive side. As mentioned in the discussion on former President Clinton, his very aggressive attacks against his opponents would not have had any chance of success if there weren't many people benefiting from his leadership and policies. His efforts at taking the offensive were at least somewhat successful because the two critical elements were there: undermining the credibility of those who sought to undo his presidency and reinforcing the benefits he was delivering.

In the public permitting debate, the positive benefits in terms of taxes, employment, construction costs, and products produced were all continually communicated, even while the debate was focused on the campaign of misinformation. The battle involving the wasting of public funds ultimately was unsuccessful in part because there was no real compelling story of public benefit to counter the myths of public risk promulgated by the opponent. However, this situation is somewhat unusual. When a company or organization is attacked and its existence or operation is put at risk, there usually is a cost to that and frequently a cost not considered while the debate is raging on another topic.

A construction executive whose company had a remarkable record of negotiated work with excellent clients reflected, "Our clients would miss us if we weren't here." That's a strong statement in a crowded marketplace such as construction. It is what every company and organization needs to be able to say: The people important to us would really miss us if we weren't here. Companies or organizations whose reputations have been tarnished need to think about who would miss them, who would lose if they disappeared. If the honest answer is no one, it is probably a good thing for the organization to go. However, if there are individuals, groups, markets, networks, governments, communities, and families that would be affected and would miss the organization, then the benefits involved become the basis for a strong and positive message.

Going on the offensive then comes full circle: It starts with those strategic relationships and a clear understanding of the basis on which they value you and what you offer them. However, when under vigorous attack, the benefits message can't be heard; put another way, it sounds quite different when coming from a person wearing a 10-gallon hat that is very dark.

Efforts must be made to remove that hat or at least change its color, at the same time strongly reinforcing the reasons why they want you to be here.

Borrowing Credibility

When it is fully understood how difficult it is to operate in the public sphere when credibility has been significantly compromised, organization leaders and communicators will do just about anything to protect that credibility. Speed, as has been repeatedly mentioned, is one of the most critical elements in this era of instant news.

When credibility has been lost, almost everything that comes out sounds defensive. Even the efforts to shift the focus of attention can appear weak and desperate. Frequently, the very best approach is to allow others who retain credibility to speak on your behalf.

In one of its better moves (although still in the "too little, too late" category), Arthur Andersen leaders appointed former Federal Reserve Chairman Paul Volcker to head an independent oversight board. The media attention then focused on him. He was not involved in any of the actions that caused the problem; he had respect; he had independence. He could clearly identify problems and suggested solutions, but he could also present the case for the existence of the company both for the benefit of the thousands of employees and the country and economy as a whole.

Following the *Exxon Valdez* disaster, a citizens' committee was established to help monitor the policies and plans of the companies operating in the Alaskan waters. Although some in the oil industry remain skeptical of this approach and suspicious of the groups, it is clear that such a group is highly beneficial when the credibility of the companies has been lost.

A forestry company operating in South America established the position of land steward. A highly respected expert in environmentally sound forestry was named the land steward, with full freedom to evaluate all planned operations and to speak freely, openly, and independently about what he observed.

Another forestry company, in a situation illustrating unusual alliances, gained the vigorous support of a strongly environmental group by negotiating a joint venture project that enabled them to manage a prime forest parcel near their communal farm. They were obligated to manage it as a commercial forest, sharing profits with the forestry company. In turn, the company would protect this land from the clear-cutting practices that its permits allowed. As a result, this environmental group became a solid supporter for the company on other issues involving the environment.

The leaders of Arthur Andersen were essentially without credibility after the shredding stories had been played out. The forestry company with a tainted environmental record was essentially without credibility. Exxon, in the aftermath of the staggering environmental loss, was essentially without credibility. Even without major crises and in the best of situations, there are people with whom your company or organization has very little credibility. The answer to them must be, "Don't believe me, believe them." Finding the people who can be believed and who will speak on your behalf is essential when the ground on which you stand has turned to sand. Now is the time when all the hard work done in building solid, loyal relationships pays off. If your longtime friends who retain credibility and believability with the audiences won't speak on your behalf, you know you are in deep trouble.

RETURNING TO NORMALCY

Deciding when it is time to return to normalcy and officially declare the crisis over is often much harder than determining whether a crisis exists or not. One thing is certain in this instant news era: It's not over just because the headlines have shifted to a new topic. One of the rules of the instant news and postmedia world is that the media no longer have complete control over the length and content of the story. As long as "publishers"—even those operating from their spare bedrooms—continue to distribute information, launch attacks, and carry on the debate, the event goes on. Legal issues resulting from the incident will also help make certain the crisis has a much longer public life than if it were only a news story that quickly came and went.

In one sense, after a crisis or a vigorous public battle, nothing is ever the same. Major crises are frequently defining moments for organizations in the same way life crises are defining moments for individuals. They become touchstones by which everything succeeding it is measured. They can deepen resolve and make an organization stronger and more sensitive to its surroundings. However, they can also weaken an organization and leave it listless and drifting. The difference, as in people, is to be found in character; in the case of an organization, it is to be found in the character and strength of the leaders.

The real question in returning to normalcy is when does the company return in the public eye to the business of brand building and business as usual? The danger of quitting too soon is that the company will be perceived as insensitive and oblivious. The danger of waiting too long is that the public exposure is unnecessarily prolonged.

Three and a half years after an incident that took the lives of several coworkers, it is clear that the tragedy is still near the surface for many employees. Although the organization's leaders cannot and should not dwell on it, to refuse to make reference to it or acknowledge that deep scars still exist would be a mistake. However, it would be an equally bad mistake to continue strong references to the incident within the community unless the issue is raised. Returning to normalcy is thus different from audience to audience.

A damaging crisis or public controversy means that credibility has been lost. Normalcy is then defined as that time when credibility has been restored. That can only be determined by measurement. The only real way of determining what the best course of action should be is through listening. The organization needs to reflect where the various audiences are at in the process and whether or not the company is believable. If mistakes are made either in carrying on too long or appearing insensitive, it is because the communication loop of listening and responding isn't there. The simple answer then is to let your audiences be your guide and make use of the direct communication tools to respond appropriately to each audience. If, despite your best efforts, credibility is still missing, leaders and communicators cannot and should not rest: The work must go on.

Identifying strategic relationships and building one-to-one, high-value relationships was the primary work identified in Chapter 10. It is appropriate that we return to that after the crisis or public controversy has ended. When a considerable part of the communication team's focus is building or rebuilding those critical relationships, normalcy has returned. Yes, the conversation might be about the events and their impact, but the precrisis work is being done. The circle is complete. When those personal and direct conversations no longer revolve around what is happening or has happened, you will know that life is going on again.

Then you can start focusing on the future, the topic of the next chapter.

ENDNOTES

1. Stephanopolous, George, *All Too Human: A Political Education*, Boston, New York, London: Back Bay/Little, Brown & Company, 1999.

CHAPTER

13 A Glimpse Into the Future

If today we live in the era of instant news, what will tomorrow bring? Of all possible futures, a few things seem certain: Change will continue and the transportation of information will continue to grow in speed and depth. Public information will be more important than ever and news will at once be more global and more local, at once faster and more in-depth. The requirements for speed and directness of information will be far greater than anything we are seeing today. Strategies for building and protecting reputations will continue to change as this postmedia world becomes more and more a reality.

Media Splintering

A quick review of media history shows there is a well-established pattern that applies to most mass media. First the new medium is introduced and there is but a single or just a few examples. It grows, its power is recognized, and it is concentrated in a few hands with the capital to control it. Then it becomes fragmented and the audiences who were once concentrated become increasingly splintered. The media respond by ever more finely defining their audiences. Newspapers, magazines, and radio provide examples, and now television is following this pattern. In television, where there were once just three major networks, now there is an almost limitless variety and number of channels, networks, stations, and video suppliers from which to choose.

The Internet might be one startling exception to this pattern, in part because its introduction has been in reverse. It was never seen as a mass medium. Only now are we beginning to recognize its impact on news, public information, and reputation management. Although it might break the pattern, it is not likely to evolve into a high degree of concentration so there will only be a few Internet sites to choose from. If it started out fragmented, its history so far shows that it is becoming even more splintered with a multitude of "broadcasters" finding new ways to create highly specific niche audiences.

The splintering pattern of traditional media was largely driven by economics. In the early days, starting a radio station was a daunting technical task. The cost of setting up for producing a magazine was enormous. Television broadcasting? Forget it. Now a magazine can be produced for relatively little; the Federal Communications Commission is licensing microbroadcasters, enabling people with limited capital to broadcast to a limited geographical area; and everyone can produce their own television program on their PCs then distribute via videotape or the Internet. If traditional media's pattern is toward democratization, the Internet started public life that way. The Internet is essentially free, uncontrolled, with few restrictions, no license to buy, and only very modest domain name and service provider fees to pay.

Competition is one driving force of this splintering effect. The new competition from the Internet, as it competes ever more strongly with traditional media for audiences and impact, will not likely reverse this process. Traditional media, particularly those accustomed to large, diverse audiences, will need to work ever harder to protect those audiences against the splintering tide.

The Ubiquitous Internet

As this book was being written, the Internet reached a milestone in the United States. More than half of all people in the country—men, women, and children—became Internet users. New users were being added at a rate of two million per month. Although the rate of adoption in the United States remains high, it has slowed considerably and has been greatly surpassed by other countries on other continents, many of which are quickly moving toward similar levels of adoption. Just because people are connected to the Internet does not make it a convenient and universal means of communication and public information. To fully realize its potential and move us more completely into that postmedia world, the Internet must become truly ubiquitous. It must be on all the time, it must be accessible through appliances that are as forgotten and close to us as the clothes we wear, and it must deliver bandwidth that enables delivery of the richest content deliverable by any medium.

There continue to be stories of having computer chips implanted in your brain and screens embedded in your glasses or on projections like bicyclists' rear-view mirrors, but it is impossible to accurately predict at this time what appliances will deliver the information on the Internet in the future. Perhaps it will not be called the Internet. Perhaps it will use a more complex form of information than zeros and ones. What is certain—barring economic collapse or some other apocalypse—is that processing power will continue to increase, bandwidth will continue to become available to more people, and appliances using the Internet will surround us. Right now two primary information devices are separated—television sets and computers. In a few years, the separation of these two will make as much sense as the antique telephones where you held the receiver to your ear while shouting into the box on the wall. There is slow but steady progress being made toward delivering high bandwidth to every home and business via fiber and satellite. Conventional television appliances are being replaced with high-definition digital screens that are capable of delivering high-quality digital information on the Internet.

Moving Internet content onto more universally used and easily available appliances is one aspect of progress toward the ubiquitous Internet. Another is the convergence of content. Today we are seeing news presented with interconnected and intertwining media. Laurence Moskowitz in *PR Strategist* stated, "The news industry began to achieve the intermedia synergy it long promised. The newspaper sends readers to the Internet for more detail and constant updates. The television station streams live on the Internet, which is often linked to a newspaper site. The radio is available on computer speakers. Call it fusion."[1]

Wireless Connectivity

There are two ways to connect the world's computers together: with wires and without wires. The same is true of telephones. Even though there have been a number of spectacular business failures in recent years related to wireless connectivity, there is good reason to believe that wireless will gradually replace wires as the means by which we talk to each other and send each other information. Already today, if you are not able to get broadband connectivity using Digital Subscriber Line (DSL) service available through local telephone companies or cable modems available through cable television providers, you can secure direct satellite broadband connectivity for a relatively low and declining cost.

When freed of its wires, the Internet becomes even more powerful, accessible, and universal. Where now we find it highly useful to be able to share work and secrets from computer to computer, convergence and wireless connectivity will make it common to communicate instantly with anyone, at any time, from any location. I can see the beer advertising already: The busy executive relaxing on the beach at Cancun removes his wireless computer from behind his ear and his liquid crystal eyeglasses and tosses them far into the ocean so he can get a few minutes of relaxation.

Replication of Experience

The Internet, wireless connectivity, converging appliances—all these are hardware issues. There are also software issues that will change public communication. Video or, more accurately computer, games are one of the phenomena of our time. One of the main factors propelling technical innovation is the fact that young people grew up on the successors to Pong. The entertainment value they derived from chasing a ping-pong ball, to Mario, to supermonsters on computer screens and television sets has required a transformation in the workplace and the entertainment value of tools such as our word processors and Internet browsers. Warfare, as we have seen in the Gulf War and in Afghanistan, is largely conducted by joystick.

Games are about replicating experience. You need not meet a 10-foot monster in a back alley to experience some of the thrill of high kicks and well-placed punches to send it to the ground. This digital replication of experience is not limited to game playing. Few houses are sold anymore without offering the opportunity to take a visual tour on the Internet, frequently with the viewer having the option of choosing which rooms to view, which angle to view them from, and how close to inspect details. Even more significant is the development of simulators. From learning to fly the most complicated military and commercial airplanes to battlefield simulation with realistic visuals of enemy soldiers shooting at you, simulation technology is becoming increasing powerful and common.

One way in which this replication of experience is seen today is through the widespread use of Webcams. Real-time cameras that the viewer can control are in place in an ever-increasing number of places around the globe. Want to watch a major construction project going up, or take a virtual tour of the streets of a city you plan on visiting? Is it hard to imagine, given military approval and a brave journalist, that in the future we might find ourselves in the middle of a battlefield being able to point and click our way around to find where the most exciting action is? Right now, enterprising Web entrepreneurs are offering views of the World Trade Center site on their Webcams as a means of driving traffic to sites such as New York City art galleries.

With continued advances in processing power and bandwidth, and by freeing the delivery of that information from ordinary computers, we are likely to see considerable expansion of the replication of experience. Tourists might stay home and tour favored places with elaborate "virtual tours." Medical professionals and technicians of all kinds will support each other globally using these technologies to share the experience of the inside look of a diseased organ or the wear and tear on the inside of a piece of machinery. News viewers will expect to get more and more visual and other data from the scene of the events so they will have more of a sense of actually being present.

Everyone Is a Writer, Producer, Publisher, and Broadcaster

Tiny digital cameras have become almost as common as cell phones. A great many home PCs have digital editing software loaded, enabling mom or dad or the Hollywood producers of tomorrow to create their own surprisingly sophisticated home movies and short films.

A recent television commercial portrayed a college student contradicting his professor, who was talking about the difficult process of getting published. The student explained that with today's technology, anyone can be an author and publisher. The class applauded.

Web logging or blogging has become one of the communication phenomena of today. Tens of thousands of would-be writers, journalists, columnists, and curmudgeons are publishing whatever they want for the rest of the world to see. The most popular of these have attracted daily audiences that rival the readership of some daily newspapers. An increasing number of Web sites are dedicated to helping people become writers and publishers and build audiences. One site, referred to earlier, helps activists make use of the latest video technology to capture police, polluters, or others they target and then get the video out to the public, where it can help stimulate change.

The Internet and computer technology are democratizing communication in all its forms from conception, to production, to distribution. This promises to be one of the most profound changes in our world and in the history of communication.

What It Means for Tomorrow's Communicators

Technology and social change combine to require new strategies, methods, and thinking about how to communicate. Although most executives and communicators are struggling to catch up with many of the changes that have already occurred, it is worthwhile to examine some of the expected changes from the viewpoint of changes in communication methods in the future. Those changes are mostly related to the fact that, like it or not, the number of publishers and broadcasters is in the process of exploding.

One factor driving the explosion of broadcasters is the tendency of today's Internet user to go directly to the source for the information they are seeking. When an airliner goes down and millions turn to the airline's Web site for information, they are no longer just the source for news, they are the news provider. When the FBI Web site is swamped with millions of hits following a terrorist attack, the bureau is now a broadcaster, like it or not. That means company and organization leaders must think like broadcasters and understand how audiences are continually changing and how they must change to adapt to evolving demands.

However, if newsmakers are becoming news packagers and news distributors, many other people are learning that they, too, can become newsmakers, packagers, and broadcasters. Some of those new voices could pose significant challenges to those who wish to protect their reputations and their public franchise.

It is reasonable to conclude that audiences will have to learn how to manage the sound and fury of more voices pushing to be heard. Credibility can only increase in importance. With so many voices, the trusted voices will win the audience and the audience's heart.

Thinking Like a Broadcaster

Speed

How can it get any faster, you might ask? Two factors drive the speed: How quickly can news organizations discover the event and bring their resources to bear to collect the information, document it with images, package it, and disseminate it? Then, how long does it take for the viewers to view it? We have seen already that collection, preparation, and distribution have undergone dramatic changes by technology and by how the news organizations do business. We have also seen that when people are at their computers and get email updates, or use text pagers with ongoing news updates, that the time to receiving this information is dramatically reduced. This is considerably different than waiting for the paper to be printed and then waiting for the time to sit down with a cup of coffee and read it. We will see incremental increases in speed in all aspects of this process, with the most significant change coming from the broader use of the Internet with wireless devices and daily appliances such as television sets. With a ubiquitous Internet and news organizations dedicated to being first, speed will increase.

What that means, of course, is that companies and organizations serving as willing or unwilling news sources must be able to respond with ever-increasing speed. Everything that has been discussed here about policies, people, and technology will be magnified in the future as expectations and demands of audiences continue to rise.

Personal and Direct

Concepts such as mass customization, technology-driven personalization, and one-to-one marketing will be transferred much more strongly into the news and information world. Mass customization is that trend in product design and manufacturing by which advanced technology enables customers to become much more involved in designing specific elements of products they want to purchase. Rather than a car maker guessing which combination of interior options should go with which hubcap style, car buyers can go to the company's Web site and literally design their own car from the many options provided.

One-to-one marketing is being demonstrated more and more frequently on commerce Web sites from many companies. If you order a book or a cigar online, you will quickly see emails that say, "If you enjoyed this book, or this cigar, we think you will also enjoy this book or this cigar, which we happen to have available today only and for a very special price." This is simultaneously personal and impersonal. The customer understands that it is the software algorithm that is doing the work, but it still can save time and effort by helping filter through the many options available.

We are seeing that mass customization and technological personalization to some considerable degree now with the options of selecting email alerts sent to your desk about narrowly categorized news topics of your choice. In dealing with the information overload that is increasing daily, news viewers will look for technological means of filtering all the things they don't want so they can concentrate their precious time on the things they do want. This puts a premium on customization of information. Investor stakeholders have a need for different information about an industrial accident than fenceline neighbors, for example. Employees' families have a different need for information about an embattled company's plans than others in the industry seeking details to help them avoid similar circumstances.

It might be tempting to try to escape this and other burdens of public information by saying that this is the job and challenge of the news organizations. After all, your company or organization is in business to accomplish something else, not satisfy the public's need for information. The problem is, this doesn't wash. Frequent Internet users now routinely turn to the news source for the most immediate and direct information. People with a high interest in what is happening with the situation or the company involved do not expect that the news media who cater to the faceless masses will have the specific information they are looking for. If this is the reality now, how much more so will it be true when Internet use increases both in number of users and frequency? Also, because some companies and organizations have placed a high priority on effective communication, they will set standards that will determine new levels of expectation and demand. The wisest course of action is to assume that more and more people will be looking for more direct, customizable, and immediate information, not from the news agencies but directly from the source of the news.

Newsmakers as Broadcasters

In the media world the roles are quite clearly defined. A newsmaker creates news by filing a legal action, announcing a major new product, having an accident at a facility, or having employees caught in a criminal cover-up. Then the news organizations take over. They collect as much information as they can from the source of the news and others who might also serve as news sources in the same story. They get the appropriate visual imagery if they are in the video presentation business and package the story to fit into a broadcast news segment. It could be a minute, it could be five minutes—the length of time and the kind of packaging are determined by the importance of the story at that moment in the eyes of the editors and producers. When fully packaged for easy consumption in the ways in which the audience prefers, it is ready for distribution, which means the content is sent to the presses and from there to the newsstands or mailboxes or the broadcast transmitters and towers.

What happens when the audience starts going directly to the source of the news? They will either have their needs and expectations met or they won't. It is likely that those who go to the Web sites of companies involved in crises right now don't expect a news broadcast-style treatment, or even a news Website-style treatment. They expect the company to put a spin on the story, argue for its point of view, and attempt to persuade the viewer that what everyone else says is wrong. What would happen if they did present their information in a package similar to news organizations?

News agencies' credibility is based on the belief that they are not personally involved in the story and offer an objective third-party perspective. When that third-party independence is compromised, the credibility of the story and the story teller are quickly compromised as well. One of the most interesting developments to watch in the next few years as public information is further splintered is to see if companies and organizations abandon their clearly subjective and self-serving presentation of public information and come closer to replicating the appearance of objectivity offered by news media. If they do, it will be interesting to see if audiences respond with credibility or incredulity to this approach.

Regardless of how far communicators are willing to go in presenting the whole and complete picture of a situation involving their companies or clients, there is little question that effective communicators in the future will more closely imitate the styles and methods of news organizations. In a relatively minor industrial accident recently, a local online news provider showed a series of still images of the black cloud rising around the facility. His images were what were presented on the regional broadcast channels and he was the one interviewed for information about what was going on. Communicators now have the option more than ever to take a higher level of control of the story by telling the story themselves rather than having others tell it for them. The company could have been the first and best source for information but chose otherwise. Some companies have policies that dictate they will not show images on company Web sites relating to news events for legal reasons. There might be good reason for this, but they are asking that others who have no interest in the long-term viability of the organization tell their stories for them.

Content and Style Changes

If communicators are going to be the packagers and distributors of the news, they must also then be aware of changing audience demands and expectations. They must think like the local news producer who watches the nightly ratings almost like my father reads his barometer. News producers now are constantly thinking about how they can engage the audience further and deeper into the story, how they can replicate the experience of being there. They search for ways to pull them in, make them a part of the story, and touch them not just with information, but with the feelings, emotions, and human experiences contained in those stories. The night anchor of CNN was recently seen in a series of promotional advertisements talking about how CNN doesn't just deliver the news, but tells the stories and conveys the character and personality of those involved to more deeply involve the audience. It was a blatant promotion for the "infotainment" approach, but it was entirely realistic. Audiences want to be touched by shared experience. When our fellow citizens in New York are grieving over personal loss, we want to be there, to hold them and comfort them and share their grief. It is the opportunity and responsibility of the news organizations to meet that deep need. However, as we move further into postmedia communication, it also becomes the responsibility and opportunity of professional communicators working for companies and organizations in the news.

We talked about the growing applications of technology for replication of experience. This is already being worked out on many news Web sites, and not just those owned by news organizations. Some leading companies were noted for having outstanding news Web sites and one of the main reasons was their extensive presentations of video footage. Video is becoming increasingly common in all forms of communication and the Internet is daily growing as a vehicle for distributing and presenting video information. Desktop video production is growing as desktop publishing grew in the late 1980s. Video as a means of conveying information and much more is exceptionally powerful and when harnessed to the instant accessibility of the Internet will become a more necessary component of most corporate communication. Communicators need to be prepared to capture, edit, and distribute video very quickly. This will not be a task turned over to video production people with rooms full of equipment. This will be part of daily work of many people in professional communication working with desktop production studios built into their Internet-based communication management systems.

A debate will likely rage within your organization about the wisdom of providing video or even still images—particularly when the story revolves around a problem—but providing images can be very beneficial. Regional television stations repeatedly used images of smoke and fire whenever a story involved a facility that had a major accident. When a small-scale event occurred, I guessed that once again the news producers would put up the horrible old images simply because the event wasn't big enough to bring out a camera crew to collect new images. Therefore, we emailed still images of the cleanup directly to the station. Some thought we were crazy to be possibly raising the profile of this small event by providing photos to the news producers. However, when the story ran that night, it showed the cleanup pictures and did not once again repeat the images of fire and smoke.

Webcasting is already becoming part of the routine of dealing with the media on larger scale news announcements. However, like all forms of public information, Webcasting will become far more common among targeted groups and even open to the public when there is high interest and relevance. Executives need to be prepared for the increasing pressure to allow outsiders to come inside the organization through these communication tools. Like all these changes, this idea of going "inside" represents risks and opportunities. The ones who understand the ultimate importance of credibility and who have nothing to hide will welcome the opportunity to increase understanding and appreciation for what they are doing. Others will shrink away, concerned about both perception and legal issues.

Think Local, Act Global

As there was a World War II generation and a Cold War generation, this current era might be characterized as the global generation. Even the current war on terrorism can be seen in this light as a war without borders and nations. It is a global war like we have never seen, where the battle lines are mostly ephemeral and the enemy is as likely to be in a remote cave as boarding a bus in our busiest cities.

Those interested in your story or those who demand information about a crisis you are involved in are not likely to be located only in your neighborhood. A recent large-scale legal battle involving companies on several different continents required the simultaneous publication of information about the situation in nine different languages. Interest groups quickly make global alliances and the global financial markets mean that investors from around the world might have a strong interest in your activities. Environmental groups, like most interest groups with deeply committed members, have alliances and friendships that extend around the globe and those alliances might be more important to the members of those cause-oriented groups than national identity. We have seen the power of special interests in influencing policy and politics in this country—we will see the power of globally connected special-interest alliances in the years to come. It will be an increasing part of life for those involved in communications for companies and organizations whose reach extends beyond national boundaries and even for some who consider themselves mostly local.

This might seem contradictory to the idea of personalization and one-to-one communication but it is not. As the global audience increases, so does the need for highly targeted, personalized information. This is a corollary to the very struggle going on as the world begins to experience the reality of a global village. There is simultaneously a trend toward a homogenous culture and a countertrend that emphasizes not so much nationalism as regional and cultural identity. Many of the world's hot spots, such as northern Iraq and Turkey with the Kurds, Bosnia, Kosovo, and Macedonia reflect deeply committed efforts to retain cultural distinctiveness as the world moves toward homogeneity. We might be moving gradually toward the establishment of English as a universal language of business and the dollar and euro as the universal standards of exchange, but we also see great efforts expended to maintain ethnic, religious, language, and cultural uniqueness.

Communicators need to understand these cross-currents, respect them, and prepare to meet the unique challenges they imply. A few years ago there was a significant trend in advertising and marketing toward global branding. This can be seen today in the establishment of simple visuals that are intended to convey meaning without language. Global brands such as Nike, Coca-Cola, McDonalds, Shell, and Mercedes employ simple universal symbols. At the same there is the understanding that communication efforts require a deep understanding of the local language and culture. It is recognized that global efforts require local involvement to be effective and to avoid offending audiences.

Audience Control

The Internet and digital communication have done more than increase the speed and directness of information. They have given unprecedented control to the audience. In the media world of print and broadcast, it is the sender of the information who controls the flow. Information in those modes is largely linear; it flows from one item to the next in the sequence determined by the presenter. With the Internet, that is changed. Information might be presented linearly, but it is normally viewed in jumps, skips, and rapid diversions. The first term applied to those who spend time with the Internet was *surfer*. The implication is one who darts about, skimming the surface, searching for those items that catch his or her fancy or which he or she finds relevant.

Print information design has gone through a remarkable change in the last few years in recognizing that readers like to skip around, scan for relevance, and settle where they are most interested. Traditional broadcast formatting is changing to make its presentation less linear by offering digital guides that allow you to quickly see what is happening on multiple channels. More significantly, change is seen in video recording and services, such as Tivo, which allow viewers to capture broadcasts in linear fashion, but then view them on their own time schedule in a more nonlinear fashion.

This increasing audience control is not something to be fought. It is a fundamental reason that it is increasingly necessary for communicators to prepare and present information targeted to various audiences. For those accustomed to taking control of their own information flow, there is little patience for wading through information you don't want to get to information you do want. All one has to do is review how Web site navigation was constructed eight to 10 years ago compared to how it is now. Professionally constructed Web sites reflect the idea that the audiences want to get to the information they are seeking very quickly. They need to see almost at first glance the relevance of the information on the site to them. This situation, which is already a reality, is a challenge to those communicators who believe it is their task to prepare a single release, post it to a Web site, and distribute it by news wire so that the job is done.

A World of Many Voices

As companies and organizations are just beginning to understand the potential of the Internet to communicate their messages to key people quickly and easily, the same is true for those who oppose those same companies and organizations. Many have already demonstrated their understanding of the potential of the Internet to communicate with large groups quickly, to make the news, to create alliances around the world, and to cause serious damage to reputations and business activities.

What is already happening is a cacophony of voices all crying to be heard and to be believed. Multiple groups and individuals, all with strong agendas, are competing for the hearts and minds of the public, which when swayed toward a point of view serve as the basis for social change and political action. News viewers will have an increasing number of options to choose from as sources for information on virtually unlimited topics and events. This is a dramatic change from the days of traditional media when there were still multiple but very limited sources of information.

How the traditional media will respond to this new competition and this increase in noise is still to be determined. The emergence of bloggers as a new form of journalism and publishing is already raising serious questions about the impact on traditional media. The *blogger.com* Web site quoted an article from *MIT Technology Review* that commented on the change being brought about by the Internet broadcasters called *bloggers*. According to the article and Web site, the traditional media will bring issues and information to national attention, but it will be up to the Internet commentators to redefine, clarify, and expand on those issues as they relate to the particular group or audience they are addressing.

The Battlefront of the Future: Being a Credible Source

This question quickly arises: Who is to be believed? The news media have been the most trusted source of information because of their real or presumed objectivity. However, that trust might be eroded by their agenda of providing entertainment. As more news viewers gain awareness of the formulaic requirements of news and entertainment, credibility and objectivity might be lost. In theater, there is the willing suspension of disbelief: a contract between artist and audience that this is not real, although it might depict real events, so that the conventions of entertainment can be fulfilled. The great danger to news organizations of so thoroughly adopting the entertainment model is they have not asked for the willing suspension of disbelief and they are pretending to the audiences that the entertainment conventions don't apply. They parade entertainment as news—one of the most serious examples being the story of exploding gas tanks of Chevy trucks that represented a serious loss of credibility for NBC's *Dateline*. When audiences gain an understanding that they are being provided entertainment without the contract of willing disbelief, the news media will lose a great deal of credibility, particularly if and when it is observed that other, nontraditional sources of information such as newsmakers and their opponents, offer better, more credible information.

Yet there is very considerable and understandable skepticism about news from a company or organization when its clear intention is to protect its reputation. Activist groups and nongovernmental organizations have enjoyed media and audience respect based on their reliance on volunteers and their commitment to a cause in the public interest. However, objectivity in these groups is also questionable when it is understood that their agenda might be driven by "profit" as well, or, more accurately, the need to develop and protect a strong base of financial supporters. The example provided earlier of an "environmental" organization opposing a pipeline project received its funding from a barge company that would have lost its business if the pipeline project were approved. Other environmental groups have demonstrated an adeptness at changing missions and targets in search of a donor base to keep the organization going.

The point is that when it comes down to it, most everyone providing information to others has some sort of ax to grind. For some it might be dominant and controlling and when audiences understand that the agenda comes first, information becomes akin to propaganda, so there is little to no trust in the source except from those already thoroughly committed to that agenda.

Another increasingly disturbing aspect of credibility is the ease with which fake information can be produced in the digital age. It used to be said that photos don't lie. The tabloid papers have proven this wrong. We have seen favorite stars with 50 years added to their lives in photos staring out at us from the supermarket checkout line. On January 22, 2002, MSNBC carried an intriguing story about the fake information on the Internet resulting from the September 11 attack. A prime example was the supposed tourist photo taken from the top of the World Trade Center with a smiling visitor facing the camera while in the distance behind and below him there is an airliner bearing down on the building. It is a chilling and powerful image. The photo was faked by a 25-year-old Hungarian who had taken the picture from the observation deck and expertly added in the photo of the airliner.

This, like many other hoaxes and misunderstandings, swirled across the world on the Internet in the days and weeks following the attacks. Other stories documented by the article include the rumor that NASA requested all Americans to step outside on the night of September 14 with a lighted candle to memorialize the victims. It is safe to presume that more than a few were standing outside with candles lit that night, although NASA issued no such request. As with most other developments involving the Internet, it is likely we have not seen the last of fakes. This trend, too, will put a premium on credibility and sources that can assure it.

There are three conclusions to be drawn from the situation of media splintering, the proliferation of voices, and the competition for credibility. First, there will be a role provided in the future that might be called *information pointer*. Second, there will be another role provided that might be called *truth filter*. Third, anyone who provides information to the public needs to understand that credibility is and should be their very first and overriding concern.

Information Pointers

Right now there is something going on somewhere in the world that is of vital interest to you, but you don't necessarily know about it. A few years ago this would not have been an issue because there was an understanding that finding out about the details that might be relevant was simply an impossibility. However, the Internet is changing expectations. Now, we have an understanding that it is quite possible and likely that things are happening or information is emerging that might be important to us and that the information is accessible. It is accessible except for the problem of how to find it in the midst of the overwhelming amount of information available.

Traditional media have played multiple roles in public information. Part of the splintering of media is the separation of roles. One critical role they have played is information pointing. I might learn from my local radio station that there has been a car accident in my neighborhood. That might be all the information relevant to all audiences who listen to that station, but I might want more, so I try to call my wife to check if she and the kids are OK. The comment quoted earlier by Moskowitz indicates the traditional media are already becoming media pointers. Both television and newspapers are bringing news viewers the highlights, but also pointing them to the Internet to gain the specifics and the details that interest them.

The Internet is a publishing medium with the lowest publication cost available. That means a tremendous amount of information in the form of audio, video, or text can be made available for public consumption at a much, much lower cost than including that in print publications or even on broadcast or cable outlets. Add to that the fact that with the Internet the audience has the highest degree of control, and it makes sense that most of the depth of details and the audience-specific information will be found on the Internet. The traditional media will use their expensive time and space to point people to where the information can be found on the Internet.

A television reporter told a group of newsmakers to make certain they gave the news outlets their Internet address when reporting a story. You might think that the news outlets would want to have such information on their news sites rather than providing another site. In fact they do. A major objective of news outlets today is to drive traffic to their Web sites, and to encourage traffic they readily use their site to point viewers to the sites of newsmakers. They don't want the cost or time lag of editing or uploading the information to their site. They simply want news viewers to get used to the idea that if they see a story they can get more information about that on their Web site. They are more than happy to simply provide links.

In a significant news event involving an industrial accident where the communication technology mentioned in a previous chapter was used, all the news outlets directed viewers to the incident's JIC site. In some cases, they mentioned that site directly in news stories, not even bothering to have people go first to the news outlet's site. They saw it as part of their responsibility in telling the story to inform their audience that more information could be found by going directly to the source of the news. They saw their role as alerting people to the story and then pointing them to where they could find more in-depth information. For the vast majority of the audience, the level of detail provided in a three-minute newscast or a two-column print story was all that was needed. However, when relevance was high, those viewers were directed to go to the source. In the days of a few national magazines, newspapers, or news networks, each major medium tried to be all things to all people as the best way to compete for audiences. However, when the media splinter and competition increases with new voices and new media, they survive by carving out distinct niches in which they can excel and lead. This is certainly true in magazines and is also true in the national newspapers we see today. As further splintering occurs, all news outlets will define themselves more narrowly. It seems reasonable that some major news media will decide their role in the marketplace is information pointing and they will seek leadership in simply alerting the mass audience they seek to the highlights and direct them to where they can get more information. If and when that occurs, if your company or organization is in the news, you will be pointed at as a source for direct information. The news outlets will have done their job of alerting interested viewers about the story. Next it will be up to you and the other sources of information about that story, including your opponents, to tell that story and tell it well.

Truth Filters

When there are multiple voices all screaming, "Believe me! Believe me!" who are you to believe? When you are not certain, you turn to truth filters—people or organizations you trust and whom you believe have the information and objectivity needed to give you the straight scoop.

People you know and trust from past experience and those who you believe have access to information about the topic or situation are naturals. The fact that strategic influencers serve as truth filters is one reason it is necessary to engage these people willingly as part of your communication effort. This concept of borrowed credibility was discussed earlier.

In the future, there likely will emerge a more formalized role in the public communication process for truth filters. We are seeing this emerge in some forms already. *Consumer Reports* serves as a sort of truth filter for consumers as it relates to products and advertiser claims. There are Web sites dedicated to helping consumers filter through information about technology products of all sorts. To some degree these kinds of sites are already emerging in public information. Their very existence depends totally on preserving their credibility and that means having absolutely no agenda other than providing the truth as well as they can determine it. *Consumer Reports*'s audience would go away relatively quickly if there was any evidence that showed a pattern of payoffs for high rankings.

A recent example involving a large oil company illustrated this truth filter phenomenon at work. In a typical Internet-based attack, activists opposing oil companies attempted to do serious damage by circulating an email that claimed purchase of Middle Eastern oil was directly helping sponsor terrorism. It listed oil companies by how much Middle Eastern oil they imported and concluded by pleading "Stop paying for terrorism!" Clearly, if a link could be made the impact could be substantial. The chain email gained momentum, as have many other such messages. The potential for significant industry and individual company risk coming from these attacks is one of the most dangerous aspects of the instant news world. However, a truth filter has emerged called *www.breakthechain.org*. In the evaluation of this email, the editor of this truth filter stated, "The most frightening aspect of this chain is its erroneous logic: 'Oil is from the middle east; Terrorists are from the middle east; Therefore, oil comes from Terrorists.'"[2] Then he went on to quote Tim O'Leary, a spokesperson from one of the companies mentioned in the chain email who expertly refuted the erroneous information and pointed out that imported oil helps provide a reliable supply of fuel to meet U.S. energy demands. O'Leary stated, "This dependable supply relationship assures the company of a steady flow of crude oil to its refineries, which serve the U.S. market. This supply stability directly benefits the U.S. consumer, providing some of the lowest prices in the world for gasoline."[3] The truth filter Web site encourages anyone who receives a chain email and questions the information in it to go to *www.breakthechain.org* for an analysis of the accuracy of the information.

There are a number of sites, usually related to special-interest public information, that examine in great detail the accuracy of media reports about a specific topic. For example, one site I reviewed was dedicated to showing the bias in Western and Israeli news reports about Palestinians. Such a site cannot be a truth filter for anyone except someone already completely adhering to the Palestinian viewpoint because they make no pretense themselves to objectivity. Their purpose, from a very subjective standpoint, is to point out the lack of objectivity of traditional media reports.

I expect that organizations and Web sites will emerge that will be dedicated to being truth filters on broader topics—perhaps on most news of general public interest. This role will be seen as important and therefore economically viable because the entrance of news sources and their opponents into the fray will almost demand it. With so many conflicting voices and so much conflicting information, the nonaligned viewer will quickly grow weary of trying to sort through the claims and counterclaims himself or herself.

It is easy and somewhat reasonable to conclude that traditional media will fill this need. However, that will be a matter of choice. It is likely that some will, but to do so they will need to abandon the melodramatic formula of much of current news. This formula is in itself an agenda and the reality that the demands for its conventions override the complexity of real life will become increasingly obvious when placed alongside truth filtering. However, truth filtering will likely remain a relatively minor niche in the economics of news presentation because, as today's media have demonstrated, sex sells, or in other words, infotainment has strong audience appeal. The difference is similar to, if not as stark as, the difference between Hollywood movies and documentaries. Both are legitimate art forms and communication vehicles, but their purposes are different. There is also no question as to which holds the greatest interest for the average moviegoer.

The Sum of All Parts: Tell the Truth

If it is true that truth filters will emerge and audiences will go to them for help in evaluating the veracity of the information provided by the many voices, then they will become an important consideration for corporate communicators. Truth filters will have a place for the simple reason that credibility or believability is of the ultimate importance. Truth filters will be needed because most companies and organizations will reluctantly abandon their efforts to spin the information in such as way as to persuade people to their perspective. This is entirely understandable. However, in the presence of truth filters, to spin the information in a way that causes legitimate concerns about credibility is to point a loaded gun at yourself; it is simply self-destructive. These truth filters will help show companies inclined toward disguise, cover-up, and legal protection that their absolute best course in protecting their reputation and their public franchise is to tell the truth, as an objective audience wants and expects the truth to be told.

There is a simple dictum that sums this up well: Tell the truth in the way in which you would want the truth to be told to you. In the instant news world, we need add just one more word: quickly.

Endnotes

1. Moskowitz, Laurence, "Call It Fusion, Call It Opportunity, It's 2002," *PR Strategist*, Public Relations Society of America, Winter 2002, p. 40. Used by permission.

2. Ratcliff, John R., *www.breakthechain.org*, May 2002.

3. O'Leary, Tim, *www.breakthechain.org*, May 2002.

INDEX

A

H

I

J

K

L

M

O

P

Q

R

S

T